THE ANTIQUES BOOK

THE
ANTIQUES
BOOK

Outstanding, Authoritative Articles on
Ceramics, Furniture, Glass, Silver,
Pewter, Architecture, Prints and
Other Collecting Interests.

Edited by Alice Winchester
and the Staff of *The Magazine* ANTIQUES

Bonanza Books · New York

DESIGNED BY GEORGE HORNBY

THE ANTIQUES BOOK

Table of Contents

CERAMICS

FURNITURE

GLASS

SILVER

FIREARMS

TOYS

THE ANTIQUES BOOK

Introduction

LIKE the subject it deals with, *The Magazine* ANTIQUES never goes out of date. Over and over people have said to us, "I just found the most helpful article in an old copy of ANTIQUES—it gave me exactly the information I had been looking for and couldn't find anywhere else." This has happened so often we have come to the conclusion that old copies of ANTIQUES are never "back numbers" and that we ought to do something about it.

We were encouraged to this decision by George Hornby of A. A. Wyn, Inc., who asked us if his house might publish an anthology of outstanding articles from the first fifty-six volumes of ANTIQUES, January 1922 through December 1949. Since many of our issues are long out of print, and since we thought it a wonderful idea anyway, we agreed — and here it is.

It was easier said than done, however. From more than 2500 articles, how were we to pick the thirty-five that are "outstanding"? We had to cover all branches of the subject of antiques, not just furniture or glass or silver. Counting them up, we found there were at least twenty-five separate categories. Obviously we had then to include all the articles that have been new and major contributions to our knowledge of these many subjects. We lost count before we had listed all of those. But we certainly couldn't leave out any of the good comprehensive articles that provide a concise, clear summary of a large and complicated subject. Not to mention the many articles directed to beginning collectors that give a sound and reliable introduction to one or another of the collecting fields. And what about the informal articles that recount personal collecting experiences and current opinion?

It began to look as though the only thing to do was toss all 2500 of them in a hat and draw lots. But we didn't do that. We weighed them all, and juggled them, and balanced them, and finally made our choice. We feel that the articles we have selected are not only outstanding, but also representative of our first twenty-eight years of publishing.

Like the Magazine itself, this volume holds something for everyone with an interest in or curiosity about antiques. It covers eleven different collecting categories. It has ABC articles, like Lura Woodside Watkins' on American ceramics, which lead the way to new collecting possibilities. It has summary articles, like W. B. Honey's on Dresden china, which provide reliable guideposts along the way. It has critical articles, like Fiske Kimball's on Victorian art and taste, which help develop independent judgment. And it has the results of profound research in many fields. Some, such as Mrs. Russel Hasting's account of a silver beaker, read like detective stories; others fit together an intricate pattern of facts gleaned from many sources, like Joseph Downs' record of the Newport cabinetmakers. All have made an important contribution to our understanding of antiques, and are still as valuable as when they first appeared. In the cases where more recent research has uncovered new information, that has been added to bring each article up to date.

The preparation of this book represents a formidable job of omission. We have grieved over leaving out whole areas of our subject, like painting, and clocks; and a long series of our "famous first" — signal discoveries that were first reported in ANTIQUES, such as the earliest surviving piece of pewter made in America, or the first labeled New York chair to be discovered, or the first genuine copy of the *Ulster County Gazette* to be identified. But we console ourselves with the promise that they will be included in another ANTIQUES BOOK.

For one who has not read any of its contents before, an anthology opens doors to new experiences, varied and full of exciting possibilities. For another, it has the fascination of an old favorite seen from a new perspective which gives it new meaning. We hope that readers of both kinds will find in THE ANTIQUES BOOK both the freshness and the familiarity that make antiques themselves enduringly satisfying.

ALICE WINCHESTER

CERAMICS

Quality in "Oriental Lowestoft"

BY HOMER EATON KEYES

IT IS DIFFICULT *to select any single article by Homer Eaton Keyes for this book, for* ANTIQUES *itself was his creation and virtually the whole Magazine was his work for the first sixteen years of its existence. As editor from 1922 until his death in 1938, he not only established the Magazine's .editorial policy, pattern, and standards, but won it the position of prestige which it still holds. He was a pioneer in publishing. When* ANTIQUES *was founded, there were relatively few collectors, fewer serious students of antiques, and still fewer experienced writers on the subject. It was through Mr. Keyes' encouragement that many of the people now recognized as leading authorities on antiques of one kind or another first set pen to paper, and it was in* ANTIQUES, *under his editorship, that their contributions first appeared. His own knowledge of antiques was vast. His scholarship was well grounded in the arts of Europe and the Orient, but his special love was for the things made and used in America in its early days. He was one of the first to emphasize the regional differences in our antiques, particularly furniture, and to identify their local characteristics.*

Mr. Keyes was a prolific writer. Besides nearly two hundred full-length articles which he wrote for ANTIQUES, *every issue that he edited contained his editorial comment, news notes, and personal observations. From all this we have selected the following article, for a number of reasons. Oriental Lowestoft — or as we now call it, oriental export porcelain — was his own favorite among antiques. For many years he had made a great study of it, and had crystallized his knowledge in a long series of articles that appeared in* ANTIQUES *from 1928 to 1937. These were the first to analyze and classify the ware in all its various types, as well as to record its history completely. The article we present here, from* ANTIQUES *for December 1937, is the last that Mr. Keyes wrote on this subject. It contains the essence of his esthetic appreciation and personal enjoyment of a ware that he helped to make known to collectors.*

QUALITY, though a word on every tongue, eludes satisfactory definition. All the more difficult is the capturing of its subtle connotations. Hence when we speak of *quality* in oriental Lowestoft, we must pick our sustaining phrases with care and enunciate distinctly, lest we be misunderstood. To most persons oriental Lowestoft is oriental Lowestoft — all out of the same pot and all of equal merit, though, for reasons of taste or sentiment, certain types of decoration may be considered more desirable than others.

For the average American collector one group of Lowestoft and one only has any significant appeal. That is the one which exhibits a blue border dotted with gilt stars, and therewith a central medallion in blue and gold depicting either a pseudo-armorial shield surmounted by two enamored doves, or, alternatively, a blue and gold urn, or a floral spray.

Porcelain adorned with the sundry variations of such motives is widely believed to have been specially dedicated to the patriotic citizens of the United States. Unhappily, the facts do not accord with the tradition. This blue and gold ware was, in its day, quite as widely used in England and on the Continent as in America. It even found its way into the bazaars of northern Africa and the Near East, where today its surviving fragments are being retrieved for export to the United States. Its golden stars, I surmise, are more likely to have been snatched direct from heaven's overspreading dome than from the flag of the new-born American republic. Having made its first appearance in the 1780's, by which time supreme excellence was becoming the exception rather than the rule in the commercial output of Chinese ceramic factories, it cannot vie in quality with the earlier export wares of the Orient.

The claim of blue and gold Lowestoft upon the affections of Americans is based on other attributes. For one thing, the ware, if not decoratively impressive, possesses the counter-balancing appeal of daintiness and refinement, both in its form and in the handling of its ornamental motives. It is immediately recognizable, and, in general, is an eminently safe purchase for the neophyte. But a still more potent consideration endears the ware to Americans. It is

to be remembered that, since direct trade relations between the United States and China were not under way prior to 1784, this blue and gold represents the type of oriental porcelain most frequently brought or sent home as gifts or as merchandise by our seafaring ancestors, our traders, and our business and consular envoys in the Far East. No wonder that surviving examples, haloed with such precious associations, are among the most revered of American penates. They deserve to be. The sentiment that prompts their cherishing is something to be praised and encouraged. It is never to be belittled or criticized, except in those instances where its virtuous essence becomes tainted with blind prejudice. However, fond though we may be of our "American Lowestoft," I fear that we must in all honesty admit that a large proportion of it fails to deserve top rating — either in its fabric or in the element of the skill and care employed in its decoration. Our armored eagles, for example, are, for the most part, ungainly sparrows. Our ships, save for a few vessels anchored in donation punchbowls, are but Chinese junks to whose sterns the stars and stripes have been appended. Even George Washington's famous and almost priceless Cincinnati items are but common Canton ware glorified by a none too competently portrayed figure of Fame.

To this general rule, of course, notable exceptions may be cited. Among these are two extraordinary punchbowls whose outward adornment consists of a careful copy of a Cincinnati membership certificate. Then, too, we have the magnificent Decatur bowl with its almost miraculously perfect transcript of a Saint-Memin profile. Several punchbowls are likewise to be highly esteemed. Outside of this group the

FIG. 1 — ARMORIAL PLATES (*1723-1735*). *Left,* Arms of Bliss impaling Bliss. Period of Yung Chêng, during whose reign occurred the transition from the *famille verte* to the *famille rose* type of decoration. Finely diapered borders often interrupted by medallions enframing floral designs are characteristic. So, too, are heavily mantled armorial designs so large as almost to fill the centre of the plates on which they appear. The diapered border here is executed in sepia and gold. The rest of the decoration is in brighter hues. *Diameter,* 10¾ in. *Right,* Arms of Izard. *Famille rose* coloring.

FIG. 2 — BOWL AND SAUCER (*1723-1735*). Period of Yung Chêng. Delicately executed European figures painted on fine eggshell porcelain by an accomplished artist. The man wears a rose coat; the woman, a blue overdress with sea-green skirt. The handsome floral scroll, balancing the figures, is gilded. Diapering in red and gold. A rare and exceptionally choice example. *Diameter of saucer,* 6 in.; *of bowl,* 5½ in.

FIG. 3 — SAUCER DISH (*c. 1740*). European figures, in brightly colored costumes, apparently examining varied Chinese merchandise. Enameled on fine ruby-backed eggshell porcelain. In spite of its western subject, this piece clearly reflects what Doctor Williamson, in his *Book of Famille Rose,* calls "the Chinese taste." That is to say, the dish is rimless, and without the surrounding ornamental bands that Europeans usually considered essential.

FIG. 4 — ARMORIAL PLATE (*c. 1740-1750*). Ch'ien Lung. The gold spearhead border here observable made its appearance about 1745. So large an armorial design as this is rare for its period. The porcelain is eggshell, unusual in armorial pieces.

FIG. 5 — HUNTSMAN PLATE (*1740-1750*). The huntsman wears a blue coat. His horn is gold. The handling of the figure is exceptionally vigorous and free from anatomical distortion, though the delineation of the hounds leaves something to be desired. The extension of the composition across the rim is unusual. No doubt the portrayal was taken from a European picture.

FIG. 6 — REBECCA AT THE WELL (*1740-1750*). Enameled in full color and more effective in the original than in photographic reproduction. The figure drawing is well above the average of Chinese delineations, but the work as a whole cannot compare with that of the earlier bowl and saucer, pictured in Figure 2.

FIG. 7 — DISH IN CHINESE TASTE (*Ch'ien Lung*). Entirely unrelated to foreign-market wares. Pictured to illustrate supposed Chinese preference in matters of both form and decoration. A rimless plate exhibiting charmingly disposed floral sprays upon a pure surface untroubled by elaborate bandings, or other distracting ornamentation.

artistically distinguished pieces of porcelain made in China for the American market might almost be counted on the fingers of one hand.

In making this statement I am anxious to be neither misunderstood nor misinterpreted. I am endeavoring simply to emphasize the difference between what is historically, and, to some extent, sentimentally important, and consequently of high monetary value, and that which is in its own character meritorious.

At this point, however, I must confess to some embarrassment. It would, I surmise, be hard to discover a serious student of Chinese porcelains, as such, who sees good in any of the eighteenth-century oriental wares specially made for export to foreign lands. These wares, the pundits contend, are neither Chinese nor European. Instead they are, virtually without exception, but mongrel products unworthy of serious consideration by persons of esthetic sensibility.

The measure of truth in this unkindly dictum is perhaps large. No one who has even a casual acquaintance with the finer examples of *famille rose* porcelain of the type produced in China for the Emperor Ch'ien Lung and his entourage will contend that the foreign-pattern products equal the best of wares made for domestic consumption. Nevertheless, two points in favor of the so-called mongrel items may pertinently be stressed: first, these items deserve attention because of their significance as mementoes of a great trading era, and because their extraordinary variety of form and decoration affords endless opportunity for studying the interplay of stylistic influences; second, granting their general inferiority to contemporary Chinese porcelains of the highest grade, they exhibit

varying degrees of excellence, or of debasement, which permit their classification and relative appraisal on primarily esthetic grounds. I might add, too, as an expression of purely personal opinion, that, while mulling over simon-pure Chinese ceramics is doubtless more edifying than consorting with their slightly vulgar relatives of the Lowestoft branch, the more cultured occupation is considerably the less exciting of the two.

Aside from the general interest which Lowestoft commands as an exotic product of mixed antecedents, the decorative motives displayed by the ware are so numerous and so diverse that one can never tell when he may encounter a hitherto undiscovered subject. In many instances, the task of determining the precise meaning and perhaps the particular source of a pictorial composition on a plate or bowl becomes a fascinating pursuit. Again, questions regarding the historical significance of a fresh find and of the latter's rarity in a given category must constantly arise. Such concerns should suffice to keep both student and collector actively alert. Nevertheless from time to time, the iconographic enthusiast should close his mind against other demands and devote himself to pondering examples of Lowestoft solely in terms of their quality. In so doing he may be surprised to observe how wide is the spread between the best and the worst, and how many gradations lie between the two extremes.

Why such gradations occur is readily explained. When European traders first began to purchase porcelain in the Orient for transport to their home markets, they acquired the native wares as they found them — for the most part the familiar underglaze blue and white types. This porcelain was of prevailingly good quality — thin, quite clear in its whiteness, compact in body, yet in tableware inclined to brittleness. Its decoration consisted of "heathen designs": lissom female figures, pagodas, dragons, flower arrangements, and the like. At the outset, the western traders had no thought of ordering utensils of special shape or of furnishing their own decorative patterns for the Chinese enamelers to copy. But their benevolent acceptance of what the oriental merchants had to offer did not endure. It is quite evident that, even as early as the decade of the 1690's, attempts to Europeanize oriental porcelain were under way. The well-known blue and white items picturing the Rotterdam riot afford testimony in point. In these and comparable pieces, however, we still encounter an excellent grade of white porcelain, carefully executed painting in the blue, and — characteristic of Chinese wares of the period — decorative devices penciled on the under side of the plate rim. When, during the beginning years of the 1700's, European customers of high estate placed orders for plates adorned with a monogram or a family crest, these elements frequently became but secondary additions to pieces otherwise predominantly oriental in design and quality. Several such items are pictured in *Armorial Porcelain of the Eighteenth Century*, by Sir Algernon Tudor-Craig. Among them we find bowls and plates displaying characteristic K'ang Hsi and Yung Chêng decorative motives amid which English heraldic devices have been ingeniously planted. The latest of these may be ascribed to about the year 1730. Throughout the same period Chinese artists reproduced many a European portrayal in the finest of eggshell porcelain (*Figs. 2, 3, and 4*).

Meanwhile commercialism was marching on. The eighteenth century was no more than fifteen years old when the profit possibilities in made-to-order porcelain in forms adjusted to western usage and embellished with designs dictated by western taste dawned upon the thrifty merchants of the East India companies. The agents of the Chinese potteries in Ching-tê Chên were responsive to the idea and the masters of the decorating establishments in Canton were equally amenable. Thus the great productive era of occidentalized Chinese porcelains was launched. So large an undertaking implied intensive and extensive effort to enlarge the western market. And this, in turn, involved a constant battle on the part of rival traders to force down what we may properly term the manufacturer's price. In so far as concerns the money side of the transaction, the West apparently defeated the East; but we may well doubt that the goods delivered were worth more than was charged for them. Perhaps, indeed, the shrewd Chinese agents profited more from these bargain orders than from those placed by really particular customers.

If one examines enough run-of-mine Lowestoft he will find ample evidence that culls from the kilns — warped or sooted in the firing, sometimes with a badly pitted glaze — were expressly preserved for the foreign-devil chiselers. Otherwise such imperfect items would probably have been destroyed as unfit for use. On the other hand, there were customers, particularly those who sought armorial sets, who demanded the best obtainable and were untroubled regarding the expense incurred. Such persons seem to have been appropriately and honestly served.

I am inclined to believe, however, that

little if any of the later eighteenth-century porcelain decorated in China primarily for the European market is so fine in body as that employed currently for oriental consumption, or as that which prior to 1730 had been embellished with western designs. A Rotterdam riot plate *(c. 1690),* if held against an electric globe in a dark room, will show almost white by the transmitted light, and will reveal in its fabric no moons due to imperfect mixing of the ingredients. On the contrary, a plate of the mid-eighteenth century or later, similarly tested, is likely to reveal a cloudy "duck-egg" hue and to be quite astonishingly moonstruck. The glaze of eighteenth-century European-market porcelain is often of quite definitely bluish cast, more noticeable on the underside than on the face of plates, where polychromy tends to confuse perception. The curdled "potato soup" glaze frequently occurring on the large platters brought home by seafaring ancestors in the late 1700's and early 1800's by no means signifies excellence, though it is frequently regarded with affection. It seems to be confined to large pieces, such as platters and urns, so heavily coated that the glaze crawled or bubbled in the firing.

Little more need be said regarding the substance of Chinese Lowestoft. The quality of potting and of glazing in one adequately decorated piece is likely to equal that in another. There are occasional distinguished exceptions to this rule; but they will be readily recognized when encountered. Pieces that are warped, or soot-marked, or seriously pitted or crazed, are usually uninteresting in other respects and should be passed by. Furthermore, enough undamaged articles survive and are purchasable at reasonable figures to remove any excuse for acquiring pieces that are perceptibly chipped or cracked or have suffered material repair.

It is chiefly in the domain of decoration that the student of Chinese Lowestoft will have opportunity to exercise his powers of discrimination. The decoration of Chinese porcelains occupied people of all ages, from infancy to senility. Some of these artisans were extraordinarily able; some were of very commonplace calibre. The best of them could copy with impeccable fidelity almost any pattern that was placed before them. It has frequently been stated, and is quite generally believed, that, even when supplied with a model, a Chinese could never achieve a rendering of the human form satisfactory to western eyes. This is not strictly true. The artisan or artisans who perpetrated the numerous robbery delineations of the Judgment of Paris, and many another mythological or religious scene, were indeed short on anatomy; but we may find no fault with the Decatur profile previously mentioned, or with the figure of a huntsman on the bowl pictured in Figure 5. The figure drawing on the Cincinnati certificate bowls, previously referred to, compares favorably with that on the certificates themselves. Decorators capable of achieving such work were quite naturally few, and their charges no doubt sufficiently above the usual level to prevent their employment save in exceptional instances.

Viewed from the purely qualitative standpoint, the finest Lowestoft wares will correspond in date closely with the finest products in the category of Yung Chêng and Ch'ien Lung porcelain, and they will exhibit much the same features of excellence — namely, a swift and dexterous linear quality in the drawing, clear and lively color, which means pinks that have not been fired to a blackish hue or even to a sullen blood color, clear luminous greens, delicate yellows untainted with a saffron tint, blues as liquid as the sky, and purples that might have been ravished direct from a lilac bush. The harsh, rusty iron reds of a later period will be notable for their absence.

Aside from a considerable measure of brilliance in drawing and exceptional purity of color, the fine pieces will reveal meticulous care in the execution of details. It is, of course, useless to attempt to describe such subtleties in words. As already suggested, not until the mind has been immunized against all sentimental or associational bias will any differences in quality be recognized — or admitted— even when strongly contrasting examples are placed side by side for comparison. An attitude of unquestioning loyalty in such matters prevents that mental and spiritual detachment which is essential to unclouded vision and unhampered judgment. Most of us may consider ourselves fortunate that our friends accept and cherish us for obscure reasons with which objective scrutiny has very little to do. We may add the corollary that what is technically the most nearly perfect work either of man or of nature is by no means invariably the most interesting. Were this not so, the phrase "beautiful but dumb" would never have been coined. Be that as it may, the eye gains critical vigor by being subjected to occasional setting-up exercises, even if considerable anguish is experienced in the process. The purpose of these notes, but more particularly of the accompanying illustrations and their captions, is to impose just such a penitential burden upon the reader.

It will be observed that nearly all the pieces here illustrated are credited to a period prior to the 1750 decade. The export porcelain made subsequent to that period is usually less elaborately and intricately decorated. Though its enameled designs are still deftly and delicately executed, they incline to sparsity. Hence, while the articles upon which these later decorations appear are often charming for domestic use or for grouping in cabinets, they yield few specimens individually so significant as to appeal to the specializing connoisseur. After 1800 elaboration is again in evidence on Chinese export wares, but it is usually elaboration of a coarse and slap-dash type in which the old-time refinement of pattern and technique yields to bolder and cruder effects more easily achieved.

FIG. 8 — EWER (*probably Yung Chêng*). A Chinese porcelain version of the French so called helmet pitchers — of silver or pewter — dating about 1700 to 1740. The decoration of this ewer, which features barnyard fowl among peonies, appears to be quite Chinese in character. Hence the piece is interesting as illustrating a mingling of European form and purely oriental ornamentation.

Meissen Porcelain

BY W. B. HONEY

W. B. HONEY IS *the great name in ceramics today. Keeper of Ceramics at the Victoria and Albert Museum for many years, Mr. Honey is the author of an impressive list of publications on the subject. He is familiar with the richest collections of pottery and porcelain in public and private ownership, and joins to his erudition a lively appreciation of the wares themselves. For many years his book,* Dresden China, *has been one of the standard references. For* ANTIQUES *he wrote in April 1946 a brief summary of this ever-popular subject, which we count it a privilege to reprint here.*

I T is not at all unusual to hear the porcelain of Meissen spoken of as if it were all pretty much alike, guaranteed, so to speak, by the famous crossedswords mark. Yet the great Saxon factory has existed for more than two hundred years — from 1710 until the present day. Many fashions have come and gone during that time, not all of them favorable to the art of porcelain, while the fortunes of the factory have varied from the greatest prosperity to a miserable following of other factories' styles and a wholesale revival of its own. It will be worth while, therefore, to define the period of the factory's best work and to describe some of its greatest artistic achievements, distinguishing them from the superficially similar work done later, both in the Meissen factory itself and elsewhere.

The great period belongs wholly to that time in the eighteenth century when porcelain was the subject of excited admiration in Europe. It was then hardly thought of

as pottery at all, but as a semi-precious substance of mysterious origin. Porcelain had been newly brought from China in quantity by the Dutch East India Company in the seventeenth century and before long was being widely imitated in Europe. But only superficial imitations in delftware and soft paste had been made before the early years of the eighteenth century, when Johann Friedrich Böttger made his great discovery.

Böttger was an alchemist working at Dresden in the service of Augustus the Strong, Elector of Saxony and King of Poland, and, with his fellow-worker Ehrenfriend Walther von Tschirnhausen, about 1708-1709 hit upon the right principle and materials for making a true hard-paste porcelain of Chinese type. As a result the great factory was founded at Meissen in 1710. Just before Böttger's death in 1719, runaway workmen managed to start two small rival concerns (at Vienna and Venice), but from this time onward the Meissen secret

[27]

was so well guarded that there was no serious rival factory for nearly forty years after the invention. Meissen kept its technical and creative lead in the world of German, and indeed all European, porcelain until the disaster of the Seven Years' War *(1756-1763)*.

Saxony was then overrun by Frederick the Great and his Prussians, and the Meissen premises were occupied. The European leadership passed to the French national factory at Sèvres, while Frederick's new Berlin factory aspired to supremacy in Germany. But it was in each case a barren lead, for porcelain by the last quarter of the eighteenth century had lost much of its novelty and glamor.

The world-wide neo-classical fashions of the late eighteenth century called for a new medium. This was found eventually in the unglazed jasper, basalt, and other stonewares made by Josiah Wedgwood in England, and at Sèvres and elsewhere in biscuit porcelain, which renounced the special charm of the porcelain material in a vain imitation of marble. The neo-classical was in fact distinctly unfavorable to porcelain; its antique seriousness and symmetry were at war with the frivolity and "modern fancies" of the essentially rococo porcelain.

The period of supreme achievement at Meissen thus dates from 1710 to 1756. It covers the periods of the late baroque with its often hard symmetry, and of the lighter asymmetrical rococo. The Seven Years' War was a blank for the factory, apart from the work done for Frederick, and from 1763 on it was either breathlessly trying, but without much success, to catch up with the French fashions, or lifelessly repeating its former successes. It sank to nothing in the time of the Napoleonic Wars, being occupied again by the invaders. An attempted revival in the later nineteenth century brought some prosperity again. But it was a dubious success; for then were made the copies of eighteenth-century models which the inexperienced collector of today often mistakes for old.

To describe even a tenth of the wares produced in the great time is plainly impossible within the limits of an article. All that can be done here is to indicate within the framework of a broad classification the general characters in coloring, design, and figure modeling of the outstanding types.

Earliest of all are the wares of the period named after the inventor himself, from the foundation of the factory in 1710 until his death in 1719. Böttger as an alchemist had sought to make porcelain by way of artificial semi-precious stones, and the first result of his research was an intensely hard red stoneware resembling porphyry and jasper. It was in fact so hard that it could be cut and polished on the lapidary's or glass-engraver's wheel *(Fig. 1)*. Böttger's stoneware is indeed one of the most thrilling of all ceramic materials.

Böttger's white porcelain is a smoky-toned or creamy color; the unfired paste was evidently exceptionally plastic, and could be finely wrought into characteristic applied decoration *(Fig. 2)*. Silver shapes were favored as befitting so precious a substance. Böttger porcelain is usually found plain white, and the painting if any is in imperfect enamels, obviously experimental and excitingly primitive.

Next comes the period of greatest achievement of the first Meissen manager of genius — the color-chemist and painter-designer Johann Gregor Herold. This corresponds with the last ten years or so *(1720-1733)* of the reign of Augustus the Strong,

FIG. 1 — TEAPOT (*c. 1715*). Böttger's red stoneware, with polished decoration.

FIG. 2 — CUP AND SAUCER (*c. 1715-1720*). Böttger's white porcelain, applied decoration.

FIG. 3 — TRAY (*1725-1730*). With Japanese (Kakiemon) decoration.

FIG. 4 — PART OF TEA SERVICE (*c. 1730-1735*). Painted by A. F. von Löwenfinck.

FIG. 5 — VASE (*c. 1725*). Marked *A. R.*

FIG. 6 — TEAPOT (*c. 1730-1735*). From a tea service painted in red monochrome and gold by C. F. Herold.

founder of the factory. The porcelain at first was, as before, faintly smoky or creamy in tone, but before long was made a brilliant, glittering, pure white. The period saw Herold's invention of his famous fantastic *chinoseries,* or pseudo-Chinese scenes, usually framed in profuse scrollwork in red, gold, and luster, as well as many adaptations actually from Chinese (early *famille rose),* Japanese *(Kakiemon) (Fig. 3),* and other Oriental wares. Developed from the Kakiemon type was the exceedingly beautiful work of Adam Friedrich von Löwenfink *(Fig. 4),* who was perhaps the most gifted of all porcelain painters. Gift tankards, often mounted in Augsburg silver, received some of the finest painting, which was occasionally by Herold's own hand. It was the period above all of the great vases *(Fig. 5)* made for the king and marked with his initials *A R* in monogram (for *Augustus Rex).* About 1730 appeared the first of the famous Meissen harbor scenes, at first "Chinese," then European, painted notably by the manager's own kinsman, Christian Friedrich Herold *(Figs. 6 and 7).* Superb colored ground — yellow, red, green, and turquoise or "sea green" — were mastered as early as 1727. The typical coloring of the period was full-toned and inclined to be hard, in the baroque manner. Powerful red, yellow, blue, and black were dominant for twenty years or more. Red and black monochrome painting, with lavish gilding, and a sonorous discord of red and rose purple were typical colors of the baroque.

Figure modeling in the 1720's and 1730's was relatively unimportant, but included, on the one hand, some small, often grotesque, models in the style of carved ivories; and on the other the life-size figures of animals and birds made as a sort of *tour de force* to the order of Augustus the Strong for the furnishing of his Japanese Palace. These last were the work of the sculptor Gottlob Kirchner, who was at the factory between 1727 and 1733, and of J. J. Kaendler (1731 onward), who eventually created the typical Meissen figure. The Japanese Palace animals are seldom found in the antique trade, but the smaller models attributable to Kirchner *(Fig. 8),* including some fountains and basins and elaborate clocks, are among the most-sought-after rarities.

The next period, from 1733, might well be named after Kaendler, though Herold was still active, but it was above all the taste of the director, Count Heinrich von Brühl, minister of Augustus III, which largely determined the styles adopted. The factory turned more and more to figure modeling. At first inclining to the monumental, the figures eventually took the form of table decorations, for display in series, such as allegories, folk types, satirical groups, and characters from the Italian Comedy *(Fig. 10).* These were modeled with superb vigor by Kaendler and his assistants J. F. Eberlein and Peter Reinicke, whose work is scarcely distinguishable. This was the period of the famous crinoline figures and groups *(Fig. 11).* The coloring was dominated by the usual strong red, yellow, and black of the baroque, changing to softer tones of mauve, green, and pale yellow with the coming of the rococo style toward 1750.

The modeling in the earlier style was powerfully rhythmical, at times even heavy and almost brutal in sentiment, with a kind of "ugly" beauty which is very characteristic. In the rococo style, toward 1750 and later, a lighter movement prevailed, and scrolled bases *(Fig. 10)* replaced the earlier pedestals and simple mounds. A

FIG. 7 — SNUFFBOXES, *Above*, painted by C. F. Herold (*c. 1735*); *right,* dates from about 1760.

FIG. 8 — FIGURE (*c. 1733*). Probably modeled by Gottlob Kirchner.

FIG. 9 — GROUP OF LOVERS (*c. 1740*). From a model by J. J. Kaendler.

new modeler in the rococo period was Friedrich Elias Meyer, whose slender elegant figures are distinct from those of his master Kaendler.

In this period Kaendler also introduced on table wares the low-relief borders in the style of silver, which set a universal fashion that is still current, while for Count Brühl he created the famous swan service, as well as others, with elaborately modeled decoration.

The painting on vases and table wares included a novelty in naturalistic "botanical" flowers (called "deutsche Blumen" to distinguish them from the earlier Oriental flowers), at first painted with a clean precision *(Fig. 12)*, which later softened and eventually lapsed into mannerism and insignificance. At the same time a new influence came from the stock of French prints sent to the factory about this time by Count Brühl's librarian. This was shown in the painting of Watteau subjects and pastoral scenes *(Fig. 13)*, as well as in fantastic rococo scrollwork *(Fig. 14)*.

During the Seven Years' War the notable work done for Frederick chiefly comprised snuffboxes *(Fig. 7, right)*, for which he had a well-known passion, and huge services ordered for his generals and friends *(Fig. 15)*.

After the War, pictorial painting inspired by Sèvres and neo-classical sentiment in the French manner marked the so-called "Academic Period" *(1763-1794)*, when the Saxon court painter and leader of the Dresden Academy C. W. E. Dietrich was adviser to the factory, and the same tendency was continued under the management of Count Marcolini *(1744-1814)*. Though some good and accomplished work was done in both periods and later, the inspiration and vitality of the earlier

time had obviously departed. Excellent work has been done at Meissen in recent years, especially in figure modeling, but this, of course, lies outside the scope of this article.

The collector's task is therefore to distinguish the productions of the greatest period lying between 1710 and 1756. First, as to marks. Until 1723 no factory mark was added to the porcelain, but the table wares of the early 1720's sometimes show an unexplained nick near the foot ring known in Germany as the *Dallwitzer Nagel*, after a collector of that name who first called attention to the feature. The marks added to the ware from 1723 on give some help, but need to be interpreted with caution. The first of these, *KPM* (Königliche Porzellan Manufaktur), dates from a year or two about 1723-1724, as does an imitation Chinese mark resembling the snake-entwined staff of Mercury. Both marks are comparatively rare. Then the famous crossed swords, from the arms of Saxony, were introduced and have remained the regular factory mark from 1724 to the present day. A dot between the hilts indicates a date in the "Academic Period" for the manufacture of the ware (but much defective ware made earlier was decorated in that period, when the factory needed funds). A star between or below the hilts indicates the "Marcolini Period"; but a star sometimes appeared in the mark on the early and usually unimportant blue-painted porcelain of the 1720's. Between 1814 and 1924 the plain crossed swords were used again. Since 1924 a dot has been added between the points. The most famous of all the marks of the great period, and one most outrageously abused by forgers, is the *Augustus Rex* monogram already mentioned; it usually indicates a date be-

FIG. 10 — SATIRICAL GROUP (*c. 1755*). From a model by J. J. Kaendler.

FIG. 11 — "CRINOLINE" FIGURE (*c. 1744*). From a model by J. J. Kaendler.

FIG. 12 — JUG (*1740-1745*). Painted with *deutsche Blumen*.

FIG. 13 — DISH (*c.1740*). Painted with pastoral scene.

tween 1725 and 1730, but was occasionally used later. Besides these marks, there are often, on early wares, gold letters and numerals of uncertain significance, and incised and impressed mold numbers which began to be regularly used not earlier than 1763, when an inventory was made.

But the mark on the ware (since it is in underglaze blue) can only give the date of making of the actual porcelain, which may have been decorated much later. This was often the case indeed with the painting done outside the factory. This *Hausmalerei*, as it is called, is of great interest but is too big a subject to be dealt with here. One much-disputed class alone must be mentioned, with decoration often in gilding only, of *chinoseries* distinct from Herold's *(Fig. 16)*. This was formerly mistaken for factory work but is now known to have been done in Augsburg about 1725-1735 on porcelain dating from 1720's. These Augsburg-decorated pieces sometimes bear pale red "luster" marks, usually initial letters. The *Hausmaler* using Meissen porcelain were as a rule unable to secure any but outmoded and defective ware, and even that was obtained only surreptitiously. Eventually (about 1760) to protect itself against loss of repute due to incompetent decorators, the factory began to "cancel" the mark on defective ware sold "in the white," by one or more cuts made on the glass-engraver's wheel. Such a canceled mark indicates that the piece was not decorated at the Meissen factory itself.

Other marks are sometimes mistaken for the Meissen swords. Some of these are eighteenth-century marks of other factories, intentionally written to resemble that of their famous rival. Such are the crossed swords and three dots of Weesp, the crossed L's of Limbach, the crossed hay-forks of Rudolstadt, and the crossed torches of the Paris factory of La Courtille. The *W* of Wallendorf and even the *C V* of Kloster Veilsdorf were sometimes made to resemble the swords. In modern times various devices of crossed swords or strokes occur alone, or with *D*, or *H*, or *T* (for Carl Thimve of Potschappel near Dresden), or *S* on French forgeries. Marks with the word *Dresden* or a crowned *D* are of course never Meissen marks but are quite often those of modern decorators, such as Wolfsohn. As already mentioned, the *A R* mark occurs absurdly on modern cups and saucers with colored grounds in panels alternating with "Watteau scenes" and the like.

But far more important for the collector is a knowledge of period peculiarities and a sense of style. These can only be acquired by familiarity with genuine specimens. A few points of detail may, however, be useful. First of all, it must be insisted that the type of decoration or the date of the model does not necessarily indicate the period in which a given specimen was made; it may be made from the original molds at any later time. Some aspect of color or style will, however, generally be found to give away its later date. As to color, the characteristic strong red, yellow, blue, and black of the baroque style, and the paler colors of the rococo have been mentioned already. The soft browns and pinks and pale and bright blues of the period after 1760 may also be noted. All are distinguishable from the pale, sickly pink and pale blue and yellowish green pervading the figures of the nineteenth-century revival of eighteenth-century models. The form of base also varies with the period. The nineteenth- and twentieth-century revivals are commonly on circular or oval pedestals with classical

Fig. 14 — TABLEWARE (*c. 1740-1750*). Decorated with fantastic scrollwork.

Fig. 15 — PIECES from a service made for General Möllendorff to the order of Frederick the Great (*c. 1761*).

ovolo and other patterns on the edges. The applied flowers are more elaborate, and naturalistic and frilly lace-work has sometimes been added. None of these criteria can, however, be regarded as infallible "rules of thumb," and a specimen may be right in almost all the respects mentioned and yet be a forgery. Greater reliance must be placed on a sense of the right sort of vitality in modeling and painting.

FIG. 16 — CUP AND SAUCER *(c. 1720)*. Decorated at Augsburg about 1730-1735, in *chinoiseries* distinct from Herold's.

French Soft-Paste Porcelain

BY JOAN PRENTICE

WITH FEW *exceptions we have limited the antiques covered in this book to those made in this country, but we have broadened our consideration of ceramics to include English, Continental, and Oriental as well as American. The reason for this is because in the field of pottery and porcelain more than in any other the products imported from abroad in early days played the leading part; American products did not achieve a quality comparable to the best of the European. Moreover, today American collectors find European and Oriental ceramics pleasant and suitable accessories to American antiques, whether or not they are exactly the kind originally used here. This article provides a résumé of the products and history of the leading French factories, in the order of their founding. It was written for our October 1944 issue by Miss Joan Prentice, at that time a staff member of the Philadelphia Museum of Art.*

FRENCH soft-paste porcelain, from its creation in 1673 until the downfall of the monarchy, forms one of the most delightful chapters in the history of the decorative arts. It was the first porcelain to be manufactured in Europe on any considerable scale and reached its highest development under Louis XV about the middle of the eighteenth century.

For a brief moment this translucent material, a mixture of glass and clay, threatened the supremacy of true hard-paste porcelain, made with kaolin, which originated in the Orient and was first produced in Europe by the Meissen factory near Dresden about 1709. Because of a tendency to crack and warp in firing, it could not be used for large pieces, but the indefinable charm of the material, its ivory whiteness and glossy texture, were exploited by the French with so much artistic talent and technical skill that it survived the finding of kaolin in France about 1765, and was not entirely superseded by true porcelain until about the turn of the century.

The rococo style which was admirably adapted to porcelain began to manifest itself early in the eighteenth century, and numerous fanciful objects, designed to please a sophisticated and luxury-loving society, came into being. Representative examples soon found their way into foreign

FIG. 1 — POTPOURRI JARS *(c. 1698)*. Made at Saint-Cloud. Decorated in dark-blue lambrequins and arabesques.

FIG. 2 — PART OF TEA SET *(c. 1730)*. Also made at Saint-Cloud, showing typical relief decoration in the Chinese manner.

FIG. 3 — PAIR OF FLOWER-POT HOLDERS *(1725-1735)*. Made at Chantilly in the Kakiemon style.

countries, and French creative genius won leadership in this as in other branches of the arts.

The first factories were founded under the patronage of a nobility keenly interested in the promotion of science and the arts. The rise of the porcelain industry was rapid. Twenty years after the establishment of the royal manufactory at Vincennes, which was later to be transferred to Sèvres, success was assured, and in the years between 1753 and 1760 no more artistic creations were produced by any factory in any country.

Transparent ware is believed to have existed in Italy as early as the fifteenth century, but only a few pieces of Medici porcelain, made between 1568 and 1620, survive. Fifty years elapsed before soft-paste porcelain was manufactured again, this time in France. Its composition was rediscovered by Edmé Poterat, a worker in one of the faience factories at Rouen, who obtained a license to make porcelain, along with pottery, in 1673. The only pieces that can with certainty be attributed to him, or members of his family, are decorated with arabesques in blue in the manner of Rouen pottery.

It was at the Saint-Cloud factory, founded in 1677 under the protection of the brother of Louis XIV, and continuing under his son the duc d'Orleans, that production on a large scale was first attempted.

In a license issued to the factory in 1702, the ware was described as "almost as perfect as the porcelain of China and the Indies." One characteristic decoration, consisting of dark blue lambrequins and arabesques reminiscent of Bérain, carried over into the eighteenth century the style of the previous era (*Fig. 1*). Typical also was a pure white porcelain, with hawthorne branches, birds,

and flowers in relief in the Oriental manner (*Fig. 2*). Oriental shapes were seldom copied, and the most usual pieces were tea sets with saucers having a raised inner rim, perfume burners, wine coolers, snuff boxes, candlesticks, and a variety of covered jars and other small objects.

A gilding process, similar to the one later used at Sèvres, was invented at Saint-Cloud, but the gold rubbed off easily, and few pieces show any trace of this kind of decoration. The factory lasted until 1766. The marks were *StC* in blue, a fleur-de-lis, a sun with rays, and the familiar *SC* over *T*, used only after 1724.

In 1725 Louis-Henri de Bourbon, prince de Condé, started a manufactory at Chantilly, hoping to duplicate Oriental porcelain of which he himself had a large collection. He employed as director a man who was familiar with the formulas in use at Saint-Cloud, and great success was achieved. The porcelain was considered superior to anything produced thus far, even, it was said, by the Meissen factory in Germany.

For the first ten years a tin-enamel glaze like that of pottery was employed, and Oriental models were assiduously copied, particularly the work of the celebrated Japanese potter Kakiemon of Imari (*Fig. 3*). Gradually, however, a style essentially French in all its elements was introduced by individual artists, and it was this style that was to bring glory to the later productions of Mennecy-Villeroy, Vincennes, and Sèvres. Soon it could truly be said, "Chinese porcelain no longer exerts that exclusive superiority which ruins and mortifies us." Forms and decorations were typical of the Louis XV period, and although statuettes were rare, sculpture as a decorative adjunct took on great import-

FIG. 4 — PERFUME BURNERS *(mid-eighteenth century)*. Ornamented with sculpture. The central one is an example of the delicate work done at Mennecy-Villeroy. The others were made at Chantilly.

FIG. 5 — VASES *(c. 1770)*. A fine pair of small vases with metal flowers. Made at Mennecy-Villeroy.

FIG. 6 — PAIR OF TURQUOISE BLUE POTPOURRI VASES *(c. 1752)*. Decorated with hunting scenes from engravings by Le Bas, after van Falens. Made at Vincennes.

ance, as illustrated by the pair of perfume burners (*Fig. 4*).

From 1760 until about 1800, quantities of table services were produced, among which there was little variation. The mark continued to be a hunting horn, incised or in color, with the initials or name of the decorator often attached.

There is some difference of opinion as to the exact origin of the "Manufactory of the porcelain of Villeroy, established at Mennecy." The most authoritative opinion seems to be that François Barbin, director of a faience factory sponsored by the duc de Villeroy, started a separate porcelain factory in the Rue de Charonne in Paris in 1734. He is believed to have kept in close touch with Mennecy meanwhile, and to have continued to use the mark *D.V.* for the duke or duchy of Villeroy. In 1748 he was refused the renewal of his license when Charles Adam of Vincennes, fearing competition, brought suit against him. The establishment was forcefully demolished, and Barbin was obliged to petition the duke to allow him to return in order to continue making porcelain under his protection.

In 1773, the Mennecy-Villeroy factory came to an end. Barbin's successors failed to renew their privileges, and moved to Bourg-la-Reine, where they continued for some years an inferior and negligible production.

A review of the factories' output confirms the apprehensions of Vincennes. Many of the pieces were equal to those of the royal establishment, both in the quality of the paste and in workmanship. Flowers and birds similar to those of Vincennes were used for decoration, and occasional landscapes like those of Marseille faience. Mennecy specialized in sculpture (*Fig. 4 center*), distinguished mainly at first by a certain naïveté of treatment, but later delicately modeled. Table services were seldom manufactured, and plates almost never. An unusual raspberry red characterizes much of the painting, and is used to heighten the relief in the small pair of vases with metal flowers, shown in Figure 5.

The combined achievements of these early factories paved the way for the establishment of the most important of them all, Vincennes-Sévres. Under Louis XV the finance administrator was charged with the responsibility of all the industries of the nation. Through his influence in 1738 two brothers named Dubois from Chantilly, who were ambitious to have a project of their own, succeeded in obtaining a large grant of money, space at the Chateau of Vincennes, even the interest of the king unofficially. Their dishonest management of affairs, however, coupled with their exaggerated pretense of knowledge and debauched behavior, led to their summary dismissal three years later. Fortunately Gravant, an able and industrious associate of theirs, profiting, it is said, by their frequent periods of inebriation, learned their formulas and proposed himself as their successor. His offer was accepted and Charles Adam was appointed director.

A special license was issued in 1745, granting extraordinary privileges to this factory, among them the exclusive right to produce "painted and gilded porcelain with figural representation in the manner of Saxe." A national interest was at stake as England about this time was beginning to make soft-paste porcelain at Bow and Worcester. Heavy penalties were imposed on any who disregarded the injunctions and workmen were prohibited from finding employment elsewhere without written permission. Skilled chemists were engaged

FIG. 7 — VASES *(c. 1752)*. A lovely pair made at Vincennes, decorated with spiral bands of blue and gold. Compare these pieces with those in Figures 6 and 8.

FIG. 8 — PAIR OF JARDINIERES *(1757)*. In the rich rose pompadour color, decorated with landscapes. Made at Sèvres.

All illustrations from the collection of the Philadelphia Museum of Art.

FIG. 9 — APPLE GREEN POTPOURRI VASE *(1757)*. Decorations in the manner of Boucher. From Sèvres.

FIG. 10 — PAIR OF TURQUOISE BLUE CORDED VASES *(c. 1768)*. Scenes represent *Jupiter in the guise of Diana making love to Calisto*, and *Apollo with Leucothoe*. From Sèvres.

to bring about improvements in the paste. Duplessis, the king's goldsmith, was placed in charge of models, and the king's enameler visited the factory one day a week. When, in 1748, a new superintendent of painting was appointed, who filled the workrooms with paintings, prints, and sculpture in a successful endeavor to do away with Oriental models, the last barrier to creative initiative was removed.

In 1753 the factory was designated the *Manufacture Royale de France,* and a new company was formed in which the king retained a one-third interest. New and even more stringent regulations were enacted, and the transfer of the factory to Sèvres was decided upon, to take place three years later. The king took a personal interest in the affairs of the concern, holding an annual exposition of its wares at Versailles, and presiding over the opening sales himself.

In the Vincennes period, 1738-1756, the popularity of porcelain flowers was at its height. A winter garden, entirely composed of these flowers, sprayed with perfume to complete the illusion, was created for Madame de Pompadour at Bellevue. In the flower workshop alone, forty-five artisans, including women and children of all ages, were employed. The most important single piece was a vase and bouquet, three feet high, composed of 470 separate flowers, which Marie-Joseph de Saxe had made for her father in 1749 at a cost of 100 louis. Vases of all kinds ornamented with garlands were fashionable (*Fig. 6*), as were a wide variety of toilette and table pieces. Representations of pheasants or water birds with long beaks were often used, and a few rare pieces were decorated with landscapes (*Fig. 8*). The style, however, changed from day to day. Decorative figure groups, taken

from Boucher, were much in evidence, and yet another aspect of the prevailing fashion is exhibited by the pair of vases decorated with spiral bands of blue and gold (*Fig. 7*).

Meanwhile great advances in technique had been made, and artists were in command of a wide range of colors. The leading attribute of soft-paste porcelain is the remarkable way in which it takes color. The richness of the ground colors, particularly the apple green, turquoise blue, rose Pompadour, and the later dark *blue du roi* of Sèvres, contributed in large measure to the factories' artistic success. Many originated at Vincennes, particularly the beautiful rose Pompadour, which ceased to be employed soon after the factory was moved. Another Vincennes innovation was the attractive use of small reserve areas outlined with gold. These characteristics are all exemplified in the boat-shaped potpourri vase illustrated in Figure 9.

The mark of Vincennes, as of Sèvres, was an interlaced double *L,* the cipher of the king. In 1753, date letters were added, one for each year, and from 1778, the letters were doubled. Decorators' marks frequently accompanied the L's.

Sculpture played an increasingly important role, and many well-known sculptors were employed. Until 1749, figurines were brightly colored, but as soon as the impossibility of competing against Meissen became evident, it was suggested that sculpture without any glaze at all be tried. Thus began an extensive output of figurines in biscuit. Sculpture with color was more or less abandoned from this time on, but a few pieces were made as late as 1777 or later.

After the factory moved to Sèvres, it passed through a long series of financial crises. Almost immediately the king was forced to take over the complete control of the organization. Conditions improved temporarily, but difficulties with workmen and competing factories continued. Meanwhile, kaolin had been found at Saint-Yrieix. The stimulus provided by this new material caused an outbreak of hard-paste porcelain factories, particularly at Paris, Limoges, and Orléans. Trial pieces were made at Sèvres, but industrial production was not attempted until 1772. On the accession of Louis XVI to the throne in 1774, new decrees were issued, but few could be enforced. Times were increasingly troubled, and small factories came to recognize no law but their own. Clignancourt called itself the *Manufacture de Monsieur,* and Vincennes, now making hard-paste porcelain under the Hannongs, the *Manufacture Royale.* Models were stolen from Sèvres, and workmen were enticed away with promises of higher wages. Trade was diminishing and money was scarce.

All during this period, the style of Boucher continued to be followed, but neoclassic elements were creeping in. As early as 1755 "Une urne d'après l'antique, bleu celeste . . ." is recorded in the list of sales at Sèvres, and Falconet, placed in charge of sculpture in 1758, further modified existing trends. A comparison of two pairs of vases illustrated in Figures 6 and 10, in regard to form and to choice of subject matter, indicates the rigid severity of the academic reactionism toward which the style was tending.

In 1789 money was again scarce, and the king contemplated the abandonment of Sèvres. Had he done so, the factory would undoubtedly have been submerged in the tumult of the revolution. He was, however, advised to reduce production by one half, and discontinue all objects of luxury. The court was ruined, and all who refused to conform to the exigencies of the times exposed themselves to insults. The production of hard-paste porcelain had increased enormously, and large pieces were much in demand. After 1780, ormolu mounts were often used to join the component parts of large pieces together, or transform ornamental objects into clocks and mirrors.

After the overthrow of the monarchy in 1792, anarchy reigned at Sèvres as elsewhere. Under changing administrations, funds were low in the treasury, and the quality of the ware, which had already begun to decline under Louis XVI, became increasingly inferior. The classic style had triumphed, and soft paste lost its vogue. Annual expositions continued to be held, but now at the Louvre instead of Versailles. Little that was new or original was created. Since 1800 Sèvres has occupied itself exclusively with the manufacture of hard-paste porcelain.

The ABC's of American Pottery

BY LURA WOODSIDE WATKINS

WHAT HARRY HALL WHITE *did for American glass, Lura Woodside Watkins has done for New England pottery. She has been studying and collecting the ceramic wares produced in America for many years, and has excavated on the site of many early potteries in New England. In this way she has established the existence of potteries at an earlier date and in greater number than anyone had suspected. The results of her investigations have been recorded primarily in The Magazine* ANTIQUES. *These have been not merely in the ceramic field; she is equally recognized as an expert in American glass and has written many articles and two books on that subject. From all this important research it is difficult to select only a single article. We have chosen this one because it reveals a profound knowledge, together with an exceptional ability to synthesize and interpret clearly for the inexperienced collector. It appeared in two parts, in September and October 1942, which are here combined.*

THERE are two distinct periods in the development of ceramic art in America. The first covers roughly the two hundred years up to the War of 1812. During that time, and in remote districts until a later date, traditional folk craft was carried on by potters working in a small way. They used native clays and made no attempt to do more than supply everyday household articles. The finer table wares were brought from England, China, or elsewhere. When the war cut off such importations, America became more self-reliant in its manufactures, and enterprising potters endeavored to produce better grades of earthenware and porcelain. In this second period potterymaking developed from a simple handcraft into a business of factory proportions.

The student of American ceramics will find the same general classification of wares here as elsewhere. He first must know the difference between pottery and porcelain. *Pottery* is opaque. It includes *earthenware* and *stoneware*. *Porcelain*, or *china*, is almost invariably translucent. It may be of two kinds: *hard paste,* a body made of true kaolin or china clay; or *soft paste,* an artificial porcelain in which bone ash or frit is incorporated. The terms hard paste and soft paste should never be applied to pottery.

Almost all American wares fall in the pottery category. Earthenware — red, yellow, or white (common crockery) — are designated according to the clays used. No matter what their glaze color, they should be classified according to the color of the

FIG. 1 — NEW ENGLAND REDWARE JAR with mottled slip glaze and lid handle in form of miniature jug. Dated *1829*. Height, 16 inches. *Collection of Charles D. Cook.*

FIG. 2 — SGRAFFITO PIE PLATE by George Hübener (*Pennsylvania, 1792*). Incised and colored design based on two-headed eagle, with two small peacocks. Diameter, 12½ inches. *Lorimer Collection, Brooklyn Museum.*

FIG. 3 — YELLOWWARE COLANDER with white slip decoration (*new Jersey, nineteenth century*). Yellowware was used chiefly for kitchen utensils except when it served as a base for Rockingham glaze. Height, 5⅛ inches. *Clement Collection, Brooklyn Museum.*

FIG. 4 — FLINT-ENAMEL STANDING STAG (*Bennington, 1853*). Attributed to Daniel Greatbach. Possibly the very example displayed by the United States Pottery Company of Bennington, Vermont, at the New York Crystal Palace Exhibition of 1853. *Formerly in the Charles H. Tyler collection.*

body. Stoneware bodies are gray or buff, although they are sometimes stained brown with red ocher before burning. American stoneware is either salt-glazed or coated with a brown slip (liquid clay) found near Albany.

Redware was the country pottery of the early period and was common in every place where potters set up their wheels. In New England it was the only ware that could be made of the native glacial clay, which was unsuitable for stoneware. Early New Englanders had to import their stoneware from England or from New York, New Jersey, Pennsylvania, or Virginia, where proper materials were found in abundance.

Redware was extremely porous and absorptive and was as a rule covered with a glaze compounded of powdered red lead mixed with clay, fine sand, and water. Plain glaze produced an orange-red, dark-red, or brownish color depending on the color of the ware itself. Brown and black could be produced by adding manganese to the glaze; green by adding oxidized copper filings. Manganese, being cheap and easy to obtain, was widely used; copper was employed sparingly. The charm of redware lies chiefly in the mottlings and colorings of the glaze, and the brushings and dribblings of brown or green flowing down the body of the ware.

Redware was made in this country as early as 1630 and perhaps before, in an infinite number of useful household articles. Characteristic are small cups, bowls, pitchers, and ale mugs. The first wares were potted with a delicacy and finesse that is lacking in the later output.

White or pipe clay was brought from England for the decoration of our early redware. Usually it was diluted and trailed on the surface of the unburned ware by pouring it through a quill inserted in a clay slip cup. In the eighteenth century, and later, this slip decoration was applied to platters, deep dishes, porringers, mugs, bowls, and other forms. Sometimes white clay was used as a coating under the glaze to give the appearance of a light or yellowish ware. In Pennsylvania the Germans incised patterns expressing their folk symbolism on plates thus prepared so that the design appeared in red through the yellow. Touches of other color were also added. This is known as *sgraffito work*. Sgraffito plates are now rare as collectibles but those with simpler ornamentation are comparatively easy to find. Many examples appear in New Jersey, New York, and Connecticut, as well as Pennsylvania. The notched-edge pie plate of Pennsylvania does not seem to have been adopted in northern New England (Barber says it came in vogue about 1790), where decorated examples in other forms are only occasionally found.

Yellow earthenware was produced for the most part from Ohio clay and was used principally for kitchen articles such as we have even today. Yellow or buff clay was also the body of the Bennington flint-enamel ware and the Rockingham types generally called Bennington, although they were made in at least twenty-five other places. The buff clay of Bennington was secured from a local deposit — virtually the only bed of the kind in New England. The name *Rockingham* indicates a brown glaze that was usually applied to the lighter-colored body in a mottled effect. *Flint-enamel glaze* was similar, except that it shows splashes of blue or green mixed with the brown. Flint-enamel ware was a hard, serviceable pottery patented by Fenton at Bennington in 1849.

Fig. 5 — STONEWARE JUG with blue decoration (*c. 1884*), by White and Wood, Binghamton, New York. *New York Historical Society.*

Fig. 6 — EARTHENWARE SAUCEBOAT by Bonnin and Morris *(Philadelphia, c. 1771)*. The first complete piece from this factory to be discovered; first recorded in ANTIQUES, January 1944). *Brooklyn Museum.*

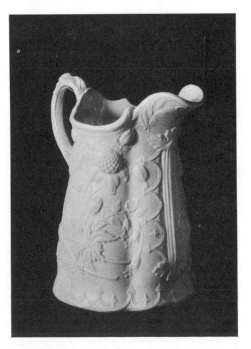

Fig. 7 — PORCELAIN VASE by Tucker and Hemphill, one of a pair, with polychrome and gilt decoration *(Philadelphia, c. 1835)*. *Philadelphia Museum of Art.*

Fig. 8 — PARIAN PITCHER in daisy pattern, marked *Fenton's Works (Bennington, c. 1847)*. *Collection of Joseph H. Park.*

White earthenware, or "C.C." ware, as it was known to the trade, needs no description. Its manufacture began during the War of 1812, but was not successful until more suitable white clays were brought from England.

Stoneware had the qualities lacking in the porous redware, whose lead glaze, moreover, was a menace to health and safety. It was burned at a high temperature with a resulting hard, glassy body. Its glaze or finish was obtained by throwing handfuls of common salt into the kiln at the time of greatest heat in burning. The cooled ware had a slightly pitted surface similar to orange peel — the characteristic mixture of salt-glazed pottery. The earliest stoneware was unglazed inside, but after 1800 it was usually given an interior coating of Albany slip.

More and more, stoneware containers replaced the less practicable redware. In New England and in the frontier states stoneware making was almost wholly a nineteenth-century development. While much of the ware was nicely decorated with incised designs or with animal and floral motifs in cobalt blue it nevertheless soon became an expression of the industrial era rather than the work of individual potters.

In collecting stoneware, unless one has the prime intention of acquiring pieces to show every mark, one should give first consideration to beauty of form and decoration. Pennsylvania and New York potters worked in this medium before 1700, and extant examples prove that the wares were quite similar to stoneware of a later date. New England and western stoneware was made after 1800, when potters used marks. Among the earliest jugs bearing place names are those of Hartford, Boston, and Charlestown. Incised motifs or bands of simple impressed ornamentation were the first types of embellishment. In 1830 it became the fashion to relieve the severity of the ware by painting with blue or brown slip a device of some sort. Designs suggested by familiar flowers, leaves, birds, or animals tended to become more and more elaborate. In the period of greatest competition, after 1850, this kind of expressionism reached its peak.

Early American porcelains are almost exclusively soft paste. Bonnin & Morris of Philadelphia succeeded as early as 1770 in manufacturing such a porcelain. In the early 1800's other potters made spasmodic efforts to establish chinamaking here, but the first American to produce the ware continuously was William Ellis Tucker of Philadelphia. His porcelains, which were markedly French in style, and those of the Jersey Porcelain & Earthenware Company represent the beginnings of present-day American ceramic art.

One of the most noteworthy, if not original, contributions in the field of porcelain making is the *parian ware* made at Bennington. Intended for figure work in imitation of Parian marble, it was fashioned also into vases, pitchers, and other objects. Some of them appear with color — blue, buff, or green — applied in the mold. Parian is defined as a biscuit or unglazed porcelain containing a large percentage of feldspar. At Bennington the quantity was regulated by formula; yet it is difficult to tell by texture or appearance whether examples come under the true parian category. In fact, the vases look like ordinary biscuit or bisque. Nevertheless chemical analysis shows that they contain the requisite amount of feldspar.

Bennington parian offers a field for new collectors. Some of the little figures, such as Red Riding Hood, the praying child, or the girl tying her shoe, are virtually the earliest porcelain figure work attempted in this country. The rarest of these small ornaments is the lamb surmounting a match-box in the form of a Bible. Parian vases, some with backgrounds of color incorporated before firing, are fairly common. They are usually ornamented with applied bunches of grapes. Small oval or rectangular boxes display similar decoration and coloring. Several types of parian pitchers can be identified by the ribbon or medallion mark of the United States Pottery Company. Since a great deal of the best parian was made in England, the novice would do well to familiarize himself with known American forms before committing himself to making a collection.

The Bennington ceramic types have been thoroughly described and illustrated by John Spargo in *The Potters and Potteries of Bennington* and *Early American Pottery and China*. The best-known examples are the fine stoneware jugs and the Rockingham ware. Unless marked, the latter cannot be dependably identified, but the inexperienced collector who leans on marks will find certified specimens. In the mottled brown and yellow Rockingham and the more colorful flint-enamel wares one may run across cow creamers, tobies, book bottles, coachman bottles, and a long list of table and toilet articles, all within a moderate price range. Rare forms are the lions, poodle dogs, and reclining deer. It must be emphasized that a large proportion of Rockingham ware was made in New Jersey, Ohio, and elsewhere, and that hound-handled pitchers, Rebecca-at-the-Well teapots, cow creamers, tobies, and many other forms originated far from Vermont.

The tendency after 1840 was to shape pottery in molds as a means to endless duplication. Nearly all Bennington wares were molded. This conversion to mass production paralleled the mechanization of the glass industry, where the machine press had largely supplanted hand manipulation.

Since the younger generation will perforce collect its antiques from the late nineteenth century rather than from an earlier time, it will be obliged to choose the products of the larger commercial potteries or will be limited to a small selection of red-ware or stoneware. In country districts, especially in the middle west, primitive potteries continued into the eighties or even as late as 1900. And halfway between the commercial and the primitive were the "art potteries."

Stimulated by the exhibitions of ceramics at the Centennial Exposition of 1876, potters with art training began to produce wares with greater variety of glazes. Their creations were a conscious endeavor to capture art as they had studied it in the ancient porcelains of China or the pottery of Greece. Up to that time beauty had been a happy adjunct of objects made for practical purposes. In the work of the art potters, utility was a secondary consideration.

The faience of Chelsea, Massachusetts, glazed in soft tones of green, blue, yellow, or the famous ox-blood red, was made by James Robertson and his sons, Alexander and Hugh, from about 1875 to 1895. In 1896 the pottery was removed to Dedham, where the same family made an excellent crackle ware. Pieces from the Robertson potteries, many of them marked, are still available. The Low Art Tile Company, also in Chelsea, made tiles and decorative panels in a variety of brilliant glazes at about the same period. They were the first ornamental tiles made in America. Numerous other concerns in New Jersey or Ohio later copied the Low methods successfully.

The later period offers prizes for the collector in choice individual pieces from the Rookwood pottery in Cincinnati or in others from shops of lesser importance, such as Keene, New Hampshire. Considerable attention has already been given the American majolica made in large quantities by Griffin, Smith & Hill of Phoenixville, Pennsylvania, about sixty years ago. Its soft coloring and curious shapes were no doubt inspired by the early Whieldon wares. The commercial products of many other works in New York, New Jersey, Ohio, and other points farther west also offer various things of interest to beginning collectors.

The problem of what to collect in American ceramics is one that depends upon individual temperament. The greatest rewards, however, go to the lover of primitive craftsmanship, who may now and then discover unusual and beautiful specimens of early redware and stoneware.

Jasperware and Some of its Contemporaries

BY ALICE WINCHESTER

WHEN HOMER EATON KEYES, *the first editor of* ANTIQUES, *died in 1938, his associate, Alice Winchester, stepped into his place. Readers of the Magazine know that she has not only kept up the high standards he set but has been quick to respond to new tendencies in collecting and to suggest fresh fields for research. She originated what has proved to be one of our most consistently popular features, the monthly picture article, Living with Antiques, which shows antiques as they are daily used and enjoyed in homes throughout the nation. Recently, she has called attention to the special interest of the nineteenth-century decorative arts — a field not exactly unexplored but as yet not generally surveyed. Obliged, as editor, to keep abreast of antiquarian activities along many lines, Miss Winchester has written for the Magazine on numerous topics, though she often remains anonymous. Her article on jasperware, reprinted here from our February 1947 issue, deals with a type of antiques which, as she points out, clearly exemplifies the change of taste that took place in the late 1700's and early 1800's. — R.B.D.*

WRITERS on English ceramics agree in hailing Josiah Wedgwood as a great innovator, and in singling out jasperware as his greatest innovation. It is the ware most commonly associated with his name among collectors, and its fame has spread so far that the veriest tyro recognizes the familiar light blue as "Wedgwood blue" and has the name "Wedgwood ware" on the tip of his tongue ready to apply to any and all ceramic objects with white cameo designs on a colored ground. But not all such objects are jasper, and not all jasper is Wedgwood.

The story of potting in Staffordshire during most of the eighteenth century is the story of a long succession of trials and errors to achieve wares that could compete with porcelain. The porcelain introduced from China and imitated with considerable success at Meissen had the desirable qualities of being white, hard, non-porous, and light in weight. The aim of the Staffordshire potters seems to have been not so much to achieve a true porcelain as to produce wares, earthen or stone, that had those desirable qualities.

The salt-glaze stonewares were a step in this direction — light-weight, non-porous, and not far from white. The cream-colored earthenwares were equally light and impervious and had a richer surface and tone. These had both been perfected by the time Josiah Wedgwood (*1730-1795*) got to experimenting with his more novel inventions — black basalt, *rosso antico* which was

[53]

really a dressed-up version of the old un-glazed red stoneware, buff or cane-colored ware, and finally, jasperware. These were all worked out primarily for ornamental uses, not for practical table wares. In developing jasper Wedgwood was still seeking a hard, white material but wanted it also to have a certain versatility: it was to be modeled in fine relief designs. He experimented with stonewares and others and by 1773 had "a fine white terra-cotta, of great beauty and delicacy, proper for cameos, portraits, and bas-reliefs." A year or two later he discovered the ingredient that gave him what he wanted. It was barite, or sulphate of barium, which has a very high specific gravity. By using more than 50% of this in his mixture with clay and flint he obtained a ware that he called jasper because it was so hard and dense that, like the stone of the same name, it could be polished on a lapidary's wheel. Strictly speaking, jasper is, it would seem, a stoneware, in that it is hard and needs no glaze to make it non-porous; but it is vitrified and in thin enough pieces it has a certain translucence, a quality that characterizes porcelain. In fact, it has often been called a porcelain or semi-porcelain. Actually jasper is jasper, for its essential ingredient makes it different from any other ware.

After achieving the ware itself, Wedgwood exploited it to the full. The details of its development from the first simple candlesticks and inkstands to such creations as the copies of the Portland vase, from the use of solid color to the dip or surface color, the gradations of the seven basic colors and the combinations in three-color effects, the extensive use of antique models for the designs and also of portraits of "illustrious moderns," and Wedgwood's vast production of imposing ornamental pieces, vases, plaques, tea and coffee services, medallions, as well as trinkets and jewelry in jasper, are amply recorded in most writings on English ceramics. Jasper became popularly recognized as the typical Wedgwood ware and has continued to be made by the firm up to the present time.

But the secret of jasper did not long remain a secret. By 1785 the recipes had leaked out and other Staffordshire potters were following them. John Turner (working c. 1756-1786), one of the ablest of the time, has been credited with inventing the jasper formula quite independently of Wedgwood. He produced pieces of various types, including the small seals, cameos, and the like, also portrait busts, and many jugs with a rather distinctive brown-glazed neck and handle. However, his earlier production of this kind lacked barite and so was not true jasper but a fine white semi-vitreous ware that was something between stoneware and true porcelain. After 1790 apparently Turner made real jasper, using the essential ingredient.

But the "secret" formula for jasper had been pirated by other potters by 1785. Perhaps one of the first to adopt it was William Adams c. 1745-1805) of Tunstall, "Wedgwood's favorite pupil." He, at any rate, was one of Wedgwood's most faithful imitators and serious competitors. His jasper was of fine quality, both the ware itself and the relief ornaments. It was of the two kinds, solid color and dip, and was made in various colors, especially a light violet-blue that appears to be a little different from that of any other potter. Adam's jasper, like Turner's, is often, though not always, marked with the maker's surname, impressed. Its manufacture ceased within a few years of William Adams' death in 1805 but was resumed by the firm, which still

FIG. 1 — BULB POT IN ALL-WHITE JASPER. One of a pair, unmarked. In two pieces, with molded decoration and applied vignettes in high relief, very well modeled and undercut. Wedgwood produced some fine pieces in all-white jasper in his early days of experimentation with the ware and was particularly pleased with them.

FIG. 2 — MARKED JASPERWARE. All with white relief decoration, all with ground color of slightly different shades of light blue. *Left to right:* HANDLED CUP, cupid motifs in high relief, marked *Turner* on rim of base. VASE in two pieces, leaf decoration, marked *Adams;* the border of interlaced circles in white relief between raised bands in ground color is typical of Adams' jasper. TEAPOT, classic decoration, swan finial, silver tip, finely modeled, marked *Adams* on base. COVERED VASE in three pieces, same shape and decoration as Adams vase but much heavier in weight and coarser in modeling, marked *Adams & Bromley;* this firm in 1873 succeeded John Adams & Co. of Shelton — no relation of William Adams of Tunstall — and till 1880 produced majolica and a jasper of middling quality, chiefly imitations of late eighteenth-century pieces. COVERED BOWL, playing children motifs, marked *Turner* on base.

exists, in the late 1800's, when jasperware enjoyed a sort of revival of favor.

Among the Staffordshire potters who are recorded as having made jasper in competition with Wedgwood are Palmer and Neale, Elijah Mayer, Josiah Spode II, Enoch Wood, Samuel Hollins. At the same time they and their contemporaries were putting out quantities of wares that were not an attempt to reproduce jasper but were designed merely to appeal to popular taste. The public was no more concerned then than it is now with the composition of its tablewares, and it probably gave relatively little thought to the particular pottery from which they had emanated. It bought what looked attractive and reasonably durable. A considerable variety of stonewares and earthenwares met these requirements.

Many of these had decoration in relief. Some were fashioned as jasper was: the ornament was formed in a plaster mold which carried the intaglio design, then it was "sprigged" on — that is, applied to the body with water. Other kinds were made by forming the entire body of the piece in a mold so that the raised decoration was an integral part of it. Sometimes the two techniques were combined on a single piece. Then, too, color was an important element of the decoration. In jasper and the closely similar wares, color was either mixed throughout the body or applied as an even layer all over the surface. In others it was provided by means of colored glazes. In others it was painted on, often in several hues.

A potter who produced so much ware with relief decoration of a certain type that his name has come to be applied generically to it was Felix Pratt (c. 1775-1810) of Fenton. He also used transfer printing and polychrome painting for decoration, but the name Prattware usually refers to jugs of light-weight, creamy earthenware with a bluish glaze which have molded relief decoration, distinctively colored — scenes, flowers, stripes or other conventional motifs — covering much of their surface. The colors, often brownish orange and dull blue and green, were applied under the glaze and appear rather blurred. Pratt sometimes marked his production with his name, but not always, and some other potters in Staffordshire as well as in Sunderland and elsewhere also produced similar wares.

The stonewares of roughly analogous type are fairly light in weight, hard and smooth, and often with a surface that has almost the mat, waxy quality of jasper. The decoration, both molded and painted, is usually rather more distinct and clean-cut than in Prattware, and the body is usually not glazed, though jugs and other hollow vessels sometimes have a glaze inside or around the neck or handle.

The name perhaps most commonly associated with such wares is Castleford. A pottery was established at Castleford, near Leeds, about 1790 by David Dunderdale. In 1803 it became D. Dunderdale & Co. Its output included creamware and a black ware like basalt, but more widely familiar are its little stoneware teapots, patterned after a contemporary octagonal silver model, with relief decoration and blue borders. Marked examples have been found, but again comparable pieces were produced by other potteries.

Despite their obvious differences, these wares may logically be grouped together in one category. It would probably be stretching a point to suggest that the earthen- and stonewares here considered were inten-

FIG. 3 — THREE STONEWARE TEAPOTS. *Left,* white body trimmed with narrow blue bands, brown medallions with raised classic figures in white on sides, all-white medallions with designs of prunus blossoms in relief around spout and handle; recticulated cover with lion finial; marked *Turner.* Similar in size, shape, cover, and prunus-blossom decoration to a marked Turner teapot in black basalt from Mr. Morris' collection (see ANTIQUES, July 1946, p. 45). *Center,* white body with white relief touched up with blue lines, classic motifs all in white; marked *Heath & Son.* Heath was an old Staffordshire name and several potters carrying it are recorded, including one Lewis Heath working in Burslem in 1802 — about the time this pot was probably made — but references list no Heath & Son. *Right,* white body with white relief, trimmed with lines of rose and blue; very light in weight; classic figures on either side; on base of pedestal on side shown the name *Clulow & Co. Fenton* is impressed. (All other marks noted are impressed on bases of pieces.) Robert Clulow & Co. are recorded as working in Staffordshire in 1802, though their location is variously given as Etruria and Lower Lane, not Fenton. Without the mark this pot might have been called "typical Castleford."

FIG. 4 — MARKED JASPER-LIKE WARES. *Left,* CANDLESTICK, white with blue bands and red and green vine, raised and colored, marked *Chetham & Woolley;* this firm worked at Lane End, Staffordshire, about 1795, producing a dry-bodied ware without glaze or smear called pearlware. *Center,* BASKET, one of a pair, white with raised blue decoration molded with the body, marked *Hackwood & Co.* This mark, and the name *Hackwood* alone, were used by W. Hackwood & Son who operated the works at New Hall from 1842 to 1856. *Right,* SUGAR BOWL, marked *D. D. & Co. Castleford Pottery.*

FIG. 5 — CREAMWARE PLATE. Dull red border, floral center in red and green. Marked *D. D. & Co. Castleford.* Creamware, comparable to that made at Leeds and in Staffordshire, was really quite as typical of Castleford's production as were the stoneware tea services.

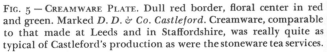

FIG. 6 — STONEWARE BOWLS. White body with molded relief decoration, blue bandings, and medallions in enamel colors, one with a landscape, the other a chinoiserie scene. Though unmarked, these are unusually fine examples of their type.

FIG. 7 — *Left*. STONEWARE PITCHERS. White body, molded relief decoration; unmarked. *Left*, with raised figures on the sides and underglaze coloring on figures and around neck. *Right*, enamel-painted scene under spout; neck and handle coated with colored glaze. These two jugs, though strongly similar, show interesting variations in treatment.

tional adaptations of the more exacting jasperware, a cheaper and more easily produced substitute for the lower-priced market. Rather, all these wares, including the jasper, expressed a certain taste of the period just before and just after the turn of the nineteenth century in England. They were undoubtedly exported in some quantity to this country and are found here today, but are rarely considered as a single category by collectors. Admirers of jasper are inclined to overlook the other types which are really quite closely related to it and to each other in source, period, technique, and taste. John B. Morris of Sauga-

tuck, Connecticut, has recognized this collecting category and has assembled a remarkable group of examples — remarkable not only for its size but for the opportunity it affords for study and comparison. His numerous marked pieces offer unsuspected revelations regarding the makers of these wares, and the entire group shows some surprising similarities as well as differences. The items here illustrated are a small sampling from Mr. Morris' collection, selected with the hope of indicating the scope of the whole and of suggesting the interest that this field of ceramics offers collectors.

FIG. 8 — *Right.* PRATTWARE. *Left,* LIGHTWEIGHT EARTHENWARE jug with raised decoration and underglaze colors: blue bands, green leaf borders, polychrome figures on sides, and *IB 1796* in dull red under spout. Though unmarked, this jug can safely be ascribed to Felix Pratt; the acanthus-leaf borders top and bottom are characteristic of his work, as is the whole piece, for that matter. *Right,* COVERED BOWL, white body with figures and leaves in relief, underglaze polychrome coloring; unmarked; probably of somewhat later date than the Pratt jug.

Staffordshire Records
of Early Modes of Travel

BY ELLOUISE BAKER LARSEN

STAFFORDSHIRE CHINA *transfer-printed with American views was one of the first types of antiques to be extensively collected in this country. Important collections of it existed by 1900, and in 1901 the first classification of the views was published by Edwin Atlee Barber. It was naturally the subject of many articles in* ANTIQUES *from its earliest days, and one of the most prolific contributors of these has been Mrs. Ellouise Baker Larsen. In 1939 she published her book,* American Historical Views on Staffordshire China, *begun as a revision of Barber's book and today the standard reference in its field. She not only listed all the known views and identified the potters who produced them but traced these views to their printed sources in early engravings. Much of this information appeared in* ANTIQUES *before Mrs. Larsen incorporated it in her book. The material that we publish here is condensed from a two-part article by Mrs. Larsen, published in April and June 1936, and illustrates one of the many amusing bypaths which may be explored by the collector of "Old Blue."*

WITH prophetic assurance the Staffordshire potters of England, a century ago, adorned their earthenware with many a portrayal of American modes of transportation. Today these quaint ceramic pictures tell a logical story of our nation's commercial progress from its crudest beginnings to the days when the railroad was well on its way to girdling the country with bands of steel. It is surprising to observe how comprehensive is the series of Staffordshire wares illustrating this development. Each picture conveys its own clear message. In the fol-lowing notes I have sought only to classify the Staffordshire designs and to supply connecting threads of history.

Travel by Land

The earliest colonists traveled on foot, following Indian trails. Pack horses, pack mules, and dog sleds were used for transporting goods. In fact, while in time roads built along the coast permitted the use of stage wagons and coaches, the crude highways of Pennsylvania allowed only pack horses and pack trains until the advent of the Conestoga wagon about 1755.

FIG. 1 — "STATE HOUSE, BOSTON" Potter, Enoch Wood & Sons. Border, floral. Plate, 10 inches. Light blue. A chaise had one seat above the wheels (two or four), no springs, a leather top to protect occupants. It was drawn by one horse. The two-wheeled chaise was similar to the modern sulky.

FIG. 2 — "BALTIMORE EXCHANGE." Potter unknown. One of a series of five views. Border, fruit and flowers. Plate, 10 inches. Dark blue. The Custom House and a branch of the United States Bank had offices in the two wings. Some private coaches used four horses. A coach had four wheels and was entirely enclosed.

FIG. 3 — "UPPER FERRY BRIDGE OVER THE RIVER SCHUYLKILL." Potter, Joseph Stubbs. Border, eagles and flowers. Platter, 18 x 14 inches. Dark blue. Notice the Conestoga wagon with six horses and the covered bridge. Such bridges are almost obsolete today. When this one was built in 1813, it was the longest of its kind in the country. In the background near the bridge is the famous Harding Tavern. The barge is heavily laden with freight. At the right is a rough farm wagon with four wheels and drawn by a pair of horses.

FIG. 5 — "LITTLE FALLS, N. Y." Marked *C.C.* This series has of recent years been credited to William Ridgway. Border, *Catskill Moss*. Deep dish, 9½ by 7½ inches. Light blue. Believed to picture the Mohawk and Hudson River Railroad, which operated the first steam-railway passenger train in New York State in 1831, between Albany and Schenectady, a distance of about seventeen miles. An engraving published in Cincinnati in 1838 resembles this scene. Both depict a locomotive faintly suggestive of an early English type.

FIG. 4 — "BALTIMORE AND OHIO RAILROAD" (*Inclined plane*). Potter, Wood & Sons, Border, shells. Plate, 10 inches. Dark blue. This track was located at the mouth of a coal mine; the windlass at the top hauled the cars up the steep grade by cable. In 1795, at a brick kiln on Beacon Hill, Boston, this idea of using a railway on an inclined plane to carry heavy materials to the bottom of the grade was first put into practice in America. The first practical model of a steam locomotive built for regular service on the Baltimore and Ohio was produced by Phineas Davis, of York, Pa., in June 1831.

The Chaise

Sedan chairs borne by servants were used by the aristocracy long before 1683. Governor Winthrop of the Massachusetts Bay Colony had the distinction of owning one of these chairs, though the Church scorned such display. The horse-drawn chaise (chair) was a development of the sedan form. We see our early nineteenth-century specimen in Enoch Wood's Boston State House (*Fig 1*).

The Coach, Private and Public

One authority states that the first wheeled vehicle in this country was the coach, privately owned, which appeared in the seventeenth century. It was used in town only, as the country roads were too rough. By 1732 coaches had become so numerous in Boston as to excite no comment. A hundred years later, when the Old Blue was made for us in England, the demand for these picturesque equipages had spread throughout this country (*Fig. 2*).

Rough two-wheeled wagons were constructed to transport goods and passengers between the larger towns whenever a sufficient cargo had been accumulated. The first regular transportation of passengers began near Boston, and the first conveyance of mail by land was between Boston and New York. In 1707 stage wagons passed twice a month between New York and Philadelphia carrying freight and people. Part of the trip was made by water. A sailboat was the conveyance from New York Bay to Perth Amboy. Thence the route was accomplished by stage wagon to Burlington, where transfer was made to sailboat bound for Philadelphia. The roads were often mudholes. About three quarters of a century later, the stage wagon was superseded by the more comfortable passenger stagecoach. In 1793 a newspaper advertisement boasted that the new Boston and New York mail coaches were "small, genteel and easy in which four inside passengers will be admitted with smart, good horses and experienced and careful drivers." From 1815 to 1825, one type of stagecoach was designed on the lines of a football. The top became flatter to accommodate baggage, seats were fitted with boards or strips of leather for backs, springs were added or seats were swung on leather straps. From 1810 to 1840 most of the important cities as far west as Pittsburgh operated a continuous line of coaches in countless designs and degrees of comfort, drawn by two or four horses. In 1831 the fastest time made by coach from Pittsburgh to Philadelphia was two and one half days, a great improvement over previous records.

The Conestoga Wagon

The unusual, typically American Conestoga wagon appeared about 1755. When the British General Braddock needed to transport his troops and supplies across the Alleghenies to fight the French at Fort Du Quesne in the Ohio region, a roadway had to be cut through the wilderness. It was thereafter known as Braddock's Road. The Conestoga or Pennsylvania wagons, later called "prairie schooners," since they were the vehicles of the western pioneers, were built for Braddock. Very powerful horses, bred in the Conestoga Valley of Pennsylvania, hauled the wagons. These were long, shaped like a bateau, and were heavily constructed to carry freight and families through the soft mud of the unbroken roads and over the mountains. The top was covered with white cloth. The lower part of their woodwork was always painted blue, while the upper portion was bright red. This coloring was a feature of this wagon,

FIG. 6 — "BROOKLYN FERRY." Potter, Thomas Godwin. Border, morning glory and nasturtium. Plate, 8½ inches. Pink. The only other picture of Brooklyn Ferry made by a Staffordshire potter. The view below, much more modern, was shown in ANTIQUES, March 1933, in an article on Thomas Godwin and the date for his production of these pictures was set between 1845 and 1850. Notice the Conestoga wagon on board.

FIG. 7 — "AQUEDUCT BRIDGE AT LITTLE FALLS." Potter, Enoch Wood & Sons. Pitcher, 9 inches, Dark blue. Border, special floral design made for a series produced to honor the opening of the Erie Canal. At Little Falls the Canal required the building of a solid wall thirty feet high across the Mohawk River. The rapids are shown.

FIG. 8 — "ENTRANCE OF THE ERIE CANAL INTO THE HUDSON AT ALBANY." Potter, Enoch Wood & Sons. Border, above series. Plate, 10 inches. Dark blue. Boat at right laden with freight. Arches in centre were used at the time of the Grand Opening ceremonies. Barge at left is one of the famous passenger boats. Sixty feet long; two cabins. One had eight beds for women. The main cabin, with a long table and lockers, was a dining-room by day and, with mattresses on the lockers, a sleeping room by night. All the buildings depicted in the background are of historical importance.

Figure 6 from the Morse Collection, American Antiquarian Society; all other illustrations from the author's collection.

FIG. 9 — "LANDING OF GEN. LAFAYETTE AT CASTLE GARDEN, NEW YORK, 16″ AUGUST 1824". Potter, R. & J. Clews. Border, large and small flowers. Plate, Dark blue. At Staten Island Lafayette, when he came to America in 1824, was transferred to the *Chancellor Livingston,* called the "pride of the river," and was escorted by a procession of decorated steamers into New York harbor, the *Robert Fulton* leading the way. In this picture, which was apparently taken from a drawing by the artist and engraver Maverick, are to be seen the *Chancellor Livingston* and *Robert Fulton,* stately vessels with masts and flags, and the tugboat *Nautilus.* The roof of Castle Garden at the right is crowded with sightseers. The minutes of the Common Council of New York City, October 11, 1824, record a resolution thanking owners of private vessels who participated in the celebration at the landing of Lafayette. Among the ships named are the *Chancellor Livingston* and the *Robert Fulton,* the latter under Captain Chase. In the picture, the latter flies two American flags, while from the central masthead floats the ship's flag. The six cannon are bravely saluting. The *Cadmus* is the rearmost vessel.

which was kept in continuous use during war and peace for a hundred years until after the rush to California for gold in 1849. The designs differed, some requiring four horses, others six; but all were sturdy and practical (*Fig. 3*).

The Railroad

The first American railroad passenger train consisted of a car like a stagecoach, with one or two stories. It was drawn by horses. From this, the passenger coach of the modern railroad was developed. Various experiments to produce a locomotive operated by steam were tried with indifferent success. According to the most authentic records, the first steam-railway locomotive to be built or to be run in this country on a track was that designed and operated by Colonel John Stevens in 1820. It was small and intended for experiment. (The first steam-railway locomotive built in the United States for regular service came from New York in 1830 for the Charleston and Hamburg Line.) All his life, Stevens worked in the realm of mechanical engineering. A few weeks after Fulton launched his *Clermont* in 1807, Stevens achieved success with his steamboat *Phoenix.*

In 1827 the Baltimore and Ohio Railway received its charter from the Maryland legislature. In 1828 work on track for railways to be operated by horsepower was begun. The next year Peter Cooper made his test with his Tom Thumb engine mounted on a flat car; the following year he had changed his model and made a successful trial trip of thirteen miles, from Baltimore to Elliott Mills, with twenty-four passengers. Thus the Batlimore and Ohio ran the first steam passenger train in America, in August 1830, and proved the practicability of this new means of transportation (*Fig. 4*).

Travel by Water
The Ferry

In early times travelers with horses forded the small rivers on horseback or waited on the bank, sometimes for days, until the stream, swollen by rains, had subsided. But when stage wagons and, later, stagecoaches appeared, it was necessary to ferry them across. The colonies provided ferries and charged toll for every kind of conveyance taken over. There were three types of ferries: first, a simple canoe, or two tied together; second, a wide, flat-bottomed boat equipped with oars or poles; third, a flat boat pulled across the stream by a rope or propelled by sail power.

Later each state built its own bridges. In 1804 Stevens designed a twin screwed propeller steamboat which he and his friends used around New York. It has been called the first ferryboat to Hoboken, though Stevens did not consider it a public ferry. In 1812 Fulton launched his first ferryboat which marked the beginning of our present ferry system.

The Canalboat

Deep interest was shown in travel on canals before the period in which this form of transportation flourished, 1817-1845. Railroads had not yet started (*1817*). On the coast and near the rivers freight was sent by boat whenever possible. But it was imperative to find a cheap overland transportation. The first American canal was dug in Orange County, New York State, in 1750. Subsequently several short local canals were opened in the states along the Atlantic. After long agitation, in 1817 the legislature of New York provided for a canal to connect Lake Erie and the Hudson. Work was begun during that year. As sections of the waterway were finished, stupendous celebrations took place. In

1819 the first canalboat to carry passengers made the trip from Rome to Utica, a distance of fifteen miles each way. The barge, which was patterned after the early keel boat, was towed by a horse on an embankment beside the Canal. Many important dignitaries, entertained with band music, rode back on the barge the following day from Utica. Thousands watched the sight.

In 1823 the Canal from Utica to Rochester was finished, and the event was duly announced by newspapers all over the country. Eighty-four passengers were entertained on the first trip between the two villages. Later in the same year the Canal was opened into the Hudson.

For years the Erie Canal was a profitable enterprise. It brought to the Hudson and thence to New York City trade from western New York and Lake Erie, to whose waters Ohio was connected by two long systems of canals, both begun in 1825 — the Miami Canal, running from Cincinnati on the Ohio north along the Great Miami River through Toledo to Lake Erie, finished before 1829, and the Ohio Canal from Portsmouth on the Ohio following the Scioto River, thence north to Cleveland on Lake Erie, completed in 1833. The Wabash and Erie Canal in Indiana, begun in 1832, and finished in 1853, was the third large canal system in the Middle West, and the longest in the country. From Evansville on the Ohio it extended north to Terre Haute, where it followed the Wabash River across the State of Indiana, joined the Miami Canal near the Maumee River in Northwestern Ohio, and entered Lake Erie at Toledo.

But the canals could not compete with the advantages of the railroads, which were now being built through the state. The Wabash and Erie came too late and was a financial failure. Pennsylvania was the first colony to agitate the idea of canals before 1700, but was one of the last to finish its large ditch from Philadelphia to Pittsburgh, built from 1826 to 1834. The third ambitious system in the East, intended to join the coastal states with the interior, was the Chesapeake and Ohio Canal, originally suggested by Washington in 1784. Begun in 1828, it was carried to Cumberland by 1850; but the plan of extending it to Pittsburgh and the Ohio was never realized. By 1854, thirty-seven years after the Erie Canal, the first important artificial waterway, was begun, transportation of passengers and freight *via* canals had diminished to insignificance.

Speed and improved facilities for handling traffic had won. The Iron Horse continued to push his way west until, in 1869, he had crossed the continent and had proved his superiority over the prairie schooner. The natural waterways became the scene of nautical expriments. Here the inventors of American sail- and steamboats wrote into our early maritime annals their varying records of fortune and misfortune.

Sailboat and Steamboat
Rivers and Atlantic Ports

The story of sail- and steamboating in America is a fascinating one, and in this realm the Staffordshire potters adhered to their early policy of recording our mechanical aids to travel. Following the universal popularity of the canoe, there appeared on the Connecticut River primitive pole boats. On the Susquehanna and the Delaware, the most important of the crude craft to drift with the current were the arks. Flatboats originated in the Ohio Valley. Keel boats, created in the East, were used everywhere along the coast and later in the

Middle West to carry passengers and freight. Gradually these developed into barges, as cabins with sleeping quarters were added. Keel boats and barges, propelled by sail, towrope, or crew using iron-tipped poles, could operate against the current.

In 1786 on the Delaware River, John Fitch successfully demonstrated his invention, the first American steamboat. The next year he was granted a monopoly of steam transportation in Delaware, New York, Pennsylvania, and Virginia for fourteen years; but, as he was unable to fulfill the conditions, he lost the privilege. He built five boats, each an improvement over its predecessor. During the summer and fall of 1790, one of his craft with a cabin for passengers, capable of traveling eight miles an hour and covering eighty miles a day, operated on the Delaware River as a passenger boat. This was the first steamboat to aid transportation. During his later life, in the wilderness of Kentucky, Fitch built a steam engine on a track. It *may* have been the first railroad locomotive built in America.

From 1802 to 1807 Colonel John Stevens of Hoboken, New Jersey, made several steamboats, but his most successful model, the *Phoenix,* being completed in 1807 a few weeks later than Fulton's *Clermont,* was compelled to operate in the vicinity of Philadelphia, since the monopoly of the New York waters had been transferred from Fitch to Chancellor Livingston and Fulton. Her trip from New York to Philadelphia made the *Phoenix* the first American steamboat to travel on the ocean.

Robert Fulton, an inventor from Philadelphia, after a fifteen-year study of engineering in England, received in 1801 the benefit of practical advice from Chancellor Livingston, who, in 1798, had been building steamboats with Colonel Stevens and Nicholas Roosevelt, a New York builder. Fulton's *Clermont* was the result. It was the first *successful* steamboat assembled in this country. The engine was brought from Messrs. Boulton Watt & Co., England. Charles Brown, a shipbuilder of New York, constructed the hull, and Fulton supervised the work. The credit for the invention of steamboats is given to Fitch, who created the designs and learned from his own mistakes. Nicholas Roosevelt received the patent for his invention of paddle wheels. Fulton improved upon all of the designs of the sixteen steamboats built in this country before the *Clermont* and produced the first practical steamer capable of giving reliable service. In 1811 the public rebelled against the monopoly of the Livingston-Fulton Company over steam navigation in New York waters. In 1824 the matter was fought out in court. Chief Justice John Marshall repealed the monopoly and declared such privileges illegal.

Twenty years before the Revolutionary War, discontented people from the East had begun to open fresh trails through the wilderness in search of new homes. During the War and for years after, white populations from North Carolina and Virginia crossed the mountains into Kentucky and Tennessee. New Englanders deserted their own states for the western sections of New York and Pennsylvania, or pushed on into Ohio. They cultivated farms and raised bountiful harvests. But the difficulty of reaching Eastern markets over mountains and through forests was serious. The Ohio and Mississippi Rivers, however, afforded travel and transportation routes for many years until, by 1860, the railroads had virtually absorbed the business of the sections

FIG. 10 — "UNION LINE." Potter, Wood & Sons. Border, shells. Plate, 10 inches. Dark blue. The Union Line apparently had most of the passenger patronage while it operated between New York and Philadelphia. Each trip occupied twenty-three hours. Boats leaving New York at 11 A.M. one day reached Philadelphia the next morning at 10. The passengers had variety added to their water trip by a stop at New Brunswick and a stagecoach ride to Trenton, where they spent the night. The accuracy of ceramic portrayals of vessels may be judged from the fact that the scenes of Figures 7 and 8 are virtually identical.

FIG. 11 — "PENNSYLVANIA." STEAMBOAT, PITTSBURGH. Potter, R. & J. Clews. Picturesque Views series. Border, flowers and birds. Plate, 10½ inches. Mulberry. This steamboat was built at Pittsburgh in 1823; the engine was high pressure; tonnage, 107. In 1827 the boat was discarded because of inefficiency. It is recorded as "worn out." Notice the two flatboats at the left and the covered barge in the right center. The city of Pittsburgh lies in the background.

FIG. 12 — "SANDUSKY." Potter unknown. Border, floral. Platter, 16½ by 13 inches. Dark Blue. Same series as Figure 10. The ship in the foreground is clearly marked *Henry Clay*. No maritime records list this boat on the Great Lakes; but at a period later than we usually ascribe to this series of Staffordshire views, *Henry Clay*, a paddle steamer, is reported, built at New York and operated on the Hudson. It was burned in 1852. A lithograph of N. Currier in that year pictures the burning of the *Henry Clay* near Yonkers.

crossed by the two rivers. The early days of river travel developed various modifications of the flatboat, a craft peculiarly suited to this locality and its requirements. An especially distinctive Ohio product was the "broadhorn," a flat-bottomed boat with an oar protruding from each side like a horn, and another at the rear for steering. From the keel boat was developed the Ohio packet for freight and passengers, equipped with a mast, sails, and a crew, who sometimes rowed or towed the boat. Louisville, Cincinnati, and Pittsburgh maintained a slow schedule of packet service. Enclosed barges with sails transported enormous quantities of produce down the rivers to agents in New Orleans, who trans-shipped the cargoes to Eastern markets.

In 1765, Pittsburgh could boast of a boatyard. Pack horses and wagons hauled timber from Philadelphia, and crude boat building became an industry of the interior. In 1817, before steamboats operated on the Ohio, the whole freight and passenger regular traffic on this river was taken care of by twenty barges and one hundred and fifty keel boats. In addition, from 1788, when the great migration toward the West began, until 1840 thousands of emigrants annually floated downstream in flatboats, each enclosed like a house. But until 1829 travel was so slow that *twelve months* was the time required for a freight barge to make a round trip to New Orleans and back to any Ohio town.

Livingston and Fulton tried to gain the monopoly of water routes all over the United States, but public sentiment against it was widespread and intense. Through the Governor of Louisiana, they received sole right to operate steamboats in that locality if Fulton would send thither one or more boats. Straightway the latter en-

gaged Nicholas Roosevelt to build a steamboat at Pittsburgh. In 1811 the *New Orleans*, with paddle wheels and two masts, was completed and started down the two rivers toward the South. But she was three months in reaching her destination, New Orleans. Her upstream record was so unsatisfactory that she was held as a packet for Southern service. However, the *New Orleans* was the first steamboat to operate on any interior stream. In 1816 Henry Shreve built the double-decker *Washington* at Wheeling, Virginia (West Virginia became a state in 1863). In 1817 he made a round trip from Louisville to New Orleans and thus proved that a steamer could navigate upstream as well as down on the Ohio-Mississippi. This feat marked the beginning of steamboating in this section. Fulton had died in 1815, but his company brought action against Shreve for violation of the Louisiana monopoly. When in 1819 the courts denied the company's claims, the rivers were open to public use. The building and operation of steamboats brought enormous increase of business to the interior.

The year 1817 is memorable in the annals of American travel. The Erie Canal was begun. The National Turnpike, financed by the government and covering part of the original wilderness route known as Braddock's Road, was completed from Washington to Wheeling. In August of that year, a stagecoach from the Atlantic Coast reached Wheeling, the first time a coach had traveled along the Turnpike to the Ohio border. Again in 1817 Henry Shreve, in his steamboat *Washington*, demonstrated that a round trip could be made between New Orleans and Louisville, and thus inaugurated a new era of interior steamboat travel.

The Atlantic Ocean

In 1838 Samuel Cunard, fifty-year-old Quaker of Philadelphia, began active development of his long-cherished plan for a mail steamship service from Liverpool to Halifax and Boston. For several years steam vessels had been crossing the Atlantic; but Cunard's innovations were so important to transportation that the year 1840, which marked the appearance of his line of steamers, is outstanding. His was the genius that opened the way for the advancement of steam transportation on the Atlantic.

Cunard, agent for the East India Company in Halifax, went to England, where he interested three men, Napier, a prominent marine engineer in Glasgow, and George and David McIver, important British steamship owners. Cunard secured from the Admiralty the contract to carry mail between England and America, at first in three steamers, later in four, sailing twice a month during eight months in the year, once only in winter, for the annual sum of four hundred and twenty-five thousand dollars. Gradually Cunard attracted the best of the passenger and freight trade. His four side-wheel steamers of moderate size built on the Clyde were exactly alike, a popular gesture since the vessels of any one company had hitherto shown no uniformity. The four Cunard ships were the *Britannica*, first to be launched; the *Acadia*, fastest of the quartet; the *Caledonia;* and the *Columbia*, the first and for years the only one to be wrecked.

The ships had two decks. The upper one was occupied by the officers' quarters, the padded cow-house for the cow that fur-

FIG. 13a — "GENTLEMEN'S CABIN" (*Three passengers and a servant*). Potter, James and Thomas Edwards. Gravy boat, 5½ inches long. Brown. No ship medallions. Border on tray, four medallions of *Caledonia*. Ladle, one of *Caledonia*. On cover, two medallions of *Columbia*.

FIG. 13b — DETAIL OF GRAVY BOAT.

nished milk for invalids, women, and children, the galley, the bakery, and coops for poultry of all kinds. (All the comforts of home.) The main deck had two dining saloons, rooms for one hundred and fifteen cabin passengers, and everything else considered essential to luxury. Two hundred and twenty-five tons of cargo, at special rates, could be transported by these ships. The Cunard Line earned a reputation for handsome ships, for regularity in sailing, and for special attention to safety.

The Cunard Line views on Staffordshire are called *Boston Mails.* They were made by the firm of James and Thomas Edwards at Kiln Croft Works, Burslem, England, before 1842. The border shows medallions of the ships, though more or less latitude in their design seems to prevail *(Fig. 13).*

Fortunate for us that the Staffordshire potters so industriously recorded the American scene of a century ago! They were, of course, prompted to the undertaking by considerations of the profits to be derived from the growing markets of the New World. But in the long march of a century they have profited posterity far beyond the measure of their own brief gains. Naturally the potters selected the scenes for their transfer pictures with an eye toward popular appeal. Scanning the range of their subjects, we find that American transportation held their attention throughout the period in which they depicted our life on their wares. A hundred years ago many of our present comfortable modes of travel existed in embryo. Fortunately, the Staffordshire potters preserved for us a more or less continuous pictorial record of travel evolution.

Early Ceramic Flower Containers

BY NINA FLETCHER LITTLE

NINA FLETCHER LITTLE's *antiquarian interest covers a broad field. Her enthusiasm for early architecture led her to a special study of the decorative painting of interiors and from there to other unexplored aspects of American painting. She has contributed articles to* ANTIQUES *on dating New England houses and on lesser-known nineteenth-century American painters. Early in her collecting days she developed a special interest in English ceramics, and by her characteristically thorough mastery of the subject established herself as an authority. From her numerous articles on that subject we have selected this one, which offers an unusual approach to the work of English and Continental potters.*

THE love of flowers seems to be innate and universal in man, whose first home, the Bible says, was where "the Lord God planted a garden eastward of Eden," between four flowing rivers. Ever since that Paradise was lost, "who loves a garden still his Eden keeps."

The rulers of Egypt, Babylonia, and other ancient states imported rare trees and plants to grace their palace grounds and halls, and their craftsmen created magnificent flower containers. The earliest songs of mankind celebrated the loveliness of flowers along with the courage of warriors; the Cuckoo Song, England's oldest (*c. 1250*). was a paen of praise for "icumen" summer with its flowers and birds. Alexander Neckan wrote in the second half of the twelfth century: "A garden should be adorned on this side with roses, lillies, and marigolds, on that side with parsley, sage, rue, and cresses. Let there also be beds enriched with onions, leeks, and garlic."

Throughout ancient and medieval times in nearly all countries flowers were the source of decorative design, were used for personal adornment, for perfumery, and in religious ritual. Flowerpots are dug up in the oldest ruins. The phrase "garden spot of the world" was used to describe Rome during the Empire, and Roman conquerors of Britain improved English gardens.

Early in the sixteenth century such flowers as the acanthus, anemone, bachelor's button, snapdragon, sweet william, and others equally familiar, were cultivated in geometrical English garden beds. About this time flowers were used for decoration in the home. A Dutch physician who traveled through England in 1560 wrote, "their chambers and parlours strawed all over with sweete herbs refreshed mee, . . . their nosegays . . . in their bed chambers and privyrooms with comfortable smell cheered mee up, and entyrelye delyghted all my sences."

[71]

Toward the end of the seventeenth century, formalism in garden arrangement began to give way to naturalism. Although containers for flowers had been used to some extent from early times, the eighteenth century, with its reawakened interest in art-in-nature, was the great era of decorative floral arrangements both on the Continent and in England. Pots and vases in many odd shapes were developed; some were embellished with very fine painted decoration executed at the great porcelain factories of Germany, France, and England. Ingenious devices were designed to hold the plants in the proper positions, some of them more amusing than esthetic.

The flower containers of this period may be classed in three main groups: those intended to display cut flowers, those made to contain bulbs or roots, and those used to hold flowering shrubs. In the first group, containers of the vase type are probably the most numerous and varied, and their popularity has continued undiminished until the present day. Mantel garnitures consisting of three covered jars and two beakers, the latter for holding flowers, were imported into Europe from China early in the eighteenth century. These were carefully copied by the Dutch in their famous blue-and-white Delft ware, whose pearly body was made to resemble as closely as possible the oriental porcelain.

Some of the flower holders may also be included in the second group, since they were devised to hold either bulbs or cut flowers, or both at the same time. These pots were made with cuplike openings to support the bulbs, and likewise with small round holes in which to place flower stems.

Of the myrtle pans and bough pots which make up the third group, the former were shallow containers of graduated sizes for holding various evergreens. The latter were large pots in which to place sprays of flowering shrubs or trees designed for use near the hearth or in front of the fireplace.

Flower holders were made during the eighteenth century at all the great German factories, including Meissen, Nymphenburg, and Strasbourg. They were also made in France, at Sèvres and Vincennes and other factories, and at all the large potteries in England. At Bow and Chelsea were made many types of vases, some in fantastic shapes, some combined with beautifully executed little figures, for use as mantel and table ornaments. From Worcester and Derby also came handsome beakers and jars.

One English potter was especially interested in horticulture, and it is through his letters, and the products of his factory, that we are given a contemporary glimpse of the important rôle that flower arrangements played in eighteenth-century England. This man was Josiah Wedgwood, whose son John became the first treasurer of the Royal Horticultural Society of London, and one of whose daughters married Doctor Robert Darwin and became the mother of Charles Darwin, the great English naturalist. Wedgwood operated his pottery in Staffordshire from 1760 until his death in 1795, and during that time lavished a great deal of time and thought on his vases and root pots. He sought the advice of his customers and friends as to the styles which they preferred, and designed his pots accordingly. Some of his titled patrons, as he wrote to his partner Thomas Bentley, liked those containers with spouts, because "they say that sort keep the flowers distinct and clever." In the same letter, dated July 29, 1772, he wrote, "Vases are furniture for a chimney-piece, bough pots

FIG. 1 — PERSIAN FLOWER VASE (*thirteenth century*). This type of vase with its tubular spouts was a great favorite, and was made in many variations, particularly at Delft in Holland. *From the Walters Art Gallery, Baltimore.*

FIG. 2 — PAIR OF CHELSEA VASES (*1753-1756*). Made in the form of eel pots with bulrushes in natural colors at either side, and modeled figures of ducks with green, yellow, and pink plumage. Red anchor mark. *Height,* 10 inches. There is endless variety in the vase type of container. Many examples of intricate design were made at the factory of Stratford-le-Bow in East London, with delicately modeled flowers applied to the body, and lavish use of scrolled curves on handles and base. Hexagonal vases and beakers, handsomely painted, and reminiscent of those imported from China were made at Worcester. The Chelsea factory made many vases of the sort illustrated here, of fantastic shapes, and decorated with examples of their famous modeling. *From the Museum of Fine Arts, Boston.*

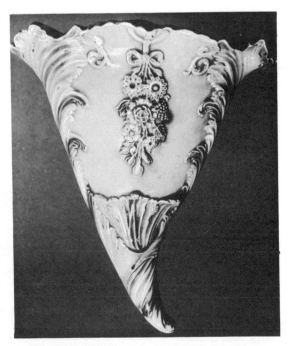

FIG. 3 — MARSEILLE FAIENCE POT FOR HOLDING CUT FLOWERS (*1760*). Chinoiserie decoration of rococo type, painted in bright colors. Marked *VP* in the familiar monogram of the factory of Veuve Perrin. *Height,* 7½ inches. Many flowerpots of this delightful type were made on the Continent during the second half of the eighteenth century, with round holes spaced at intervals to hold the flower stems. Note the holes in edge of back rim so that the pot might be either hung on the wall or placed on a table. The back is flat. *From the Museum of Fine Arts, Boston.*

FIG. 4 — FLOWER HORN OF WHIELDON TYPE (*1760-1780*). Cream-colored earthenware with a variegated glaze. *Height,* 8 inches. These flower horns are also found in white salt-glazed stoneware. They were made to hang on the wall. An example holding hyacinths appears in an eighteenth-century print. *From the Museum of Fine Arts, Boston.*

FIG. 5 — FIVE-SECTIONED FLOWER
HOLDER, PROBABLY BRISTOL (*late
eighteenth century*). *Height,* 7½
inches. These odd containers are
found with slightly differing
forms and decoration, but usually
painted in the browns, greens,
and blues peculiar to the old Bristol Delft decorators. Five-pointed
flower horns were also made at
the Leeds Pottery toward the end
of the eighteenth century, copied
from earlier designs in queen's
ware. Although at first glance
they appear stiff and angular,
they lend themselves to surprisingly graceful floral effects. *From
the Author's Collection.*

FIG. 6 — WEDGWOOD JASPER BOUQUETIER (*late eighteenth
century*). Mauve ground with figures in white relief.
Height, 8¾ inches. Wedgwood specialized in flower containers of all sorts, and many patterns which were popular on tableware were used also for flower, root, and
bough pots. Animal heads, masks, and dolphins were
used for handles. Adaptations of classical subjects were
employed on his famous jasper pieces. In 1781 large lots
of Wedgwood's myrtle pans and bouquetiers were sold
at Christie's in London for very moderate prices. *From
the Museum of Fine Arts, Boston.*

for a hearth, under a slab or marble table. I think they can never be used one instead of another." Of the materials which he used, creamware — perforated, festooned, or enameled — was one of the most popular. Cane color, black basalt with reliefs in red, and jasper in many different shades were used. We find such descriptions as "bouquetiers of red and white biscuit," "myrtle pans of cane-leaf pattern," "flower jars of purple and green enameled," and "bulbous root-pots in pebble and gold." The wholesale price of the latter in 1775 was seven shillings six-pence each. Other prices varied from "dice-worked flower pots at one shilling," to "blue-ground flower pots with griffin heads and laurel festoons, eight inches high, at fifteen shillings each."

After the first quarter of the nineteenth century many of these delightful flower holders went out of fashion, vases alone holding their popularity through the Victorian era. If some of the old shapes could be revived, they would lend charm and originality to flower arrangements of our twentieth century.

FIG. 7 — PAIR OF BOW-FRONT TULIP POTS BY WILLIAM BADDELEY (*1800*). Unglazed buff body of very fine texture, ornamented with delicately molded reliefs in white, blue, and chocolate brown. Dolphin knobs in bright green. Marked *Eastwood. Height,* 7½ inches. Mantel garnitures were frequently made in sets of three, one large pot or vase for the center, and smaller ones for either end. So many of these have become broken or separated that we rarely find a complete set today. This illustration shows the two end pieces of such a garniture; the center pot is somewhat larger, and has slightly more decoration. These semicircular pots could be combined into one round piece, and used to advantage as a center decoration for the dining table. *From the Author's Collection.*

FURNITURE

The Windsor Chair

BY WALLACE NUTTING

No other piece of American furniture has inspired so much affectionate regard and enthusiastic research as the Windsor chair. Wallace Nutting, whose name is probably better known to the public than any other writer on American furniture, made a special study of Windsors in the early days of collecting, and published his book, American Windsors, *in 1917. He was among the contributors to the first number of* Antiques *in January 1922, and this article appeared the following month. Along with the preparation of the numerous publications which occupied him during the 1920's, Mr. Nutting found time to send contributions to* Antiques *about once a year during that period. His activities as collector, student, and writer were of great influence in inspiring others to explore the then little-known field of American antiques. The Wallace Nutting collection of American furniture was purchased by J. P. Morgan and given to the Wadsworth Atheneum at Hartford, Connecticut. His three-volume* Furniture Treasury *(1928 and 1933), with its five thousand illustrations, comes closer to being the American equivalent of Macquoid & Edwards'* Dictionary of English Furniture *than anything else we have except Miller's* American Antique Furniture, *which appeared in 1937. Wallace Nutting also wrote* Furniture of the Pilgrim Century *(1921 and 1924) and the* Clock Book *(1924). While the extent of our knowledge of specific cabinetmakers and local styles has broadened greatly in recent years, Nutting's work offered a secure foundation on which to build, and all students must feel a sense of personal debt for his indispensable contribution to the history of American furniture.*

THE origin of the Windsor chair is not certainly known, but its English home is in Bucks, the center of its manufacture being High Wycombe in that shire, a little north of Windsor. As the chairs spread, in their use, to Windsor, and as they went down to London by boat from Windsor, in some cases, it is apparent that the name may have originated in that way.

The English Windsor is very crudely turned by a foot lathe, which cuts only on the down stroke. A spring board attached to a tree reverses the motion of the lathe when the foot pressure is released. The turners work under tepees of boughs in a beech wood, a section of which they have bought. They are called bodgers or botchers, and it may be owing to their rough work that the meaning of that word has been extended. Up to recent years they sold the legs for two pence apiece to the assemblers. The wood for the legs is not sawed but split out and rough shaped by a boy helper. The seats are roughly sawed and put out to be shaped as a cottage industry. They are quite often made of elm because it does not split easily. The seat is thin, and consequently cannot be boldly shaped. The leg is placed near the corner of the seat and is more nearly perpendicular than in the American chair. Some of the finer designs had cabriole legs in front and rather handsome middle stretchers. These features established a probable date of the first distinctive English Windsors in the Queen Anne period.

The plain stick leg driven into a wooden seat like a milking stool is a true, though crude, Windsor, and its origin in this simple form without a back dates from remote antiquity and is still in common use in benches and stools in frontier districts or in old eddies of civilization like the Tennessee mountains, where true Windsor forms are still used for dining table settees without backs.

The English Windsor seems to have attained its majority in adapting for the center of its back a pieced splat, taken from the more elegant early Dutch or Queen Anne type.

A Windsor may be defined as a stick-leg chair, with a spindle back topped by a bent bow or comb.

The English type soon added to the central splat plain turned spindles on each side to form a "sack-backt" chair convenient for sustaining an outer garment like a shawl, or even a plain sack, as a kind of temporary upholstery to ward off the cold.

In America the Windsor chair appears first to have been made in Philadelphia. It speedily acquired a great popularity, and was copied by many makers in New York, New Haven, Providence and Boston in some of its forms. One form, the so-called blunt arrow leg, with a somewhat crude base turning above the foot, was the earliest

pattern and seems to have failed to appeal to New Englanders. The American makers entirely abandoned the English splat. In fact, some English examples, like Goldsmith's chair, had already abandoned it.

The back as made in America was all spindles. Owing to the great abundance of pine in America, a rarer wood in England, the American type became established with the pine seat, two inches in thickness as against the English inch or less. This thickness was primarily adopted to guard against splitting. For the same reason the holes for the legs were bored farther from the edge than was the English custom. But to secure an equally broad and stable base with the English it was then necessary to insert the legs with a much greater rake in the pine seat. Thus incidentally the two greatest charms of the American Windsors were discovered through necessity. They are the deep, fully-shaped seat made possible by the use of pine, and the sharply raked (splayed) leg made necessary by the use of pine.

The spindles in America were usually of hickory (white walnut). In the north they usually tapered both ways from a bulb, and were whittled, not turned, in the early examples, before the invention of the back rest for the lathe made possible the turning of long, slender spindles. In holding the spindles in the hand for whittling them down, or even in placing them in the vise of a shaving horse, it was natural to whittle or shave each way from the hand that held the spindle; hence the bulbous spindle became naturally established. Stocky Philadelphia spindles could be turned. The bow, hoop or round back as it is indifferently called was bent from hickory saplings or white oak, when green, without the softening assistance of water or steam.

Fig. 1 — GROUP OF CHAIRS showing the six variations of backs, of which all other American types are variants. Four of them — *a, b, c,* and *d* — originated in Philadelphia. New England types are represented by *e* and *f,* the latter a direct copy of an English Windsor back. *Formerly in the collection of J. Stogdell Stokes.*

The seasoning took a longer time by this old method. Often no form was used, but a withe was bent and the ends thrust through the post holes of a fence in the pasture in the spring, to be gathered in the fall for making chairs when nothing else pressed for action.

The shape of the side bulbous rungs was adopted to afford plenty of wood where they were bored for the middle rung or stretcher. The bulbous middle stretcher, adopted after the early elaborate Queen Anne stretcher went out, was doubtless an accident, a side spindle seized in haste to complete a chair, and found graceful after the fact. Of course the stretchers were tapered to secure lightness, strength at the center, and to afford a neat connection with the leg.

In the Windsor chair as it got its full American development the three points of importance are the legs, the seat, and the back.

The legs in good styles are fully two inches in diameter at the largest bulb, that is the bowl of the vase, and the vase shape must be very bold and graceful, tapering at the small points to seven-eighths of an inch.

These and other dimensions are given after the measurement of a vast number of the best old chairs.

The taper, or lower end of the leg, may be a plain straight taper (conic section) or in the Rhode Island variant, which we do not count as quite desirable, a slightly hollowed taper. The legs rake about four inches from a point on center, two and a half inches from the edge of the seat. The shaping of the seat should cut a full inch, that is, half way through. The saddle should be the full thickness of the seat. A great variety of backs are found, most

of them good. Many of the best types have two bracing spindles running into a bob-tail in the seat. This extension of the seat in side chairs is a part of the seat. In wide chairs, as most arm chairs, the grain of the seat runs cross-wise rather than from front to back; consequently when the bob-tail for the brace is used, it must be mortised into the seat.

The spindles are graduated to the size of the chair. Coarse spindles, or a small number, are a demerit, nine for a plain-backside chair, and ten including the two bracing spindles for the bob-tailed chair, being the ideal number (though there is no objection to one more).

The construction of the Windsor involves many delicate adjustments. The best cabinet maker was driven distracted by the effort to get all the curves and angles. The chair could only be made in fine form by specially-trained men. For instance, the seat slants backward. The arm rail slants still more. Every spindle from the center of the back to the last under the arm is bored at a different angle, and is slanted in two directions. An eighth of an inch too much or too little in the bow gives coarseness or weakness.

The bow when bored for the spindles is very much cut away, and will break unless the best wood, carefully worked, is used. Most of the old bows cracked.

The New England arm, the only thing contributed to the Windsor outside of Philadelphia, was a beautiful piece of work—the one-piece bow and arm, which added only four ounces to the weight of a side chair. But at least ninety per cent of them broke at the bend of the arm, where it was bored for a spindle. The low double back, that is the style having a bow above the arm rail, was the commonest and the most

FIG. 2 — WRITING-ARM WINDSOR CHAIR (*pre-Revolutionary*). An interesting example, with comb back and slide below drawer. Originally belonged to the Reverend Richard B. Salter of Connecticut. *Collection of Mrs. Frank J. Sheldon.*

FIG. 3 — ARMCHAIR with braced one-piece back and arms (*New England, c. 1760*). In its original condition except for refinishing, this chair combines all the finest qualities of the Windsor. It has the rare knuckle arms, braced back, continuous arm, nine graceful spindles with slight swelling, and quite perfect arm supports, leg turnings, and underneath stretchers. The bow back has a delicate beading. *Davenport Collection, Lawrence Art Museum.*

FIG. 4 — COMB-BACK ARMCHAIR, a fine example of this type. Seven spindles pass through the shaped low back to support the gracefully curved top rail with scrolled ears. The double-curved arm, with knuckle entirely carved on the thin arm itself, is most effective. The incut at the sides of the seat is so far back that the armposts are necessarily sharply raked, contrasting with the less pronounced splay of the legs. *Davenport Collection, Lawrence Art Museum.*

FIG. 5 — FAN-BACK, BRACE-BACK WINDSOR, which shows a well-shaped tailpiece.

uncomfortable chair ever made. The seat was often only thirteen and seldom more than fifteen inches deep.

The great Philadelphia comb back was a fine man's chair. The seat was from twenty to twenty-three inches wide. The arm as a rule was not carved but boldly scrolled. The ear of the comb was generally carved with a strong spiral, having one more whorl than the other types. The spindles were usually plainly tapered rather than bulbous, as in the type which became popular in the north. The arm rail was either bent or sawed. If sawed it was in three parts, the center piece overlapping the other two, and being shaped. The chair was sometimes made with no comb or bow above the arm rail, and in that form was the ancestor of the very common degraded office chair, made and used even now.

The so-called flare back was secured by springing out of the spindles after they left the arm rail.

The arm termination was often spirally carved in a rude manner suggesting a knuckle joint.

It would be impossible short of a volume to describe the variants of the arm and back. The higher backs are the more desirable.

Some backs have been found with two combs, one superimposed above another on four or five spindles extended for four inches above the lower comb. The writing arm chair is a large and fascinating chapter by itself. The best forms have the visible arm carved; have two drawers, and some have a folding or sliding candle stand extension. The spindles are specially turned to support the writing arm.

Settees with four, six, eight, or ten legs are found, the last in two known examples with triple bow backs intersecting or cross-

ing, and running into the main or arm back.

The bamboo turning is a later and poorer style though in some cases, when carefully done, is fair. The bent stretcher with spoke-like side stretcher is an interesting and much-sought variation. Windsor cradles are found, and combination settees and cradles, also stools, high and low, but no beds. A few tables having all the features of the Windsor base are known. They should not, however, be confused with the tables called Windsor, from the town of that name in Connecticut.

In the nineteenth century, machine-made chairs began to appear, with rungs running around the outside. The seats were always shapeless. They are unworthy to be called Windsor. They are numerous, coarse, uncomfortable; in every way an extreme degradation. Some have a top rail suggesting vaguely a Sheraton back.

Windsors in America, made so as to be worthy of the name, are included in the extreme dates 1725-1825, but all pine examples appeared before the end of the eighteenth century.

The merit and special charm of the Windsors are so often overlooked or unknown that we wish here, with almost brutal emphasis, to say that lightness was the chief purpose of the Windsor, to follow the heavy late Gothic furniture which a woman could not move without a struggle. Hence an American Windsor means a pine seat if it means anything good. Also delicate lines to secure lightness throughout. This includes strongly bulbous legs and a light back. Such chairs well made were durable because they were elastic and bore falls without breaking.

In a good Windsor, lightness, strength, grace, durability, and quaintness are all found in an irresistible blend.

The wood of the legs, stretchers, and arms, when sawed, was maple, or birch. Beech has been found, and rarely, oak. Maple turned smoothly. The front turned spindle of the arm chair, and the long side back spindle of the fan back, a side chair, was also maple, or at least of the same wood as the legs.

When the style began to decline, after 1800, we often find, as in the bamboo arm chair, an arm scrolled vertically, the beginning in a smaller form of the Boston rocker arm—which, by the way, is probably the most popular chair ever made, and is a very much degraded Windsor, of the "early Buchanan" or "late Lincoln" period!

The small scrolled arm was invariably attached to a bow back or the large side rear spindle. This was a very weak and poor support. This arm was in some cases made of mahogany, but no old Windsor, of thousands examined, was ever found with mahogany in any other part. The fad of making modern Windsors in that wood shows complete ignorance of the genius of the chair, for no graceful back can be made in mahogany, as that wood lacks the strength of hickory and only a coarse back of mahogany could be strong enough.

The finish of Windsors was usually, and always in the early patterns, bottle green, or at least green paint, not a stain. The chair was primarily designed and advertised as a "garden chair," and required paint. If a "natural" Windsor chair was ever discovered, it was because the maker used it at home. It was not a recognized finish. Then came in red and yellow paint, the latter often in children's high and low chairs. Black was rarely used. White is in wretched taste for Windsors.

FIG. 7 — WINDSOR WITH BAMBOO TURN-INGS, following a fashion that came in about 1810. Believed to have been brought from Connecticut by a pioneer family to Clinton County, Ohio, early in the nineteenth century. The seat is chest-nut, the rungs and legs maple, and there are nine spindles in the back. Stamped on underside of seat with the name *S. Tracy.*

FIG. 6 — TRIPLE-BACK ARMCHAIR with comb rising above the double back. The arms with delicate three-finger ends and side scrolls matching those of the ears on the cresting are points to be noted. *Davenport Collection, Lawrence Art Museum.*

The Furniture of Goddard and Townsend

BY JOSEPH DOWNS

FURNITURE WITH blocked front and curved shell has engaged the attention of collectors and writers for at least fifty years. It is the closest thing we have to an original American style of cabinetmaking. A succession of facts and opinions about this furniture and its makers, by a succession of writers, has appeared in ANTIQUES. In December 1947 we published this article by Joseph Downs which, though brief, is the definitive treatment of the subject. He has sifted the previous published material and separated fact from fiction, to give us the most valuable record we have of the Newport Goddards and Townsends, makers of blockfronts. Joseph Downs is one of the most highly respected of American antiquarians. His knowledge of the many other aspects of antiques is no less formidable than his knowledge of furniture. Formerly Curator of the American Wing of the Metropolitan Museum, he is now Curator of the du Pont Collection at Winterthur, Delaware.

FOR forty-five years and more, the legend about Newport cabinetmaking has been growing, fostered by books, magazines, and word of mouth until the corpus of information is elephantine. Now obsolete in part, it has all contributed to widen interest in the superlative furniture made by the Goddards and Townsends. These two families, bound by the ties of Quaker faith, intermarriage, and pride in fine workmanship, embraced twenty craftsmen in four generations, forming a unique school of furniture makers. Only one other American family, that comprised by the thirteen Danforth pewterers of Connecticut and elsewhere, can in any way approach their record.

Contrary to previous opinion, the genesis of the Rhode Island blockfront and shell design, on which early Goddard and Townsend fame is based, appears to have been European. The fanciful curves of baroque Italian, Dutch, and French furniture are richer versions of the serpentine, kettle-shape, and blockfront case furniture made in colonial America. Shells, too, were the stock in trade of Continental *ébénistes*. Do not the words "rock" and "shell" combine in French to form *rococo*, that term so aptly describing the spirit of eighteenth-century European fashion? Yet the reputation of the Goddard and Townsend cabinetmakers is justly founded, for no exact foreign protoype for the blockfront and shell design as it developed in Newport and Connecticut exists. They have given us their own version of the baroque style, in the spirit of the original, but new in

FIG. 1 — MAHOGANY DRESSING TABLE. Made by Job Townsend, 1746, and mentioned in his bill to Samuel Ward, later the governor of Rhode Island. Lining of tulip poplar wood. The profile of the top is the early type on many Queen Anne tables. *Collection of Mrs. John Elliott.*

FIG. 2 — MAHOGANY SECRETARY-BOOKCASE. Inscribed *Made by Job Townsend in Newport.* An early example of the block and shell design in the writing cabinet, that later was enlarged on the exterior surfaces of Newport furniture. First published in 1923, this piece has been a key in the attribution of other case pieces to Newport. The lining is tulip poplar and white pine. *Museum of Art, Rhode Island School of Design.*

conception, and calculated by its restrained elegance to suit colonial patrons. Their work continues to be one of the most outstanding expressions in wood made anywhere.

In a curious rather than aspersive mood, it is rewarding to trace the Newport story from its beginning to the present, reviewing various comments already made and furniture signed by seven of the Goddards and Townsends. Moreover, in addition to examining material published earlier, it will be interesting to consider several pieces of furniture which have not appeared before.

The legend begins as far back as 1902 when a secretary-bookcase *(Fig. 12)* was illustrated by Luke V. Lockwood in the first edition of *Colonial Furniture in America,* pp. 272 ff., figs. 233-234, and attributed "presumably to a cabinetmaker at Newport." In the next edition of the same book, published in 1913, many examples of blockfront case furniture with shell decoration were pictured and points of difference noted, but no attributions, beyond that of Newport or Connecticut, were made. A blockfront chest-on-chest appeared in the first issue of ANTIQUES (January 1922, p. 18), and was described as "probably made by a Newport cabinetmaker, supposed by some to have been John Goddard." The story grew mightily in the next few months. Goddard was said to have come to Newport from England, straight from Thomas Chippendale's own shop in St. Martin's Lane, returning to his native country at the outbreak of the Revolution (ANTIQUES, May 1922, pp. 203 ff.). Goddard's great-grandson strengthened this belief by pointing out that a copy of Chippendale's *Director* had been owned by his able ancestor. Moreover, late in the same

year, a dressing table unique among all fine kneehole dressing tables was published (ANTIQUES, September 1922, pp. 111, 112), combining an extraordinary number of Newport details of design. Little is known of its history other than that it was found in Virginia in a dilapidated condition, and shortly afterward passed into the John C. Toland collection in Baltimore.

The next discovery was announced in 1923 when two pieces of furniture by John and Job Townsend appeared in ANTIQUES (February, pp. 63-66), documented keys for future guidance in the attribution of Rhode Island furniture. One was a blockfront chest of drawers with three carved shells signed *Made by John Townsend, Newport, R. I.,* and the second was a simple secretary-bookcase *(Fig. 2)* with a writing cabinet of blockfront and shell design. Not content with this important contribution, the author also attempted to solve the origin of the blockfront style, studying furniture from Massachusetts, Connecticut, and Rhode Island, and concluding that the style was a late phase of the serpentine, and of rounded blockfront furniture seen in localities other than in Newport. This reasoning was based on the combination of claw and bracket feet, supposedly earlier in date, that does not appear on Rhode Island pieces, as well as the three-drawer style of chest, thought to be indigenous to Connecticut.

Four years later, a blockfront chest-on-chest with the label of John Townsend, Middletown, Connecticut, was illustrated in the third editon of *Colonial Furniture in America,* p. 357. A note accompanying the illustration seems little short of clairvoyant in the light of recent information about the connection between Rhode Island and Connecticut furniture (AN-

FIG. 3 — MAHOGANY PIER TABLE. Believed to have been made for Abraham Redwood in Newport, who was married in 1724 and in 1747 founded the Redwood Library. The shell carving and feet are similar to Figure 10. The lining is all tulip poplar. Brass handles of later date. *Collection of Mrs. E. Maitland Armstrong.*

FIG. 4—MAHOGANY DRESSING TABLE. The shell upon the skirt is the type used by Job Townsend on Figures 1 and 2. The combination of claw-and-ball and pad feet is also shown on Figures 8 and 10, a Newport feature. The undercut claw is a *tour de force,* typical of Newport carving. The lining is all of soft pine, except red cedar for the bottom boards of drawers. *Collection of Mrs. J. Insley Blair.*

FIG. 5 — KNEEHOLE DRESSING TABLE OF MAHOGANY. Identical to one inscribed by Edmund Townsend (*1736-1811*), son of Job Townsend. The petals at the base of the shells, and the bar below them, are exactly like those on the one in the Karolik collection (Catalogue no. 38). This type of chest was also made by Goddard, which he called a "buro table." *Collection of Mrs. J. Insley Blair.*

TIQUES, April and May 1946): "As his pieces closely resemble the Goddard pieces from Newport it is fair to assume he first worked in Newport, and either worked with Goddard or was familiar with his work, and that he subsequently moved to Middletown." Mr. Lockwood also recognized variations in the blockfront furniture he pictured from Massachusetts, Rhode Island, and Connecticut.

In a long and analytical study of a special loan exhibition of Newport furniture held at Providence in 1927 *(Bulletin of the Rhode Island School of Design,* April 1927, pp. 14-24), Norman N. Isham attributed the whole blockfront group to John Goddard, using three letters between Goddard and Moses Brown in 1763 to prove his point. However, none of the furniture in the exhibition was definitely known to be that mentioned in the letters. The author also illustrated in his study a kneehole dressing and writing table with three carved shells *(op. cit., fig. 2)* identified by an inscription as the work of John Goddard for his daughter, Catherine Weaver, who was married in 1778. Goddard's will notes "The account I have against my daughter Catherine Weaver of household furniture." Mr. Isham's conclusion was that ". . . it is the work of a great craftsman and a great artist. It is useless to talk of him as merely one of a school. No matter who trained him or in what tradition he was trained, no one can study the pieces in this Exhibition without feeling that they are the work of one who leads, not follows, who is a master and not a disciple."

A few months later, in 1927, three first-rate examples of furniture, namely a clock *(Fig. 7),* a chest of drawers (ANTIQUES, April 1946, p. 228), and a card table, each with the signature of John Townsend, were purchased by the Metropolitan Museum of Art. They came from a descendant of Christopher Champlin in Newport; the pieces were believed to have been made at the time of his wedding in 1763. An imposing addition to the galaxy of Townsend accomplishments, this furniture considerably diminished the glory earlier accorded Goddard. At the same time, no credence was given to the relation between the Townsends of Newport and Connecticut cabinetmakers (Charles Over Cornelius, *Metropolitan Museum Studies,* I, 1928, pp. 72 ff.).

A detached trade card inscribed *John Goddard Cabinetmaker No. Bridge Street on the Point Newport* was found in the Newport Historical Society also in 1927. Illustrating a sideboard and two chests in the Hepplewhite style, this card was a fresh clue to the type of furniture made by later Goddards and Townsends. This John Goddard was the son of Stephen, and a grandson of the earlier John Goddard; he worked until 1843, the last of the dynasty.

In 1929 a secretary-bookcase appeared in ANTIQUES (April, pp. 274-277) with a penciled inscription to the effect that it was *made by John Goddard in 1761,* and *repaired by Thomas Goddard in 1813.* Thomas Goddard was a son of the early John, and Stephen Goddard was his brother. A printed label fixed to a card table bought by the Metropolitan Museum in 1929 advertises that *Stephen and Thomas Goddard Cabinetmakers Carries on said Business . . . in Newport.* This half-round table with satinwood inlay in the Hepplewhite style must have been made prior to 1804 when Stephen died, and differed from all other Goddard or Townsend furniture then identified.

In 1930 at the epoch-making auction

FIG. 6 — CHEST OF DRAWERS. A very fine example made in Connecticut. This is perhaps the nearest of any known blockfront and shell-carved piece to the type made at Newport; the chief differences are in the heavy gadrooned skirting, and lengthened bracket feet without scrolls, unlike those used in Newport. The dish top is a notable feature, rarely seen on case pieces. *Collection of Reginald M. Lewis.*

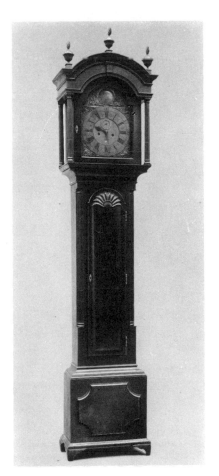

FIG. 7 — MAHOGANY TALL CLOCK. Inscribed *Made by John Townsend in Newport, 1769.* The works were made by William Tomlinson, London. The cross-hatching at the base of the shell is also used on a table by Townsend. The lining is chestnut and tulip poplar. The toes of the feet are missing. *From the Metropolitan Museum of Art.*

FIG. 8 — MAHOGANY CARD TABLE. In design it belongs with the tea table John Goddard made for Jabez Bowen in 1763, now in the collection of H. F. du Pont. The framing is cherry. A similar table, without the carving, was illustrated in ANTIQUES, June 1930, p. 288. *Collection of Mrs. J. Insley Blair.*

FIG. 9 — MAHOGANY ARM-CHAIR. From a set of chairs owned in Newport that has the same gadrooned carving, the reeded and fluted legs employed by John Townsend (see Fig. 11). *Collection of the Misses King.*

FIG. 10 — HIGH CHEST OF DRAWERS. This highboy has several features of Job Townsend's labeled work, in the shape of the skirting, the pediment, and moldings (see Fig. 3, ANTIQUES, April 1946, p. 229). All the details of the shell carving are like those of John Townsend's signed chest of drawers (Fig. 2, ANTIQUES, May 1946, p. 292). The combination of pad and claw feet, and the carved knees are like the card table in Figure 8. Here is a merger of various features observed on several Newport pieces, by Goddard and Townsend alike. *Collection of Mrs. J. Insley Blair.*

FIG. 11 — MAHOGANY PEMBROKE TABLE. Almost certainly the work of John Townsend, if compared with a similar table signed by that craftsman in the collection of H. F. du Pont (see Catalogue no. 472, Philip Flayderman Sale, New York, 1930). This table is inscribed *J. T. No. 31,* and was originally owned by Christopher Champlin in Newport, together with Figure 7 and a mahogany card table not shown. Oak, red cedar, and maple are used in the framing. *Collection of Mrs. J. Insley Blair.*

sale of the late Philip Flayderman collection in New York, the name of the early John Goddard again appeared in connection with an elaborate tea table (Catalogue no. 450), from the family of Jabez Bowen. This table was mentioned in one of the letters between Goddard and Moses Bowen, and quoted by Mr. Isham in 1927. The sale also included a Pembroke table (no. 470) in the Chinese Chippendale style with the label of John Townsend. This piece, similar to his signed card table in several respects, was nearly identical to an unsigned table in the Boston Museum of Fine Arts (Karolik Collection, no. 66).

In 1936 the secretary *(Fig. 2)* first published in 1923 was presented to the Rhode Island School of Design and led to further theories that Job Townsend, the father-in-law of John Goddard, might have originated the blockfront style. That same year a relatively simple slant-top desk (ANTIQUES, September 1936, pp. 120 ff.) came to light, with shells in the writing cabinet unlike those on the Job Townsend secretary, inscribed *John Goddard*. A similar one, with the outlines of the Goddard name still upon it, was recently added to the collection of H. F. du Pont.

In 1937 (ANTIQUES, June, pp. 308-310) some heirlooms of John Townsend were published, including a straight-front desk having a shell and block writing cabinet, and a dressing table with pad feet, and a shell on its skirting; the details of the serpentine-edged shells were similar to those used by John Goddard, a fact that gave substance to the theory of one carver for all of this school of furniture. James Townsend, who had been assigned to this task, would not have been old enough to have originated the shell designs on Figure 1 or perhaps Figure 2.

In 1941 the name of Edmund Townsend first appeared on a blockfront knee-hole desk (Karolik Collection, no. 38, Museum of Fine Arts, Boston). He was the son of Job Townsend and cousin of John. A piece identical to that one, even in all of the details, the moldings, and shells, is shown in Figure 5.

In 1946 (ANTIQUES, April and May) the whole genealogy of the Townsend and Goddard clan of craftsmen, and the story of John Townsend's removal to Middletown and Norwich, Connecticut, during the Revolution, and his return to Newport afterwards, was finally cleared up. Likewise the most recently mentioned cabinetmaker, Townsend Goddard, working in Kingston, Rhode Island, was credited with making the blockfront furniture for the Potter family there. It may be noted, however, that a Newport-type secretary from this family, recently given to the Newport Historical Society is inscribed *John Goddard*. Two pieces now in the Newport Historical Society stand at the antipodes of the Newport school; one a highboy labeled by Job Townsend, with the same type of shell that he used upon the secretary-bookcase *(Fig. 2)*, and a cabinet in the Empire style of 1825, attributed to John Goddard, the son of Stephen and grandson of John (ANTIQUES, April 1946, p. 228). The author illustrates, too, the divergence from the Newport style by the Connecticut cabinetmakers Benjamin Burnham and others.

During August 1947, a loan exhibition of heirlooms held at the Colony House in Newport revealed several important pieces of furniture hardly known before. One was a dressing table *(Fig. 1)* which is mentioned on a bill to Samuel Ward, later Governor of Rhode Island, from Job Townsend, dated *July 1746*, which is quoted in full in ANTIQUES (April 1946). Now we begin to recognize the typical Job Townsend shell, cut within an arc without a serpentine edge, that he used upon his signed highboy and secretary. A second piece in the exhibition was a pier table *(Fig. 3)* originally owned by Abraham Redwood, gentleman, philanthropist, and botanist in Newport. Although the Townsend account book does not mention Redwood, unquestionably the table belongs to the early Townsend-Goddard group.

Quantities of simple chairs, desks, and tables in red cedar, maple, and pine were turned out in Newport in addition to the handsome mahogany furniture. Captain Bunker "bought of John Townsend 3 desks and 4 maple tea tables at 23 pounds each" to carry to the West Indies. A maple tavern table with the so-called porringer top, pad feet, and round at the corners, may well be like them. It originally stood in the Finch house on Easton's Point in Newport and is still owned by the Finch family. A dining table in the same collection has the same inlay on its apron as the labeled card table by Stephen and Thomas Goddard.

There seems little stylistic progression in Newport furniture, to judge from a comparison of certain blockfront examples made before 1710 with those of twenty years later. The earlier ones are as highly developed as the others. Both the type of design, and principles of construction, became crystallized early and lasted until the classical revival.

In almost every piece that was examined, blocking was cut from the solid wood of drawer fronts and wherever the concaved sections cut too deeply, extra wood strengthened the interior surface. The convex shells, on the contrary, that so often ornament the top drawer, lid, or doors of secretaries and chests, were nearly always glued onto the surface.

The details of the shell carving differ on almost every piece, the exception again proving the rule *(see Fig. 5)*. Not only are the concave and convex lobes of varying number, curve, and depth, but the outer edges and centers are treated in a variety of ways. The detail of the petals at the shells' center gives an immediate clue to the excellence of the entire work; some are curved, others are stiff; some are hollowed, others are solid.

In the colonial period, the bombé or kettle shape and the serpentine-front form held little favor in Newport. Only the flat blocking answered the need for a "sweld" shape in case pieces, as Goddard described his finest furniture.

Regional characteristics are easily observed in the feet of a piece of furniture. In Newport, the claw-and-ball foot is elongated, the claws having an extended grip, with no webbing between the talons. The rear feet of tables and chests of drawers often do not match the front ones; on several handsome pieces, that were made to stand against a wall, the claw-and-ball and pad feet are used together *(Figs. 8, 10).* The undercutting of the claw *(Fig. 4)* appears on several pieces probably made by John Goddard, but its fragility, no less than the difficulty of carving it, precluded frequent repetition. Even the tiny spiral that curves outward on the bracket foot, whether closed as on the Joseph Brown secretary *(Fig. 12)* or open *(Fig. 5)*, is not seen beyond the bounds of chests which were made in Newport.

Wide chamfering to lighten square sections of leg, piercing of stretchers with open frets, and gouging table-top edges to relieve their abruptness are the usual devices of the cunning makers of Newport's furniture.

The secret locks of case pieces were ingeniously contrived. The top drawers of a high chest *(Fig. 10)* are locked by strips attached to the undersides which drop down and hold the drawer when it is pulled forward. They may be released only from inside the drawer below them.

The interior lining of case furniture was made chiefly of tulip poplar, with occasionally some chestnut, red cedar, and soft pine. Cherry, and maple, too, are pressed into service for underframing and swinging gates that require strength, but the exposed surfaces are almost always fine mahogany, from Cuba and Santo Domingo.

Drawers are lightly built, with a delicacy of dovetailing and thinness of framing that are a revelation. In a recent comparison of case pieces of Philadelphia, New York, Connecticut, and Newport, of comparable quality and period, in Mrs. J. Insley Blair's collection, those of the last group were in a class apart. Strength was given to the long drawers by carrying the bottom board across the width to support the sides and fixing runners to the under edges. This construction was not followed in other cities.

FIG. 12 — MAHOGANY SECRETARY-BOOKCASE. First illustrated in 1902 (see *Colonial Furniture in America,* p. 272). The carving on this piece shows marked differences with others of block-front and shell design, and refutes the earlier theory that all the carving is alike on various pieces. This is the most highly developed of the secretary group and is most like the chest-on-chest (see ANTIQUES, January 1922, p. 18) in its pediment treatment, type of bracket feet, and detail of shell design. It was made, like the chest-on-chest, for Joseph Brown in Newport, one of four brothers who are known to have patronized John Goddard for furniture, and was owned until lately by Brown and Ives, Providence bankers. *From the Rhode Island Historical Society.*

Benjamin Randolph of Philadelphia

BY S. W. WOODHOUSE, JR.

IN THE 1920's *early American furniture was for the most part assumed to be crude, and anything elaborate was attributed to England. When Dr. Woodhouse advanced the claim that six extremely elaborate sample chairs which had begun to attract attention were not English but were the work of the Philadelphia cabinetmaker Benjamin Randolph, he met with rather violent opposition. This first article appeared in May 1927, and he further amplified his claim in an article in January 1930. Some of the introductory statements made here do not hold today, since our knowledge of southern furniture as well as that of New York and Boston has greatly increased in the intervening years. But the attribution of these chairs to Randolph is now generally accepted, though they are more elaborate than any signed examples of his work. Probably they were actually "samples," designed to show to clients. The present location of the chairs, all of which have changed hands since original publication of this article, is given in the captions.*

Dr. Woodhouse was a pioneer in original research in the American antiquarian field. Through his association with the Philadelphia (then Pennsylvania) Museum of Art, and his numerous writings in ANTIQUES *and elsewhere, he made a notable contribution to the history of the American decorative arts.*

I. PHILADELPHIA, LEADING CITY OF THE COLONIES

IT is interesting to remember that pioneer collectors called a certain type of high chest of drawers a *southern highboy* until there was discovered, in Baltimore, a walnut lowboy with the label of William Savery, of Philadelphia, in the bottom of the upper drawer. This piece was afterwards purchased by Luke Vincent Lockwood for the Colonial Dames at Van Cortlandt Manor, New York. Thereupon dealers and collectors, in the flush of discovery, styled all fine American Chippendale furniture *Savery*.

Though there were, undoubtedly, good makers in Annapolis, Baltimore, and Charleston, comparatively little important furniture was, as a matter of fact, produced in the South.

Philadelphia, however, in the latter half of the eighteenth century — larger than New York or Boston — was, for some time, the center of wealth and luxury in America. As late as 1765, New York had not progressed far beyond the position of a Dutch trading post; and Boston was a small town of prim and Puritanic character — certainly not a place where luxury prevailed. Concerning Philadelphia, on the

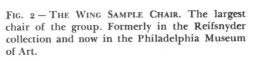

FIG. 1 — ONE OF THE SIX SAMPLE CHAIRS. These chairs, now quite definitely attributed to an American maker, represent the highest achievement of Philadelphia furniture makers. *Collection of the Philadelphia Museum of Art.*

FIG. 2 — THE WING SAMPLE CHAIR. The largest chair of the group. Formerly in the Reifsnyder collection and now in the Philadelphia Museum of Art.

FIG. 3 — THE FIRST OF THE SIX CHAIRS. Said to be the finest chair yet found in America. *Collection of the late Henry W. Erving and still owned by his family.*

other hand, it should be remembered that there were men of wealth amongst the early settlers in Pennsylvania. Their numbers were later increased by the advent of younger members of distinguished English families who, thanks to the opportunities afforded in the new land, were, in due time, able to emulate the elegant and refined surroundings to which they had been accustomed at home.

The significance of the fact that Philadelphia always boasted an important group of fashionables — spoken of as "World's people" in distinction to the plain Friends or Quakers — has not been sufficiently appreciated. During the years prior to and during the Revolution, many Tories, Quaker pacifists, and so on, lived in Philadelphia; and, though the city was occupied by the British, relatively little was destroyed during the war. Hence it is easy to understand why the major part of the choice American furniture that follows a style which, in a loose way, we may call Chippendale, has come to light in Philadelphia — as is indicated by the Pendleton collection at the Rhode Island School of Design, and the Palmer and Myers collections in the Metropolitan Museum.

II. The Six "Sample Chairs"

Twenty-five years ago "Jimmy" Curran heard rumors, hunted up and bought a fine chair. It was one of six that old wives' tales had frequently referred to as "the six sample chairs." By judicious efforts the entire six were ultimately unearthed, though one still remains in the family of original ownership.

The first was bought by the Doyen of American collectors, Henry W. Erving, of Hartford. He found it in Curran's treasury one hot summer's day as he was returning from his son's commencement at Johns Hopkins. Of this chair Luke Vincent Lockwood says in his *Colonial Furniture in America*, "It is the best chair that has been found in this country." Three others of the six, one wing and two side chairs, are in the collection of Howard Reifsnyder, of Philadelphia.

Other pieces of furniture showing points of resemblance are the fine chair illustrated on page 91 of Lockwood, owned by Mrs. Ingersoll of Hartford and formerly in the Bulkley Collection; the chairs from the Charles Wharton house; the Cadwalader card table and console table. [The Cadwalader family card table is illustrated in Hornor's *Blue Book of Philadelphia Furniture*, Pl. 104; the console table is now in the American Wing, Metropolitan Museum.—Ed.] The question which has constantly lain before all collectors is: are these pieces of American or English make? The great connoisseurs have vaguely suggested American, perhaps English; or English, perhaps Philadelphia; and we get nothing more definite.

After the publication of the Metropolitan Museum *Bulletin* (Vol. XIII, No. 12, 1918) in which my friend R. T. H. Halsey rescued the name of one of Philadelphia's brilliant galaxy of cabinetmakers, all were naturally searching for a clue to some of the others, or seeking to discover which of the various kinds of furniture following the general fashion of Chippendale was made by which individual of this group. The next considerable contribution to our information came in the form of the very splendid engraved business card of Benjamin Randolph. Yet from that time until a chair was discovered bearing Randolph's actual label, we were still at sea, though there had been various efforts to connect the "six sample chairs" with this maker.

III. BENJAMIN RANDOLPH, CABINETMAKER

Little has been published about Randolph. He was supposed to have come from New Jersey, and it was known that, when he retired, he went to his place *Speedwell Mills,* on Wading River, near Burlington, in that state.

Gradually, however, I have acquired some data concerning this interesting cabinetmaker from the records of the Genealogical Society of Pennsylvania. He first married on February 18, 1762, Anna Bromwich, only daughter and sole heiress of William Bromwich, stay maker of Sassafras Street. As William Bromwich was buried in Christ Church graveyard, November 19, 1763, it would seem that, by his marriage, Benjamin Randolph came into close association with "World's people."

In his early transactions he is noted as "joiner." He possessed one horse, some cattle, and one servant, and paid a tax of £42.16 in the Middle Ward. Soon, however, we find his taxes increased, and he styles himself "cabinetmaker" in 1768.

By regular progression he climbs in the scale as a "carver and gilder," and then as "merchant," until, in 1786, he pays a tax of £176.11, and has property in the High Street Ward, in the Mulberry Ward, in the Middle Ward, in the Northern Liberties, and out in Abington. He is now possessed of two horses, cattle, and one Negro. Finally, at the time of his retirement, he styles himself "gentleman," a term not lightly used in the eighteenth century. It would be well to remember that Benjamin Randolph was a cabinetmaker in such a position as to secure Thomas Jefferson's patronage, and, as Jefferson states, to make for that statesman the desk on which the Dec-

laration of Independence was drafted, now in the Library of Congress.

Several of Randolph's old property transfers are very interesting, and shed further light on our maker of fine furniture. In 1767, when purchasing his shop in Chestnut Street from one Thomas Shoemaker, a carpenter, Randolph, we find, acquired a lot twenty-four feet wide by one hundred and seventy deep, "through to the lots on High Street," with a seven-foot cartway at the side, adjoining the property of Henry Mitchell, "joiner." We observe that these men, most of them woodworkers, were meticulously accurate, for this deed expressly states "to be paid in dollars — that is to say sixty-six Spanish milled dollars commonly called milled silver pieces of eight, each piece weighing seventeen pennyweights, six grains, fine coined silver and eleven-sixteenth parts of a dollar." So shin plasters, currency depreciations, and what-not may come and go, but Thomas Shoemaker, Quaker carpenter in Philadelphia, is certain to receive full value in silver bullion.

In 1781, Randolph purchases property, adjoining Benjamin Franklin's lot, for £775 "in gold and silver coins." Of more interest than the fact of sale is the quaint phraseology of the deed when he transfers some of the old Bromwich property on Sassafras Street. It begins:

"TO ALL THE PEOPLE, I BENJAMIN RANDOLPH, Carver and Gilder send greeting. Know ye that the said Benjamin Randolph in consideration for £100 gold and silver coins do sell on the north side of Mulberry Street "formerly belonging to William Bromwich." William Bromwich died intestate, leaving his only issue a daughter named Anna, upon whom the same descends as heiress at Law, who intermarried with me, said Benjamin Randolph, and by whom I had issue two daughters named Mary and Anna, now living and in their minority and my said wife Anna some years ago died intestate, whereby her estate in the premises descended to my said two daughters, Mary and Anna as co-partners and Heiresses at Law, subject to the life estate of me, the said Benjamin Randolph as tenant by courtesy, — ." (*Deed Book,* Recorder of Deeds, Philadelphia, D-19, p. 514.)

IV. HERCULES COURTENAY, CARVER

We find that in 1767 the witness to one of the many real estate transactions of Benjamin Randolph is Hercules Courtenay. Now what do we know of Hercules Courtenay? He married Mary Shute, May 18, 1768, at "Old Swedes," Gloria Dei church. He advertises from his house in Front Street between Chestnut and Walnut, where he paid taxes in 1769, at that time styling himself "carver." The advertisement reads:

"Hercules Courtenay, Carver and Gilder, from London, INFORMS his Friends and the Public, that he undertakes all Manner of CARVING and GILDING, in the newest Taste, at his House in Front-Street, between Chestnut and Walnut Streets. N. B. He is determined to be as reasonable as possible in his Charges, and to execute all Commands with the utmost Diligence." (Alfred Coxe Prime, *Colonial Craftsmen,* from the *Pennsylvania Chronicle,* 8/14/1769.)

After the Revolution, apparently, he gave up his artistry and became a "tavern-keeper."

Now we enter the field of conjecture. One seldom goes far out of his way to hunt up a witness to his signature. It would seem probable, therefore, that Hercules Courtenay was in the employ of Benjamin Randolph at the time of delivery of the previously mentioned deed. It is even more probable that, when young Courtenay came out from London, as his advertisement states, he was employed by Benjamin Randolph. Yes, you may say, but what reason is there for connecting Benjamin Randolph with six elaborate sample chairs? — To discover that we must follow the story of Randolph's second marriage.

V. ESTABLISHING A LINE OF DESCENT

Benjamin Randolph, after his retirement, married Mary Wilkinson, widow of William Fenimore. Benjamin Randolph's will, dated 1790 at Trenton, New Jersey, recites:

"Whereas there was a verbal agreement between me and my wife, Mary, previous to marriage, that neither of us would claim any right in any property of the other, in consequence I have not meddled in her real or personal estate, therefore I bequeath to my said wife, Mary £20."

Such ante-nuptial agreements were common usage. The supposition that Benjamin Randolph came from the Fitz-Randolphs of New Jersey is strengthened by the fact that his only surviving daughter, Anna, after her father's death, went to live in Morristown, New Jersey, in which vicinity the name of Fitz-Randolph is prevalent.

Randolph's second wife, Mary Wilkinson Fenimore, survived him by some years. In her will, dated June 1, 1816, in the fifth paragraph, occurs the statement: "All the remainder of my household goods I give unto my son, Nathaniel Fenimore" (her son by her first marriage). By the second clause of the first paragraph, her daughter Priscilla is to have a home with her brother Nathaniel Fenimore as long as she remains single. Nathaniel Fenimore, who inherited under this will, married Rebecca Zelley, and had a daughter Rebecca Zelley Fenimore, who was born in 1831, and eventually married her cousin Samuel Stockton Zelley.

Five of the six sample chairs have been purchased from the descendants of Nathaniel Fenimore, stepson of Benjamin Randolph. Benjamin Randolph was living with Mary Wilkinson Fenimore Randolph at the time of his death, and, though his will makes no mention of his personal effects, it seems reasonable to suppose that these prized pieces of household gear — the six chairs — remained in possession of his widow. From her they would naturally, by descent, pass to her heirs, after Benjamin Randolph's only surviving daughter Anna had gone to live in another part of the state; for, in those days of poor roads, one endeavored not to transport household furniture over long distances.

VI. THE ARGUMENT FOR AMERICAN WORKMANSHIP

It has generally been accepted that chairs of the latter half of the eighteenth century showing rounded, stump rear legs, or those so constructed that the seat rails completely pierce the stiles at the back, are, by those signs, to be classed as products of Philadelphia craftsmanship. Some of our six sample chairs display these characteristics; some do not. On that point, more presently.

In proportion the six chairs follow English rather than American precedent — the precedent of the *Director*, Plate XVI. American chairs tend to be smaller in the seat than English chairs, especially narrower at the rear of the seat. American

chairs, however, have higher backs than contemporary English pieces.

The fact that our specimens follow English precedent in proportions is by no means evidence of English manufacture; though it does argue close regard for English methods. It is, therefore, to be noted that, in the Pennsylvania Museum, there is a very simple chair, bearing the label of Benjamin Randolph, which follows English proportions and in which the seat rails do not pierce the stiles. While the carving and structure of the splat of this chair are fine, they are extremely simple, for this is a much less elaborate type of chair than those pictured in the *Director*.

The only plates in the *Director* showing chairs with the splat spreading widely to connect with the sides are the three with ribbon-backs, and those in Gothic and Chinese taste. Mr. Erving's chair (*Fig. 3*), in its essentials, resembles the ribbon-back. The carving of all is of a peculiarly soft, rounded character, which has been spoken of as French carving. The second sample chair (*Fig. 4*), closely resembling Mr. Erving's piece, has the back splat widening at its upper third so as to become attached to the stiles. Very similar, again, is a hall chair exhibited by the late John D. McIlhenny at the Pennsylvania Museum in the Chippendale Show of 1924.

The two latter chairs present so many features in common that their close study is well warranted, though the modern upholstery of the sample chair quite alters lines that are intensified by the wooden seat in this superb example of Mr. McIlhenny's.

The Erving chair has rear legs following the English fashion; the two Reifsnyder side chairs, previously referred to as part of our sextette, have back legs with rounded

Philadelphia stumps; the second chair has back legs with rounded Philadelphia stumps; the sixth chair likewise shows the Philadelphia stumps. In the chair at the Philadelphia Museum the side rails do *not* pierce the stiles; in the two Reifsnyder chairs, the side rails do *not* pierce the stiles; in the second sample chair, the rails *do* pierce the stiles; in the sixth sample chair, the side rails *do* pierce the stiles.

Comparison of illustrations will make it clear that the leg of the Cadwalader card table (Hornor's *Blue Book of Philadelphia Furniture,* Plate 104) is merely the leg of the second chair elongated. The carving of the skirt of the card table and of the skirt of this second chair are virtually identical, and show, further, close similarity to that of the skirt of the Erving chair. Very similar handling is revealed in the carving of the Cadwalader pier table in the Metropolitan Museum, the Washington sofa in Independence Hall, and the Louis Myers piecrust table in the Metropolitan Museum, the pier tables in the Philadelphia Museum, the Pendleton collection at the Rhode Island School of Design, and, lastly, with the less ornate chairs from the Charles Wharton house. Mrs. Ingersoll's chair and Miss Esther Morton Smith's, exhibited at the Philadelphia Museum, December, 1920, in varying degree, exhibit the same construction, timber, and carving.

It is interesting to note the English professional point of view as embodied in the opinions of Herbert Cescinsky, who states that, in English chairs, one seldom finds the side rails of as heavy timber as in American analogues; that the rounded stump legs do not occur in fine English furniture of the second half of the eighteenth century; that the side rails of our sample chairs are of heavier timber than is customary in English pieces; and that the bracing of these pieces is done in a manner peculiar to Philadelphia.

In his advertisement, Benjamin Randolph not only draws attention to the fact that he makes all these fine things, but likewise does "Carving, Gilding, etc., performed in the Chinese and modern taste." As Hercules Courtenay seems either to have been in Randolph's employ or to have enjoyed specially friendly relations with him, I do not think we go too quickly in suggesting that all these chairs — as well as other similar pieces — were probably carved by Hercules Courtenay.

At least five members of the Carpenters Company of Philadelphia were possessed of Swan's *British Architect,* published in 1745. The third edition of Chippendale was bought by the Philadelphia Library Company in 1762. The Loganian Library had a copy of Battie Langley's *Treasury of Building and Working Men's Designs,* published in 1745. When Benjamin Randolph bought his shop in Chestnut Street. Smithers, who engraved his business card, was working in Philadelphia. There is no doubt that this engraver had access to the copy of the *Director* owned by the Library Company, or, more probably, to one of the several copies that I believe were in the possession of individual craftsmen in the city. It is significant that where we do find Philadelphia-made Chippendale furniture, it is from plates in the third edition, the copy owned by the Library Company.

Whatever the place which history ultimately reserves for Benjamin Randolph or Hercules Courtenay, it is quite certain that these six chairs, now considered together for the first time in more than one hundred years, are outstanding examples of work in the Chippendale fashion, and have undoubtedly had their home on the banks of the Delaware since before the Revolution.

FIG. 4 — THE SECOND OF THE SIX CHAIRS. The splat so broken as to engage the stiles of the back is an unusual feature. *Collection of Henry F. duPont.*

FIG. 5 — THE SIXTH CHAIR. The least ornate of the group. Designed in the Gothic style. The rear stump legs and their relationship to the lines of the chair-back should be compared with those of Figure 4. *Mabel Brady Garvan Collection, Yale University Art Gallery.*

Federal Furniture of Baltimore

BY ELEANOR C. PINKERTON

UNTIL THE *Baltimore Museum of Art held its loan exhibition of Maryland furniture in the spring of* 1947, *it was difficult to get any clear view of the style of the Baltimore and Annapolis cabinetmakers, based on comparative study. When Eleanor C. Pinkerton (Mrs. A. M. Stewart) began some ten years before to compile records of Baltimore furniture, her work was in the nature of pioneering. It resulted in the article reprinted here from our May* 1940 *issue, the first account of the subject to be published, and one of the many articles in* ANTIQUES *which have developed the theme of regional characteristics in American antiques. Mrs. Stewart was a member of the committee that arranged the* 1947 *exhibition, and this analysis of Baltimore furniture was brilliantly substantiated and amplified in the exhibition catalogue,* Baltimore Furniture 1760-1810. *The nine pieces illustrated here were included in that exhibition; seven of them are from photographs kindly made available for this purpose by the Baltimore Museum of Art.*

BALTIMORE'S history began late as compared with that of Annapolis, New York, Philadelphia, and Boston, but once impetus was provided in the form of lucrative trade, its cultural development was rapid. The taste of the time manifested itself in elegant, well-designed, spacious homes, equipped with the handiwork of a number of local silversmiths, painters, and cabinetmakers, working in a distinctive style.

From 1708, when its municipal charter was granted, until after the Revolution, Annapolis was the commercial metropolis of Maryland. In 1790, about twenty cabinetmakers and importers of furniture were advertising in either the *Maryland Gazette* or the *Maryland Journal*, both published in Annapolis. Among the advertisements of

May 6, 1773, was: "John Shaw and Alexander Chisholm just imported from London and to be sold by Shaw and Chisholm cabinet and chairmakers in Church St. near the dock, a neat and general assortment of joiner's and cabinetmakers' tools. . . ." The notice lists the various tools in detail. In 1776 the dissolution of the partnership of Shaw and Chisholm is announced. Still later, in 1828, a notice records the death of Shaw, with an inventory of his possessions and his will.

When Annapolis was given its charter, Baltimore was not even "the little town up the Patapasco River." Not until 1729 did "the inhabitants of Baltimore county" ask the General Assembly to consider the erection of a town on the Patapasco. A watercolor sketch of 1752, now in the Maryland

FIG. 1 — SWELL-FRONT SIDEBOARD. Mahogany, with side compartments decorated with large ovals of dark crotch wood, outlined in crossbanding of light wood within mitred panels. Similar ovals, elongated, on center drawer. The use of contrasting tone in ovals is characteristic of Baltimore, as is also the large bellflower inlay on the leg. The urns containing flowers and leaves have been noted on other Baltimore pieces. *Collection of Mitchel Taradash, photograph courtesy Metropolitan Museum of Art.*

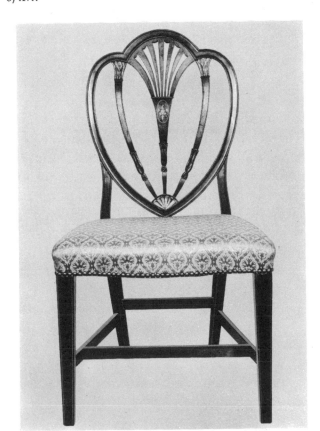

FIG. 3 — CHAIR WITH INTERLACING HEART BACK. Central splat decorated with inlaid oval eagle medallion; a segment of a shell inlaid at the base of the splats; square molded tapering legs. Formerly owned by the Keyes family of Baltimore. *Collection of Mrs. Harold Noel Arrowsmith.*

Historical Society, shows Baltimore, thirty-two years after its founding, as having only twenty-five dwellings, one church, and two taverns. In 1768 Baltimore Town became the county seat of Baltimore County, and in 1797 its municipal charter was granted. By the census of 1790 Baltimore had a population of 13,503, and in 1800, 26,514 — about 4,000 more persons than the whole of Anne Arundel County, Annapolis included. In 1799 its exports were equal to those of Philadelphia and New York. Baltimore merchants were becoming rich, and they were building beautiful mansions in and around the town. Great quantities of mahogany were imported from the West Indies, and used for stairways, doors, and furniture by the 300-odd cabinetmakers who were advertising in Baltimore's newspapers. Some of this furniture was shipped to the West Indies, and to the southern cities on the United States seaboard, but most of it went into Baltimore's own homes.

As a wedding gift to his namesake son, Charles Carroll of Carrollton gave $10,000 with which to build and furnish a house. Young Charles began building his mansion, Homewood, in 1801; in 1809, when it was completed, he had spent $40,000, in the face of parental protest. Close by Homewood was Homestead, the mansion where Betsy Patterson and Jerome Bonaparte lived the first year of that disastrous international marriage. Well within the present city limits of Baltimore was Belvedere, the home of Colonel Howard of Revolutionary and 1812 fame. Parnassus, the home of Doctor Henry Stevenson, was converted into a hospital and started Baltimore on its road to medical fame. Green Mount, Belmont, and Hampton are a few of the homes built in or near Baltimore

which were centers of elaborate entertaining, particularly between the two wars. It is not surprising that a considerable group of cabinetmakers found patronage in Baltimore at this time, and that, while developing a local character, they worked in the Hepplewhite and Sheraton styles learned from the English designers.

The Library Company of Baltimore was founded in 1795. Its first catalogue, which appeared in print in 1809, lists such volumes as *Cabinet Maker and Upholsterers' Guide*, with plates (Hepplewhite's, of course, though the author is not named); Winkelman's *Histoire de l'Art de L'Antiquité;* an *Account of Herculaneum, and Reflections concerning the Imitation of the Grecian Artists in Painting and Sculpture;* Palladio's *Architecture;* Paine's *British Palladio*, with plates; *Plans, Elevations and Sections of Noblemen and Gentlemen's Houses in England;* Robert and James Adam's *Works of Architecture*, with plates; and Hamilton's *Collection of Engravings from Ancient Vases.*

The cabinetmakers of Baltimore had ample opportunity to use these books, and obviously did. For example, one feature characteristic of Baltimore furniture is the insertion of painted glass panels in the doors of secretaries and even in the aprons of tables. Prototypes of these paintings appear in Hamilton's *Collection of Engravings from Ancient Vases,* and in sketches in the Winkelman volumes. Homewood is purely Adam in character, as are some of its original furnishings. The influence of Palladio on Baltimore architecture is patent.

Although there were at least three hundred and sixteen cabinetmakers in Baltimore from 1790 to 1820, few labels have appeared on pieces of furniture. The late Doctor Henry Berkley mentioned only

FIG. 4 — TALL CLOCK with
dial signed by Charles
Tinges, Baltimore, listed in
city directories 1787-1816 as
watch and clock maker.
High scrolled pediment
ornamented with pierced
fretwork and fine inlay in
vine and leaf design on
hood. The inlaid frieze
simulating fretwork is seen
on other Baltimore clocks
and on a secretary by
Stitcher & Clemmens. *From
the Edgar G. Miller, Jr.,
Collection of Baltimore tall
clocks, given by Miss Ethel
M. Miller to the Maryland
Historical Society.*

FIG. 2 — LABELED SECRETARY by John Shaw of Annapolis, made
for John Randall of Annapolis. Combines carving, inlay, and
finely patterned wood for full decorative effect. *Privately owned,
photograph courtesy of Baltimore Museum of Art.*

four in his article *Early Maryland Furniture* which appeared in ANTIQUES in September 1930. I have seen the label of John Shaw of Annapolis on a Hepplewhite sideboard, a secretary desk, an inlaid card table, a side chair, a pair of Chippendale card tables, a sofa, and a Chippendale serving table. Other labels that are mentioned by Doctor Berkley are those of Stitcher and Clemens, Thomas Renshaw, and John Simonson. Stitcher and Clemens are listed in the Baltimore directory of 1804 as cabinetmakers on South Street. Their label appears on a typical Baltimore inlaid secretary with glass doors, in the possession of Mrs. W. W. Hubbard. Thomas Renshaw is listed in the directories of 1814 and 1815. His signature and address, 37 Gay Street, with that of John Barnhart, "ornamenter," are painted on a Sheraton settee decorated with scenes of Baltimore. I do not know the source of John Simonson's label, but his name is in the 1810 directory.

I have seen the label of John Needles, cabinetmaker, 54 Hanover Street (directories 1812 and 1820), on a Sheraton pedestal table; I have owned a gilt Sheraton mirror with painting on glass, bearing the label of John M. Barrett, cabinetmaker, 5 York Street (directories 1812-1817); and I have seen a solid-door secretary with the label of William Brown, cabinetmaker, 109 N. High Street (directory 1800). A set of four chairs now in the possession of Joe Kindig, Jr. came from a Baltimore family who claimed that they were made by Warwick Price, cabinetmaker, 136 High Street (directory 1800-1810).

A distinctive feature of Baltimore furniture is the very high quality of the wood used and the interplay of veneered surfaces. Crotching is used in geometric shapes, sometimes bordered by line inlay.

Inlay is the favorite decorative device, used in a great variety of ways. A flattened feather design and an elongated sunburst appear, especially on chairs. The acorn or the horn of plenty in a medallion worked in varicolored woods is seen on many pieces — on the top or back of a table, or on the fall board of a desk, as well as on smaller forms. The medallions are composed of olive wood, satinwood, ebony, holly, and burnt or dyed light-toned woods, so that the inlay takes on an almost three-dimensional quality.

Most typical of all the inlay motives used in Baltimore, however, are the bellflower and the eagle. The bellflowers are usually separated by a dot or a loop, and never, in all the pieces that I have seen, joined together or telescoped as they are in New England furniture of the period. Whether in inlay or carving or a combination of the two, the bellflowers tend to fill completely the space allotted to them. (*Figs. 1, 5*). When a motive is not enlarged to cover a whole chair splat or leg, it is confined within a given geometric design in a double inlay (*Fig. 6*). The use of the eagle was generous in every respect. Its neck, wings, legs, or claws are usually stretched to anatomical capacity if not beyond.

Curly maple is used in large strips and bandings, often as an inset for the more intricate inlay but also for its own decorative merit. When used in its own right it is usually outlined with narrow strips of dark and light geometric patterns. The use of color in reverse on the lower part of a leg is another characteristic of the Baltimoreans. The tassel is an appropriate supplement to the bellflower. I know of several tables, each with a long Baltimore history, which have maple inset, tassel, and bellflowers used in combination. Frequently

FIG. 5 — MAHOGANY CARD TABLE, semicircular, with satinwood cross banding on both horizontal and vertical edges of the top, also on skirt, where a geometric inlay appears on lower edge. Ovals inlaid with lily of the valley on the stiles, while the bellflower drops inlaid on legs appear on three sides of front legs and two sides of back legs in a lavish manner of ornamentation characteristic of Baltimore. *Collection of the Hon. & Mrs. Breckinridge Long.*

FIG. 6 — MAHOGANY CARD TABLE of modified D-shape with cross-banding of satinwood on edge of top and the skirt outlined with a broad band of satinwood. Characteristic are the panels on the legs in the shape of elongated teardrops containing small drops, affording the contrast of woods so much desired by Baltimore cabinetmakers. *Privately owned. Photograph courtesy The Maryland Society, Colonial Dames of America.*

FIG. 7 — OVAL-BACK CHAIR, combining carving and inlay. Seat upholstered half over skirt and inlay along lower edge, typical of Baltimore. *Collection of Mrs. Frederick Leiter.*

Fig. 8 — Secretary in Sheraton Style, decorated with painted glass panels of Hope and Temperance found on other Baltimore pieces. *From the Metropolitan Museum of Art.*

Fig. 9 — Mahogany Chair from a set made for Charles Carroll of Carrollton. Shield back combines details from Sheraton's *Drawing Book*. Prince of Wales feather motif (with five feathers) at the top of center splat with carved bellflowers below. Festoons of drapery and acanthus leaf carving at base of splats. Swell-front seat upholstered half over frame. On two sides of the legs are recessed panels carved with half rosettes, to which bellflower drops are attached. *Collection of Mrs. Dorothea Harper Pennington Nelson.*

carving and inlay were intermingled on a single piece. They merge and augment each other time and again, providing contrast of color, texture, and plane (*Figs. 2, 3, 4, 7*).

At the height of the Hepplewhite period in Baltimore, inlay was used to the greatest possible extent, and in the hands of a poor craftsman a piece of furniture became a monstrosity of patchwork. But there was another type of decoration used by skilled workmen to elaborate the surface: painting. It was combined with inlay or carving or both, or used alone. And if three forms of decoration were not enough, an inserted panel of painting on glass was added (*Fig. 8*). Certain pier tables combine painting, inlay, and glass work, with the added splendor of a marble top. Painting was used by itself on a large group of Sheraton and Adam-type chairs, tables, and benches which were decorated with conventional designs or with scenes of Baltimore, both architectural and natural.

Two other features that appear in Baltimore furniture are herringbone inlay and the inlaid decoration of an entire top. The herringbone is usually a contrast of two shades of mahogany, bordered with a line inlay. Baltimore craftsmen often inlaid two or three sides of table or sideboard legs. This feature appears on so many Baltimore tables and so rarely on those of other regions in America that it becomes an outstanding local characteristic.

In construction Baltimore furniture is very close to English, perhaps closer than any other American school — a fact which has led to its being frequently classified as English. The chairs were usually made with small stretchers across the corners, or two large stretchers across the seat, instead of the usual American corner blocks. Al-

most all the tea tables and card tables have one or sometimes two stretcher supports under the top from the centers of the apron crosswise. Again in the chairs, the frame of the seat often has a band of veneer edged with inlay along the lower part instead of being overupholstered or slip-seated (*Figs. 7 and 9*).

The shield back rounded at the bottom was the favorite of the Baltimore chairmakers, but we also find examples of the round back and of the modified shield (*Fig. 9*), which can easily be traced to Hepplewhite's designs. Sideboards were sometimes made with an intricate beehive construction under the top to strengthen them and to prevent them from warping and splitting.

Mahogany is almost always used for fine Baltimore furniture of the Hepplewhite period, though I have seen both cherry and walnut treated in a very sophisticated manner. In the interiors of drawers and the backs of sideboards, desks, and chests of drawers a general selection of woods was used. A very coarse-grained yellow pine known as Anne Arundel pine, from the county adjacent to Baltimore, often appears. Poplar is the most common, but a great deal of Maryland oak and chestnut were used. Ash appears frequently and elm occasionally. Often a mahogany piece will be mahogany throughout, and a walnut piece walnut. I have a Baltimore serving table with drawer which is walnut throughout and veneered with mahogany.

Baltimore-made furniture of the Hepplewhite period is not only very light in effect but usually of the lightest possible construction. Yet with this delicacy the cabinetmakers used many different shapes. In sideboards we find serpentine and bow front as well as the more usual break front with convex ends. The kidney shape appears in sideboards and tables. There are a complete clover leaf table with typical Baltimore inlay; a very deeply serpentined chest-on-chest with characteristic crotched and inlaid surface treatment; and a group of intricately shaped chests of drawers — a combination of serpentine and break front. The examples chosen for illustration here are, on the whole, representative rather than unusual.

The craftsmen of Baltimore of the period around 1800 made every kind of furniture: beds, cupboards, sofas of exquisite refinement, secretaries and other case pieces, benches, liquor boxes, small tables, and mirrors. Some of their best workmanship is exhibited in sideboards and hunt boards, chairs, tables, and clocks. The dining room, particularly, can be completely equipped with Baltimore furniture at its finest.

Almost every feature of Baltimore furniture appears in some other American school of cabinetmaking, but when several of them are combined in any one piece, it is almost unmistakably Baltimorean. Moreover, the Baltimore inlaid bellflower and eagle medallion have characteristics as distinctly their own as a Philadelphia carving above a ball-and-claw foot, or a Rhode Island shell on a block-front desk. Baltimore furniture of the Federal period should not be confused with contemporary Salem pieces, which it resembles in fine workmanship and, superficially, in style. Nor should it be loosely classified as "southern." It deserves to be recognized and appreciated as the distinguished work of a distinctive school of cabinetmakers, about whom there is doubtless much additional information awaiting discovery.

John Seymour & Son, Cabinetmakers

BY MABEL M. SWAN

As indispensable to antiquarian research as archeological excavation is the kind of "digging" that Mabel M. Swan has done in the field of furniture. Delving into all sorts of early records and documents, seeking out primary sources of information whose existence was not even suspected, she has established the identity of innumerable early craftsmen who would otherwise have remained in obscurity. Notable among her discoveries recorded in ANTIQUES are cabinetmakers and joiners of Newport, Newburyport, Boston, and Salem. Her series of articles on Samuel McIntire is particularly noteworthy. This account of John Seymour, which appeared in our October 1937 issue, is representative of the type of contribution that she has made. It not only established the man himself in terms of vital statistics, but identified his work on a stylistic basis.

JOHN SEYMOUR, or his more aggressive son, Thomas, affixed the label *John Seymour & Son, Cabinet Makers Creek Square* within the lower drawer of a secretary formerly in the Philip Flayderman collection and now in that of Henry F. du Pont. Had he failed to do so, the two able craftsmen might have remained forever unhonored and unsung. Their names, certainly, would not have been retrieved from oblivion, for a year of searching uncovered almost no public mention of them. Hence in preparing the following notes, I have had to piece together from newspaper advertisements, directory entries, and little else.

Seymour is distinctly not a Massachusetts name, though countless members of the clan are to be found in Connecticut and New York. Four successive John Seymours in Hartford suggested investigative possibilities; but not one of these men followed the cabinetmaker's trade. Records in the old Boston Court House quote the administration papers of a Thomas Seymour, merchant, who died in Boston in 1757, leaving a multitude of debts as his sole legacy to his "two minor children Mary and Thomas J.," both "above fourteen years of age."

These children were placed under the guardianship of James Boies, a prosperous farmer and paper manufacturer of Dorchester. On his death in 1796, his property was left to Jeremiah Smith Boies, who, in 1798, is listed as the owner of a wooden building on Creek Lane, where, at the same time, one John Seymour, cabinetmaker, had a shop. The location of John's shop in this short lane, and the fact that he named his son Thomas, suggest some connection between John and the bankrupt merchant on the one hand, and the Boies family on the other. The fact that Stephen Badlam's cabinetmaking shop with its numerous apprentices was close by James Boies' paper mill is also suggestive. Badlam's will records that Thomas Seymour, probably the son of John, owed him over $1,300. However, such connection as may have existed between Badlam and Seymour I have thus far been unable to define. Since supposition is valueless, I shall confine myself to assured findings.

The death notice of Jane Seymour, published in the *Columbian Centinel* in 1815, states that the deceased was the wife of John Seymour formerly of Axminster, England. Axminster, be it said, is a small market town in the county of Devon, and noted for its carpet manufacture. The 1789 Boston directory contains no mention of John Seymour, but the issue for 1796 records a cabinetmaker of the name on Creek Square. The 1798, 1800, and 1803 directories list him on the same square, which, until 1803, constituted the south side of Mill Creek, back of Union and Ann Streets. Seymour's shop was actually on a short lane, Creek Lane, which is described as running from "Brooks Corner in Marshall's Lane by Mr. Bulfinchs to Scottoms Alley." From the preceding evidence it would appear that at some time between 1780 and 1796 John Seymour came to Boston with his wife Jane and son Thomas. As we find Thomas in business as early as 1805, he must have been at least ten years old when he accompanied his parents to this country.

The first newspaper mention of John Seymour's work that I have found appears in *Russell's Gazette* for June 28, 1798. Its wording suggests that already Seymour was in high repute as a maker of excellent furniture:

"To be sold at Public Auction at the house of Dr. J. Flagg, next door to Rob't Hollowell, Esq., north side of Fort Hill near Oliver's Dock all the Household Furniture viz. Bed Carpets Chairs China Mahogany Dining Pembroke and Card Tables of the workmanship of Mr Seymour four post & Field Bedsteads Looking Glasses 1 pair Stones 38 by 14, plates of a Lapidary cut; 1 hand mirror Mahogany Bureau & double key'd Harpsichord with four stops in good order & with improved jacks.

"Josiah Flagg"

The first mention of Thomas Seymour, son of John, that I have found in the Boston directory appears in the issue for the year 1805. The listing is as follows:

"Seymour Thomas furniture warehouse Common Street."

Thomas married Mary Baldwin on December 2, 1804. Two days later the following advertisement appeared in the *New England Palladium:*

"Boston Furniture Warehouse

"The Subscriber respectfully informs the Public that he has taken and fitted up in a most commodious manner those extensive premises at the bottom of the Mall (lately occupied as the Washington Museum) for the purpose of a Commission Furniture Warehouse where he now offers for sale a handsome assortment of Cabinet Furniture, Chairs, Looking Glasses; and from the daily addition to his Stocks and to the prices of the Furniture he flatters himself that persons purchasing any of the

FIG. 1 — SEYMOUR SECRETARY (*1790-1800*). In many respects the most exquisite Seymour piece yet discovered. Note particularly the tambour doors, the vertical figure of the mahogany veneer, the delicacy of the inlay, the ivory-bound keyholes, and the Bilston-enamel drawer pulls. The interior of the cabinet compartments is painted a curious robin's-egg blue — a frequent but not invariable mark of Seymour workmanship. The labeled piece in the du Pont collection is very similar. Details of inlay differ, and the drawer fronts show a different selection and handling of the mahogany. But the enamel handles and ivory keyhole escutcheons recur. In size and proportions these two labeled Seymour secretaries are to all intents identical. *From the collection of Mr. and Mrs. Andrew Varick Stout.*

FIG. 2 — SEYMOUR SIDEBOARD (*1790-1800*). Less richly decorated than the preceding secretaries but exhibiting a similar fondness for tambour work, applied pilasters, and the use of ivory inlay. Note particularly the scrolled apron piece, which will presently reappear. We have already seen enough to observe that, in this period, the Seymours had a recognizable manner, but were inclined to vary the details of their pieces. *Formerly in the King Hooper collection.*

FIG. 3 — HERE ATTRIBUTED TO THE SEYMOURS (*c.1800*). Here the Seymours have stepped out of Hepplewhite and into Sheraton, and produced a very fine piece of furniture. In the main, carving and reeding supplant inlay; but the favored pilasters recur in conjunction with tambour doors; so likewise do the scrolled apron piece and attractive keyhole insets. The leg blocks adorned with bosses are something new. So are the turned and reeded legs. Note particularly the foot with its three rings and slightly concave extremity. *From the collection of Ginsburg and Levy.*

FIG. 4 — HERE ATTRIBUTED TO THE SEYMOURS (*c. 1800*). The finest known Seymour sideboard. Here salient features appear. The reeded legs are extended to the top board as engaged reeded columns, whose upper sections show carved floral forms in relief. But we again meet the familiar tambour doors with flanking inlaid pilasters, the apron piece, here carved with heads of grain. The heavier top board is inlaid with a curious pattern of half circles, a motive repeated along the skirt. Note that while the reeding of the legs is capped with an acanthus carving, the feet are precisely like those in the preceding piece. The cupboard interiors are painted a robin's-egg blue. *From the collection of Mr. and Mrs. Andrew Varick Stout.*

above articles will find it to their advantage to call as above.

"Thomas Seymour

"N.B. As it is his intention to keep constantly on hand a general assortment of every article necessary to furnish the house completely, those who may have second hand furniture to dispose of will have an opportunity of obtaining its full value by depositing the same at the said warehouse where the Cabinet business is carried on in all its branches and any article made on the shortest notice."

Young Thomas showed business enterprise in his frequent advertisements, which, indeed, were probably necessary, for several other furniture warehouses in the neighborhood offered him plenty of competition. While he was located at the foot of the Mall, his most formidable competitor was "at the head of the Mall." This was one William Leverett, who advertised even more extensively than did Thomas, and even took occasion to broadcast to his conservative Boston patrons that his furniture was "made of the best material and by the first town workmen; whatever may be said by *some cabinet makers* to the *contrary,* notwithstanding."

But in spite of Leverett's boasts of superiority, the Seymour warehouse or Boston Warehouse, as it was also called, flourished. Early in 1805 appeared the announcement of its enlargement to include "upholstery in all its branches executed in a superior manner by a Person from London." Also "Chintz Furniture made in Plain and French Style, Stuffing of all kinds, Bordered Italian and French Paper Hangings in Stiles and French Pannels, Carpetings

of every description and in the neatest manner and at the shortest notice at Seymour's Boston Furniture Warehouse where is constantly on hand the largest assortment of furniture ever offered for sale in this Commonwealth by retail or for exportation." Seymour, too, could boast.

Three months later, in May 1805, our progressive young cabinetmaker still further enlarged his business and advertised that he had "fitted up a convenient place for the reception and sale of Carriages and has on hand a few handsome Coaches and Chaises cheap for Cash." As a further inducement for patronage he added, "A Cart purposely for carrying Furniture hung on springs — any Gentleman moving his furniture may be accommodated with the cart and a careful driver." A second postscript followed: "Wanted as above — a Lad, about 15 or 16 years old."

December 1805 found Seymour's furniture warehouse still doing a thriving business. To its usual advertisement of cabinet furniture, chairs, beds, and so on, was added the announcement of a sale of various kinds of carpeting and looking-glasses, which the young owner had purchased at a sale of the stock of Smith & Parker. Thomas' customary postscript announced "a very pleasant House to be let and entered into immediately." Apparently this was his father's house, for the next address of John in the directory is given with that of his son on Common Street.

The popular furniture warehouses of the day, besides facilitating the purchase of household furniture, became natural centers about which cabinetmakers inclined to settle. Thus in April 1806 Charles Tuttle, a well-known Boston craftsman, advertised that he was moving his shop to a place "adjacent to the Boston Furniture

Warehouse." The next advertisement of the Seymour warehouse appeared in May 1806, and called for two good workmen and one apprentice to the cabinet business. The Boston directory issued for the year 1807 carries the two following entries:

Seymour Thomas furniture warehouse
    Common Street
Seymour John house Common Street

No Boston directory was issued for 1808. From the business disasters of that year, due to the great embargo on all commerce, the cabinetmakers were by no means immune. They naturally abandoned newspaper advertising. Thomas Seymour's warehouse was obliged to close its doors, not again to be opened. The directory for 1809 records Thomas as still dwelling on Common Street, but he is now in partnership with James Coggswell, a cabinetmaker on the same street. There were two Coggswells, both cabinetmakers, John, the father, and his son James. As early as 1789, John Coggswell had a shop on Middle Street. Twenty years later he is listed as a surveyor of mahogany as well as a cabinetmaker. His high reputation is implied in an advertisement for the sale of 10,000 feet of very fine Santo Domingo mahogany which had been surveyed by Mr. John Coggswell.

Perhaps it was because the Coggswells were members of the Massachusetts Charitable Mechanics Association that Thomas Seymour joined that organization. But his new partnership was of but brief duration; nor did his membership in the Mechanics Association last much longer. He was discharged in 1812, a procedure usually consequent upon non-payment of dues. Apparently undaunted by his previous

misadventures, Thomas advertised, May 30, 1812, as follows:

"On Tuesday next the
WARE ROOM of the
BOSTON
CABINET
MANUFACTORY
Congress Street

will be opened when will be for sale Useful, and Ornamental Cabinet Furniture all made by or under the direction of Thomas Seymour. Ladies and Gentlemen particularly the former customers of Thomas Seymour are respectfully invited."

Whether or not this undertaking was successful is a matter of conjecture. We know, however, that at this time business in Boston was virtually at a standstill. However, in March 1813, Thomas advertised for an apprentice, "a lad of correct habits, docile and healthy, about 14 years of age as an Apprentice to a cabinetmaker where he can learn the business in all its branches."

Thomas was now living on Milk Street and his father on Portland Street between John McHeron, a soap boiler, and James Bracking, a laborer. Two years later John's wife Jane died, aged 77, and we find no further mention of him in the Boston directories. It was in this year that Stephen Badlam's will records a debt of over $1,300 owed him by Thomas Seymour. The only other death of a Seymour in the Boston death records is "Seymour —— Alms House" in 1818. Can this have been John?

As for Thomas, he shifted his abode to Portland Street, while apparently continuing his shop on Congress Street until 1821. His next shift carried him to 837 Washington Street, where he was a close neighbor

FIG. 5 — HERE ATTRIBUTED TO THE SEYMOURS. In ANTIQUES for March 1931 this splendid commode is credited to Samuel McIntire. The propriety of transferring the honor to Seymour begins to be apparent when we compare the reeding of the engaged columnar supports with that of the sideboard of Figure 3, and note the character of the floral carvings, and the form of the feet, which is but a well-scaled modification of that in the two preceding examples. The lion's-paw toes will be found on some other pieces, attributable to the Seymours but not here illustrated. *From the Museum of Fine Arts, Boston.*

FIG. 6 — HERE ATTRIBUTED TO THE SEYMOURS. Later than the preceding sideboards. The tambour doors have disappeared. The only inlay is a double line of half circles around the top. Handles are of handsomely cut glass. Form and treatment of the legs closely similar to those of the sideboard of Figure 4. The foot, though in contour very like that in previous examples, assumes a pear shape owing to the omission of the usual three rings. Again we encounter a flamboyant floral carving more elaborate than the preceding, but analogous in spirit. Note how closely the base line of the centre section corresponds to that of the sideboard of Figure 4. *From the collection of Townsend H. Soren.*

to Aaron Willard. Here he remained until 1842, doubtless doing some work for the Willard clockmakers. Thereafter his name disappears from Boston directories. Of his death, which must have occurred about this time, neither the Boston nor the Roxbury records make mention.

Among documents in the Bostonian Society I have found the following note, which I quote in the hope that it may call forth additional information concerning the two Seymours. It reads:

"Given by Mrs. Mary A. Carter a Knitting Bag and needles used by daughters of Thomas Seymour a Boston Cabinet Maker from 1805 to 1828. His home was on the old Mill Dam now Beacon Street."

John Seymour was an excellent craftsman. From whom did he learn his trade? What became of him? These are but two of the many questions the answers to which we should like to have help in discovering.

A NOTE ON THE SEYMOUR MANNER

By HOMER EATON KEYES

MRS. SWAN has accomplished what at the outset seemed an impossible task — the collecting of shreds and scraps from the life fabric of John Seymour and his son Thomas and the reweaving of them into a pattern, which, though fragmentary, is at least coherent. Perhaps it suffices to know that the family name in association with the cabinetmaking trade appears in the Boston directories as early as 1796 and is to be encountered here and there in public print until as late as 1842.

During this long period of years the Seymours suffered sundry vicissitudes of fortune. There may have been occasions, like the ghastly days of the embargo, when they were virtually idle for weeks, or months, on end. Nevertheless, even discounting their productive opportunities to the greatest calculable limit, these men, individually and jointly, must have turned out vast quantities of furniture, of which it is fair to assume much more has survived to the present than has been identified or even dimly recognized as of Seymour workmanship.

The purpose of this note, supplementing Mrs. Swan's excellent narrative, is if possible to determine whether the Seymours exhibited either constant or recognizably sequential mannerisms in the design of their furniture. If they did, a reasonably intimate acquaintance with their general and specific treatment of detail should enable us to extend materially the list of pieces attributable to the Boston masters. Hence an attempt in the direction indicated appears to be justified. One difficulty of such an undertaking is removed by the fortunate circumstance that we may begin our study with pieces whose Seymour authorship is attested by printed labels. On the other hand, however, we are hardly embarked upon our enterprise than we find our course confused by the fundamental change in furniture design which, early in the 1800's, marked the quite general adoption of the Sheraton mode and the consequent relegation of Hepplewhite to a secondary position.

The earliest and in so far as I am aware the only labeled pieces of Seymour furniture, made probably somewhat before the year 1800, betray their makers' allegiance to Hepplewhite. They are dainty in proportions, and delicate in every detail of workmanship. Carefully selected mahog-

FIG. 7A — SEYMOUR DETAIL: CARVED APRON PIECE AND ACCOMPANYING INLAY FROM FIG. 4.

FIG. 7 — SEYMOUR DETAILS: *b*, LEG FROM FIGURE 4. *c*, FLORAL DESIGN FROM FIGURE 6. *d*, CARVED CAP FROM LEG OF FIGURE 6.

any veneers, satinwood inlays, ivory key-hole escutcheons emphasize the almost feminine elegance imparted by the slender taper of rectangular legs, the close crop-ping of overhanging elements, and the neat elimination of elaborate moldings (*Fig. 1*).

But this kind of design and workman-ship could not long continue. Fashion was demanding something different. Away with inlaid rectangular legs. Henceforth such members must be turned, and either fluted or reeded. Away, again, with all but a min-imum of inlay. Let carving supplant it. Away also with flush surfaces and the clean simplicity of joints so perfect as to need no concealing moldings. Henceforth let there be salience of major members, variation of relief achieved by panels and moldings, and, therewithal, a constant play of al-ternating light and shadow. Disobe-dience to so insistent a command was not even to be contemplated.

Even had we no tangible evidence that the Seymours clambered aboard the Shera-ton bandwagon, the very nature of the situ-ation would convince us that they did that very thing. Yet for men of their refinement

and exactitude in craftsmanship, the shift from one style to another may not have been readily accomplished. We should ex-pect it to have been gradual: here the sub-stitution of a new form for an old one, there the retention of a long-time favorite motive, but, on the whole, a steady drift toward complete acceptance of the new vogue. This, evidently, is what occurred.

Between the work of John the father and Thomas the son it seems unwise to try to differentiate, at least for the present. We shall do well enough if we succeed in dis-covering some indices of what we may call the Seymour manner, that will be accepted by the serious student and that will prove applicable in validating some new and rather surprising attributions. The best way in which the task may be accomplished is by means of an orderly sequence of pic-torial demonstrations, beginning with the known and acknowledged and progressing step by step to embrace the hitherto un-known and unidentified. It is objects, not words, that must tell the story, though words must be used to direct attention to such features as constitute the important links in the chain of argument.

The "Style Antique" in American Furniture

BY RUTH RALSTON

NOT LONG AGO collectors refused to accept as properly antique the furniture that was made after about 1815. As the twentieth century advanced, however, the period known as the Greek Revival came to be taken more seriously. Attention was focused on it by an exhibition held at the Metropolitan Museum of Art in November 1943, which emphasized architecture with some reference also to interior furnishings. Developing this study, Ruth Ralston of the staff of The Magazine ANTIQUES investigated the sources of Greek Revival design, sifting out the French and English influences which contributed to an American style. Miss Ralston had been well equipped for this type of investigation through her years at the Metropolitan Museum as Associate Curator of the American Wing, and through her later work on the editorial staff of ANTIQUES. This article, which appeared in ANTIQUES for October 1945, is illustrated largely with pieces included in the Metropolitan's 1943 exhibition, originally published in an ANTIQUES article by Joseph Downs.

THROUGH the work of furniture designers in France and England at the end of the eighteenth and the beginning of the nineteenth centuries, the classical revival in furniture reached its ultimate development in the antique style predicated upon an adaptation of classical forms. American cabinetmakers were, as always, selective in evolving their own unmistakably American versions of the style. Their models were both actual pieces of imported furniture and the illustrations in books of designs. It is not always easy to tell whether the French of English strain is dominant in the American product, especially as in the parent strains themselves there was so much borrowing back and forth. In this exchange the French con-

tributed more to English furniture design than they borrowed from it.

But the antique style, once it appeared in this country, did not immediately sweep the boards. Traditional eighteenth-century English structural outlines did not go completely out of fashion in either England or America until well toward the middle of the nineteenth century. The simple, basic patterns of Hepplewhite, of the Sheraton of the *Drawing Book*, and of the *Cabinetmakers London Book of Prices*, which in 1793 shows nothing in the newest versions of the classical style, were followed, as well as the more modish and eccentric shapes of the antique style.

In America a great deal of furniture in what may be called the Sheraton tradition survives. Although it carries on the earlier forms made in this country, it displays that heaviness in outline, lack of delicacy in the turning of members, and coarseness in the carved decoration that marked the taste of the period. In this category are the pedestal table supports with outsweeping tripod legs; the pembroke and card tables with straight legs, twist-turned or acanthus-carved; dressing and work tables of similar form; tall or short bed posts, often with acanthus and "pineapple" carving; chests of drawers and other case pieces with attached three-quarter columns at the front angles extended to form the feet. Particularly in New England we find attractive pieces of this Sheraton-tradition furniture with variations in the turnings and carvings that mark local centers of manufacture.

At the same time furniture was being made in America which clearly marks the advent of the antique style. French influence on this American furniture is both direct and indirect. The Directoire style in France — which covers the period from the beginning of the Revolution to the beginning of the Empire in 1804, not merely the political period of the Directoire — established forms, particularly in chairs and sofas, characterized by flowing curves in the structural members inspired by classical seating furniture. Some of their basic outlines became current in England and eventually in America. Among them are the stool or chair with supports composed of two meeting segmental curves or crossed reversed curves — the so-called curule type — and its various derivatives; the simple classical or "Greek" chair with incurved legs, the back either rolled over or with a wide back rest; sofas of the backless type with outcurved arms and legs; a similar form with high back; the couch or chaise longue with low rolled foot piece; and tables which imitated the classical tripods and low stands.

Certain decorative motifs as well as basic outlines were also popularized by these French pre-Empire pieces, such as the stiffly conventionalized water leaf and a flattened acanthus leaf running partway down the supports of tables and chairs, and along the arms of all kinds of seating furniture. Reeding was applied to the frames of chairs and couches. Light but muscularly carved dog and lion forelegs and paws firmly uphold seats of chairs and benches. Small winged-paw feet appear on sofas. The lyre, anthemion, and lattice cross-bars fill the backs of chairs.

Although the introduction of these antique forms in modern dress and the new and popular rendering of long-used motifs of decoration may be credited to French designers, all of these ideas were warmly received across the Channel. The American interpretations often appear more closely related to early English Regency versions than to the fundamental Directoire conceptions (*Fig. 1*). There were, however, numerous purely French decorative motifs which our cabinetmakers must have taken directly from French models.

There is Directoire influence on American furniture, possibly a greater amount of direct influence than has yet been discovered. But it is a little misleading to label "Directoire" every American chair or sofa with a simple, flowing, "classical" outline, unless it is understood that the French inspiration may be several removes from the accomplished piece, and the more immediate ancestor to be found in the English branch of the family.

If the recognition of the influence of

FIG. 1 — A "GREEK" CHAIR. The back posts, side rails, and front legs are joined in flowing curves. The concave lines of the legs were adapted from the familiar classical chairs. This chair, made in New York in the early nineteenth century, is closer kin to English chairs of the Regency than to the Directoire versions of the Greek chair. *Courtesy Ginsburg and Levy.*

FIG. 2 — AMERICAN CHAIRS of this type closely followed the French models. The legs of this chair have a slight reverse curve which indicates a date toward the end of the classical revival period. *This and Figures 4, 6, 9, 11, courtesy of the Metropolitan Museum of Art.*

FIG. 3 — CLASSICAL SOFA with legs derived from the stool with crossed legs. This ancient form had never suffered total eclipse even in the Medieval period. *From the Boston Museum of Fine Arts.*

FIG. 4 — THE MIXTURE of Roman massiveness and Greek detail is apparent in this labeled bed by the French cabinetmaker Charles Honoré Lannuier, who worked in New York between 1805 and 1819. The placing of the bed against the wall, and the crown supporting the curtains, continue an eighteenth-century French fashion. *From Bartow Mansion.*

FIG. 5 — A CARD TABLE of Empire derivation made in New York. The strange beast, apparently part eagle, part lion — minus forelegs — has his counterpart in the anatomically curious animal supports of French tables. *From the collection of Mrs. May Harris-Hamersley.*

FIG. 6 — THIS MARBLE-TOPPED rosewood and gilt pier table, probably the work of Lannuier, is in the Empire style. It is elaborated with winged caryatids and dolphins, and ormolu mounts. *From the Brooklyn Museum.*

FIG. 7 — CHEST OF DRAWERS fairly typical of the veneered American Empire bedroom pieces. The top drawer, with curved front, projects to the line of the blocks above the columns. Lines of inlay, as shown here, are unusual on case pieces of this kind. *From the collection of H. B. Henscher.*

French pre-Empire design on American furniture has led to some exaggeration of its importance, this is a healthy corrective to the opinion held some years ago that French influence was not apparent in this country until about 1810. A stream of refugee aristocrats who began to arrive in the cities of Baltimore, Albany, Philadelphia, and New York in the early 1790's brought French culture to our shores. The prominent Americans who had made long sojourns in France acquired a taste for the elegant and graceful furniture of the last years of the monarchy. Thomas Jefferson's eighty-six crates of the contents of his Paris house with which he furnished Monticello are a case in point. In the early years of the nineteenth century French artisans were appearing in many American cities. At present we know more about the Gallic artists and craftsmen in New York than in other American centers. The most famous of the émigré furniture makers, Charles Honoré Lannuier, who was working in New York by 1805, is a good example because his work displays the successive changes in styles from Louis XVI to Empire with which the average French cabinetmaker was familiar. Other French cabinetmakers were working in New York, in Boston, Philadelphia, Baltimore, and Charleston. They disseminated their native styles, and in turn borrowed ideas from their Anglo-American brethren.

A good deal of French Empire furniture of the simpler sort entered the country in the first three decades of the nineteenth century, and it was considered very fashionable. An entertaining entry in Philip Hone's *Diary* under date of April 29, 1835, witnesses the continued popularity of the French fashions, at least in New York. "A sale of French mahogany furniture recently imported took place at the City Hotel today. This being considered an interference with the regular journeymen's business, some of them went to the place where the furniture was exhibited, and cut and scratched it in such a diabolical manner that the injury exceeds a thousand dollars."

Besides actual pieces of furniture, American cabinetmakers by the early 1800's could draw upon design books for models of French Empire fashions. Percier and Fontaine's *Recueil de décorations intérieures* of 1812 presented some of the models created by these Imperial architects. The plates of the valuable *Meubles et Objets de Goût* brought out by Pierre la Mésangère between 1802 and 1830 show designs published by Percier and Fontaine in their book as well as drawings based on the pieces they had executed. But Mésangère also illustrates many patterns in the current French fashion of less than Imperial splendor suitable for the nouveau riche bourgeois who had succeeded the pre-Revolutionary aristocrats. These fine engravings offer precise models. The plates must have been immediately available as they came out because so many trails from England, Germany, and America lead back to them. While Mésangère's plates do not necessarily depict every design for furniture introduced in France during thirty years, an examination of the engravings must give a pretty clear idea of types and of the development, or, more properly, the degeneration of furniture styles during the period. Some unexpected findings in connection with what has been known as the "American Empire" style result from an inspection of Mésangère's collection.

The sweeping curves of the front legs and outrolled back of the classic chair of the Directoire soon give way in popularity before other shapes. Most of the chairs have square front posts with paw feet, winged figures supporting the arms, and solid square or rounded backs. However, in the Restoration, to judge from published drawings and from photographs of French furniture, the incurved lines for chair legs returned to popularity in France. The simple "Greek" chair is shown in a plate dated 1818. It may have been reintroduced from England where it had never gone out of fashion. Likewise the form of couch with high outrolled head rest and low foot rest, the back extending part way to the foot as a half-back, is conspicuously absent. The essential form of this graceful chaise longue, originally attributed to France in the time of the Directoire, is always presented in the English design books of the first quarter of the nineteenth century. American couches on this order were also made from the early 1800's until at least the middle of the century. The sofas with high backs and arms of scrolled outline made in England and America do not find their immediate prototypes in Mésangère's plates. The bold paw and wing foot for sofas and couches is not developed there to any extent. Even on the case pieces the paw feet so characteristic of so-called American Empire chests, sideboards, and wardrobes are also disappearing by 1806 in favor of straight, short, turned or stump feet.

But if among the hundreds of designs in Mésangère we do not find the immediate ancestors of some American furniture forms supposed to be of direct Empire derivation, there are many plates which could very easily have been the inspiration for furniture makers in this country. The hairy foreleg and paw support is carried on for a time, appearing in the 1802 plates on high tripod lamp or candle stands which have a circular top resting on small beaked heads. High stands of this type were favorite "American Empire" parlor or library pieces. In 1802 the outlines of "taborets" with square incurved legs and small paw feet suggest the shapes of American window benches and low stools.

The "fauteuil de bureau," a chair with back rounding to form the high solid arm rests, was made here, but usually in a simplified and later version than those illustrated in the first years of the French publication. It is not until around 1806 that the Empire side chair that was to become so popular in America begins to make its appearance (*Fig. 2*). This is the chair with vertical splat and wide head board or cresting, the arms sweeping in a concave line from the front rail. From such chairs were ultimately developed the ubiquitous "fiddle-back" side chairs made by the thousands in America. Toward the very end of the period the upholstered chair with swan head, or scrolled arms, more comfortable than beautiful, was a common parlor or library chair.

By 1810 a type of rectangular sofa had been published which was taken over to some extent in America. It is built on straight rectangular lines, with stout posts at either side of the front terminating in heavy round knobs. There is usually a necking of brass around the top of the posts. A great many American sofas have carved arms in the shape of cornucopias filled with fruits and leaves. The extravagantly luxurious bed executed for the Empress Josephine must have started the fashion for this cornucopia furniture.

The French beds, with their great sweeping curves in head and foot boards, and

Fig. 8 — Sheraton's Grecian Sofa. While English and American furniture makers undoubtedly were familiar with this plate (*a*) from Sheraton's widely circulated *Dictionary*, they improved on the design as the graceful American sofa (*b*) reveals. Furniture craftsmen seldom followed published plates in detail. *Sofa from the collection of P. B. Rolfe.*

Fig. 10 — A Center Table made in New York (*c. 1830*). A good example of full Greek Revival style following English precedent. The fine stenciled decoration as a substitute for ormolu mounts is an American invention. Rosewood with touches of gilding in the leaf carving. *From the Museum of the City of New York.*

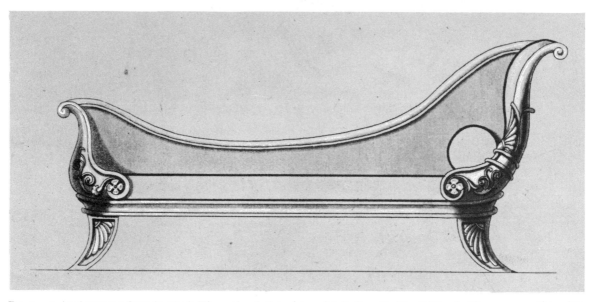

Fig. 9 — a, An American Sofa (c. 1820). The maker followed two details from Smith 1808 book. The arms are after plate 63 (b), the winged feet are after plate 65. The composition does not have the graceful harmony of the earlier classical sofas.

their heavy plain bases, inspired the American "sleigh bed" as well as a similar English version of the form. A "French bed" in its native land and in England is one placed against the wall, the head and foot boards seen in profile. While adapting the French design the French custom of placing the bed is not often followed in this country, although we occasionally find beds intended to be set sidewise to the wall *(Fig. 4)*.

Many American tables were based on French models. The Imperial furniture bristled with winged lions, griffins, and sphinxes balancing the slabs of tables on their heads. Some of this menagerie found its way into American furniture *(Fig. 5)*.

Designs for the side tables with column supports in front begin as early as 1804. The back is often fitted with a mirror. Tables of this type were taken over from Empire forms *(Fig. 6)*. There were many French and American versions of these side tables. In following the pattern through the thirty years of Mésangère's publication we find the beautiful applied brass mounts with their griffins, swans, goddesses, amorini, bees, flowers, and conventional wreaths, leaves, and anthemia disappearing in the early part of the second decade of the century. Even the severely plain brass bands or neckings of the columns of furniture are going out. By 1820 the marble-top tables upheld by great scrolling brackets are making their appearance.

From about 1820 on quantities of chests and drawers, dressing tables, "escritoires," bookcases, and wardrobes were made in America much like the heavy case pieces which had been in fashion in France through the second decade of the century *(Fig. 7)*. Moldings are dispensed with. A heavy cornice either flat or in the form of a cyma curve tops some of the tallest American pieces. An architectural turn is given by engaged or by free-standing columns with plain capitals. The most elaborate of the American pieces, unlike the late French Empire prototypes, show a good deal of carving in capitals of columns, and paw feet with acanthus leafage which is sometimes gilded. Elements taken from the Empire style were adapted to American pieces like sideboards and slant-front desks for which there was no analogous French form.

A charming and distinctively American invention of the early nineteenth century had been the substitution of stenciled and painted designs in gilt and bronze powder for the expensive metal mounts of the early French Empire furniture. Decorations in these media did not go out of fashion in America when the bronze embellishments were no longer used in France.

French furniture had become plain and ponderous during the Restoration *(1814-1830)*. By the time that Louis Philippe came to the throne in 1830 the cycle of the classical style was complete. Mésangère's plates show the slippery descent of the style just before it glides into the revived rococo. A great many of these late patterns seem to have been used in America, as they were in England and Germany.

Much "American Empire" furniture remains. When it parallels, in American guise, the French examples of the earlier years of the style, it fits the roomy interiors of our Greek Revival houses. Its worst fault is that it shares the obese decadence of the style which it imitated. The artistic pit from which the fashion could not raise itself is well illustrated in the designs in John Hall's book published in Baltimore in 1840.

In recognizing the influence of France

on American furniture of this period, we must not underestimate the continuing influence of England. American furniture makers of the first four decades of the 1800's referred to English precedent as they had for two hundred years. The parallel borrowing between England and France is what complicates analysis of the American product.

In England influential followers of the French late eighteenth century fashions had already introduced the antique style when Sheraton's *Cabinet Dictionary* appeared in 1803. But neither in the *Dictionary* nor in the *Cabinetmaker and Artists Encyclopaedia (1805-1806),* which was unfinished at the time of his death, did Sheraton succeed in catching the real spirit of the archaeological style of the 1790's, though there are in the *Dictionary* the basic outlines of some of the forms which were destined to last the period out in America as well as in England. Among the structural shapes that have American counterparts are Sheraton's high-backed "Grecian sofa" which has rolled arms forming a continuous line with the seat rail *(Fig. 8, a and b).* The frame shows the reeding which became one of the marks of Regency furniture. He calls his couch with the high outrolled headboard, low foot roll, and half-back, a "Grecian squab," a name which persisted. He also has in the *Encyclopaedia* a drawing of the classical chair with curved back rest on which he displays flat acanthus-leaf carving extending partway up the reeded arms. Possibly it was a plate from Sheraton that inspired the fearsome animals which uphold some American sofas made in the South. The more extravagant designs of the *Dictionary* and *Encyclopaedia* were, however, ignored by American furniture makers.

The London *Chair-makers and Carvers Book of Prices* (supplement of 1808) must have been very useful to American cabinetmakers. Its simple and explicit plates give line drawings of all the furniture in the early Regency antique style made here in the beginning of the nineteenth century. There are several versions of the popular classical chair. The chairs and stools with meeting curve and crossed curve supports are entitled "Grecian cross Fronts." There are sofas and couches with all the various types of rolled and straight arms and backs; details of arm rests and supports of all kinds.

Such early Regency furniture was currently called Greek or Grecian. But it remained for Thomas Hope with the publication of *Household Furniture and Interior Decoration* in 1807 to crystallize a more strictly archaeological mode for which the term Greek Revival can be reserved. By this time fashionable London society, following the lead of the architects and wealthy amateur collectors, had become possessed of an archaeological enthusiasm embracing Greek, Roman, and Egyptian classical remains. The Greek phase was the most persistent and important in interest. How much Hope owed to the French Empire designers it is difficult to decide. He did not hesitate to lift some of his designs from the executed work of Percier and Fontaine. He also copied or modified slightly a number of patterns for beds, chairs, and sofas that had appeared in Mésangère. But he also contributed to the English furniture repertory new shapes, more exotic and varied decorative motifs, and an insistence on archaeological scale and correctness. The light flowing lines of the earlier Regency furniture are tightened.

Our Greek Revival architects left us few sketches of the furniture which they would have considered suitable for their interiors. We have, however, a good idea of what Alexander Jackson Davis would have designed in the way of furniture from his well-known watercolor drawing of the reception rooms in a New York house. The tables, chairs, sofa, screen, and mirror are all of the most severe classical shape. And they hark back directly to Hope's *Household Furniture*.

George Smith was a commercial designer and cabinetmaker. His *Collection of Designs for Household Furniture,* with plates dated 1804-1807, was published in 1808. A specific evidence that this book was used in America is afforded by the details of a sofa of Massachusetts origin *(Fig. 9, a and b)*. Smith quite evidently picked over the plates of Mésangère, and he also knew the interiors which Hope had created for the display of his collections of antiquities, for he faithfully reflects these sources of his inspiration. He followed all the decorative trends of his time, including the Chinese and Gothic fashions with the Greek, Egyptian, and Roman, in order to omit nothing that was currently popular in Regency England. Smith conceived some fantasies in furniture. But in the drawings in his first book he managed to simplify ornament, a great deal of which is of Greek derivation, and to suggest a scale that befitted the substantial Regency houses. He shows circular tables with a heavy column support resting on a platform upheld by great paw feet. These big columns, often coarsely fluted and surrounded at the base with a deep cup of leaves, were characteristic of the Greek Revival style in England *(Fig. 10)*. They were probably suggested by the shafts of Roman candelabra. Smith's

book includes among the simpler designs parlor chairs with the incurved "Greek" legs, and with dog-leg supports; "French" beds, couches, and sofas, of straight Empire type, as well as the characteristically English forms of sofas and couches with classical lines. Duncan Phyfe might well have used Smith's "window seat" as a suggestion for an ottoman *(Fig. 11)*. The lion paw with wing and the curved "saber" foot, both much used for sofas in America, are developed in this book.

By 1820 the English furniture in the Greek Revival style made for the average householder had become more angular and simple. This tendency can be noted in the American pieces which are related to English designs. On the typical "Grecian chair" straight, substantial front legs, often reeded, were substituted for the incurving legs of the earlier classical chair. The "Grecian squab" couches, and the sofas with high back and curving arms lines, continued in fashion. Sofas of rectangular shape made their appearance. The front posts of those sofas may have been evolved in deference to the shaped rectangular supports of late Greek and early Roman thrones and couches. In any case sofas of this type properly belong to Greek Revival furniture.

The single column of heavy dimension or a substantial three-sided shaft, although not new inventions, now become the common supports for tables. The case pieces such as secretaries, bookcases, and wardrobes are high and severe in outline, with architectural embellishments confined to pilasters or columns. By this time Gothic and classical elements are often combined in the same piece. Greek ornament — the fret band, the Greek form of acanthus and water leaf, acroteria, paterae, and above all the anthemion and a great deal of acanthus leafage — appear in the carved decoration of furniture in the classical style. Paw feet, especially on tables, are still popular. The winged animals as well as the Egyptian sphinxes are going out of fashion.

It is Regency furniture from Hope on that coincides in period with the widespread Greek Revival architecture in America, and its inherent qualities make the term Greek Revival furniture particularly applicable to it.

Some of the American pieces which are most satisfactory in design combine structural lines and decorative motifs from several traceable stylistic antecedents plus distinctively American contributions. These indigenous products deserve special study of their makers and of their characteristics as regional expressions in cabinetmaking. It is possible to trace developments in American furniture paralleling the changes of French furniture from the style of the 1790's through the Restoration, and English furniture from the early Regency through the 1820's. What evidence remains, however, from houses completed in the heyday of our Greek Revival architecture shows that there was less consistent furnishing in a particular version of the antique style than a legitimate mixture of furniture, some in the Sheraton tradition, some early Regency, some Empire, and some in the later type of "Greek" style.

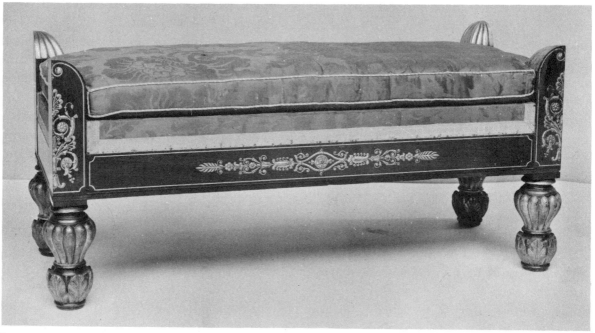

FIG. 11 — ONE OF A PAIR OF OTTOMANS signed by Duncan Phyfe. Upon its rosewood frame, pure Greek forms are applied in gold leaf — the anthemion or honeysuckle, the patera, and spiral foliated with acanthus. The acroteria at the corners also suggest the ancient classic finial. *From the Brooklyn Museum.*

Random Notes on
Hitchcock and His Competitors

BY ESTHER STEVENS BRAZER

ESTHER STEVENS BRAZER *(formerly Esther Stevens Fraser) was one of the numerous leading authorities in specialized fields who made their writing début in* ANTIQUES. *Her earliest articles in the 1920's were about painted furniture in America, particularly the painted chests of Pennsylvania. Painted decoration, in fact, became her specialty, from the practical as well as the scholarly point of view. She mastered the all-but-lost art of stenciling and free-hand painting on wood, metal, walls, and floors, and through her teaching passed it on to many followers. She was tireless in recording authentic early designs wherever she found them, and conscientious in restoration work, of which she did a great deal. Since her death her endeavors have been perpetuated in the Esther Stevens Brazer Guild. Her book,* Early American Decoration, *is a guide to the old techniques and a valuable record of her researches. The field of painted decoration in America has been proved much greater than previously recognized, but the Hitchcock chair still remains its most widely known manifestation. That is why we have chosen from Mrs. Brazer's numerous writings in* ANTIQUES *this article from August 1936, which shows the type of original research that she did, even in a relatively familiar field.*

FOR the reader's convenience, these notes may as well begin with a brief résumé of the already familiar events in the life of Lambert Hitchcock, chairmaker. Hitchcock was born in Cheshire, Connecticut, June 28, 1795. He died, apparently at Unionville in the same state, in 1852. In 1818 he settled in the village of Barkhamsted, where he established a chair factory. In 1821 the community was rechristened Hitchcocksville; in 1866 it assumed the name of Riverton, evidently a satisfactory appellation, since it has not since been altered.

Hitchcock is said to have engaged first in the making of chair parts which were shipped to Charleston, South Carolina, and other southern coastal cities. This does not mean that he turned out fragments of chairs, but the unassembled elements — backs, seats, slats, stretchers, and so on, which were easily and inexpensively packed and shipped

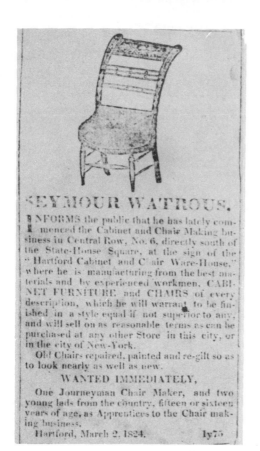

FIG. 1 — ADVERTISEMENTS OF SEYMOUR WATROUS (*1824*).

FIG. 4 — THE STENCIL KIT OF Z. WILLARD BROOKS. From Hancock, New Hampshire. Velvet dauber at extreme right. The stencils, cut from copybook paper, are late. *From the collection of Maro S. Brooks.*

FIG. 2 — CHAIR APPARENTLY BY WATROUS (*c. 1824*). Compare with illustration in the Watrous advertisement. Back shows better proportions, better turnings, and greater delicacy of detail than we find in Hitchcock chairs. Leg turnings less fussy. Shaping of lower part of front legs more carefully treated. *From the collection of Mrs. Madeline Wiles.*

and could be put together by the ultimate purchaser. This method is said to have been widely adopted by manufacturers of cheap furniture, who in the heyday of the traveling peddler and of the country store used such agencies for the distribution of their product.

After a few years, Hitchcock seems to have abandoned the selling of knocked-down furniture. At any rate he embarked on the more ambitious project of manufacturing completely constructed and more or less elaborately painted chairs for middle-class homes. Such articles were known to the trade as "fancy chairs." Fancy chairs had enjoyed a considerable measure of popularity since the 1790's, though with the passing of time the delicate early forms were supplanted by sturdier designs, and quickly applied stenciling superseded the more delicate and costly process of hand painting.

In 1826 Hitchcock had reached his peak of prosperity, which he celebrated by erecting a new factory employing upward of a hundred hands, including women and children. In 1829 financial reverses compelled a reorganization of the business. Arba Alford, who was previously general manager of the concern, was admitted as a partner, and manufacturing continued under the name of Hitchcock, Alford & Company. The arrangement thus made continued until 1843, when Hitchcock withdrew to establish a business of his own in Unionville. The old establishment was, however, carried on by Arba Alford and one Josiah Sage under the name of Alford & Company until 1853, when a new and different industry supplanted chairmaking in the old shop. Meanwhile, Hitchcock's venture in Unionville had proved unsuccessful and was gradually abandoned.

As we pass from personal biography to a study of furniture, it is necessary to emphasize the fact that the term "Hitchcock chair," as usually employed, is generic rather than specific. In other words, most persons use it to designate a wide diversity of chairs whose only common characteristic is a painted surface adorned with stenciled designs in gold or colors. Such chairs were turned out by many shops, in many places, over a long term of years. Among these shops, the one owned and operated by Lambert Hitchcock was apparently the most consistent in labeling its products. Despite the wear and tear of time, many fancy chairs of the 1820-1840 period still retain the inscription clearly lettered on the back strip of the seat: *L. Hitchcock, Hitchcocksville, Conn. Warranted.* So by virtue of his enterprise in advertising himself, while most other manufacturers were content with anonymity, Lambert Hitchcock has been popularly accepted as the originator of the general style exemplified in the painted chairs of his day, and as the genius from whose creations his contemporaries derived their inspiration.

One hesitates to hurl down the statues of the gods, and thus incur punishment for sacrilege. If now I seem to be embarking on such a perilous adventure, let me defend myself in advance by saying that, while Lambert Hitchcock was evidently a good citizen, an honest man, and a conscientious chairmaker, he is not to be reckoned among the deities who have ruled the tastes of humankind. All the essential motives discoverable in his earlier chairs — notably the turned top rail with a rectangular bar in its midst — will be found in Sheraton's design book of 1803. The leg turnings of Hitchcock's chairs are decadent versions of those to be found in Sheraton's drawings. Other makers of fancy chairs in America apparently had a hand in developing the type prior to Hitchcock's advent. Two newspaper advertisements dated March 2, 1824, by Seymour Watrous of Hartford testify to this probability. One portrays a round-seated chair of a type that we incline to associate with the modes of 1815, the other a chair with rectangular seat — much cheaper to construct than the round type, and in its major features very like the early Hitchcock product.

Again we find that one William Moore, Jr., a man old enough to be Hitchcock's father, was a resident of Barkhamsted at least twenty years before Hitchcock set up business. Moore was a manufacturer of chairs and so continued, more or less in competition with his new neighbor, until forced out of business in 1829. An inventory of assets filed at the time of Moore's insolvency affords an interesting view of the business ramifications of a country manufacturer more than a century ago. The inventory in question lists 100 chairs on their way to Philadelphia; 46 in the hands of G. & I. Wills, Northampton; 30 with Lewis Baily in New York; and many others in less distant communities. The wholesale valuation of these pieces was 62 cents each. It is appalling to think that anyone should have to conduct business at the meagre margin of profit implied by such a figure.

Thus far I have found only two chairs by William Moore, Jr., both in possession of one whose family lived in Westfield near Springfield, Massachusetts, when the chairs were purchased. The decoration of both is adequate, and the striping exceptionally fine. An edging of braided cane around the seat of the caned example is a touch of elegance seldom encountered. The second of

these Moore chairs is signally important because of its resemblance to the labeled Hitchcock example of Figure 3. The stencil units of the two are so nearly identical as to suggest that they are the work of the same painter working for two manufacturers. If this is not the case, we must assume that one shop was actually tracing the designs of its rival. One leaf in the two patterns precisely matches a leaf in the other — a circumstance not to be explained on the ground of pure accident. It may be that Moore joined forces with Hitchcock. Mrs. Mabel Roberts Moore, author of a pamphlet on Hitchcock, thinks she remembers seeing the name of William Moore, Jr., in a list of Hitchcock employees.

In this connection it is worth observing that, though Lambert Hitchcock is said to have established himself in Barkhamsted in 1818, I find his first recorded purchase of local property to have been in 1820. Mrs. Moore, his recent biographer, states that he built his large factory about 1826 and thereafter changed from manufacturing chair parts for foreign shipment to producing complete chairs. Fully decorated Hitchcock chairs would therefore date from 1826 or somewhat later, if they carry the label *L. Hitchcock, Hitchcocksville, Conn. Warranted.* Such early chairs, in my opinion, exhibit a finer sense of line and proportion and a keener appreciation of good turnings than contemporaneous chairs by William Moore, Jr. Their bronze stenciling is unsurpassed — well designed and superb in its brilliance. Such excellence is not apparent in Hitchcock's later products. We cannot say when Moore began making chairs of the style exemplified in Figure 3. But we know that Hitchcock was turning out virtually the same article in 1829. Evidence supporting this state-

FIG. 3 — DETAILS FROM CHAIRBACKS. *Right,* William Moore, Jr. *Collection of Mrs. Gilbert Jones. Below,* Lambert Hitchcock. *Collection of Mrs. Arthur Oldham.* The stenciled decorations of the two chairs are almost identical. The Moore Chair is stenciled *Wm. Moore, Jr.* on back of seat rail.

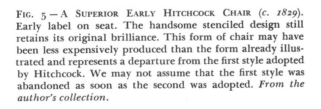

FIG. 5 — A SUPERIOR EARLY HITCHCOCK CHAIR (*c. 1829*). Early label on seat. The handsome stenciled design still retains its original brilliance. This form of chair may have been less expensively produced than the form already illustrated and represents a departure from the first style adopted by Hitchcock. We may not assume that the first style was abandoned as soon as the second was adopted. *From the author's collection.*

ment is afforded by a receipted bill for nine chairs. Five of the original set recorded in this bill still survive, identical with the example pictured in Figure 3. At the time of this sale, October 1829, Lambert Hitchcock was suffering financial reverses. The retail price of his chairs was $1.50 each. William Moore's wholesale figure, we recall, was 62 cents each.

A finer labeled Hitchcock than that pictured in Figure 5 would be hard to find. The stenciling is in almost mint condition, lustrous as if burnished. Around the frame of the caned seat runs a braided-cane border. Even before Hitchcock's business was reorganized the lustre of his stenciling began to fade. Evidence of a timid use of bronze is found in the chair of Figure 6. The design on the slat is compressed and relatively uninteresting, while the urn and scroll motive in the midst of the upper rail is wholly inadequate to the space occupied. The previously mentioned braid about the seat is missing.

In her biography of Lambert Hitchcock, Mrs. Moore tells us that the application of stencil patterns was accomplished by women. In this process, she says, the workers first dipped their fingers in oil, then in dry bronze powder, which they forthwith rubbed through the stencil apertures on the still slightly damp painted surface of the chair. As a result of this constant rubbing, the women's fingers in time became hard as boards. Though I have had much practical experience in stenciling, my attempts to emulate the practice described have been so unsuccessful that I fear Mrs. Moore may have been misinformed by someone anxious to withhold the jealously guarded secret of stenciling. A book whose fifth edition was published in 1826, and available to Hitchcock, directs

the manipulation of stenciling powder with a pad of soft glove leather stuffed with cotton wool. The ninety-three-year-old craftsman who taught me the art and mystery of stenciling used a similar dauber covered with velvet instead of leather. Likewise a stencil kit recently found at Hancock, New Hampshire, is equipped with a velvet pad (Fig. 4). With such an apparatus the texture and shading of the old-time bronzing may be perfectly reproduced. The horny handedness of Hitchcock's female employes may have been due to a process known as "handing," which calls for rubbing a foundation coat of paint with pumice and water under the bare palms of the worker.

After the reorganization of the Hitchcock enterprise under the name of Hitchcock, Alford & Company (1829), the factory continued chairmaking very much in the old manner. However, we now find pieces in which a fine irregular graining is superimposed upon a black ground. Formerly, the two-tone effect had been achieved on a red undercoat — a circumstance responsible for the erroneous assumption that all Hitchcocks were given a preliminary brushing of red. During the period beginning about 1829, a basket of fruit was added to the firm's repertoire of stencil patterns. We find it alike on chairs bearing the label of L. Hitchcock and of Hitchcock, Alford & Company (Fig. 7).

A Hitchcock and Alford rocker in my collection displays a flower and leaf pattern and scrolled ears that hark back to earlier designs, though evidently a later and, in the scrolls at least, less careful cutting. On the legs, front stretcher, and back posts occurs a conventional vine pattern in freehand stroke whose cost at today's wage scale would be more than the Hitchcocks-

FIG. 6 — A LESS SATISFACTORY EXAMPLE (*c. 1829*). Compare the pinched and timid stenciling with the rich design shown in the preceding illustration. Because of the shape of its solid slat and the associated protuberances, such a chair is popularly termed a "turtle back." The resemblance to a turtle is more pronounced in some other examples. *From the author's collection.*

FIG. 7 — MARKED HITCHCOCK, ALFORD & COMPANY CHAIR (*c. 1829*). With basket of fruit and flowers. *From the collection of Mrs. Marean.*

FIG. 8 — HITCHCOCK, ALFORD & COMPANY ROCKER. Compare scroll design applied to top rail with that of the chair of Figure 7. The deterioration is evident. *From the author's collection.*

FIG. 9 — CHAIR LABELED BY J. K. HATCH. Perhaps a New Hampshire item. Heavy seat and nondescript legs. *From Higgins Antique Shop.*

ville concern received for the chair complete *(Fig. 8)*.

While Lambert Hitchcock had many competitors and some imitators, few of them marked their products. Figure 9 pictures a stenciled chair with heavy wood seat and nondescript legs, which exhibits the branded label *F. K. Hatch, Warranted.* I believe it to have been made in New Hampshire. To the advertisements of the Hartford chairmaker, Seymour Watrous, I have already referred. The pictured example of what may well be his work is from a set which, strangely enough, was purchased by the present owner in Seville, Spain *(Fig. 2)*. Of their American origin I have never entertained the slightest doubt. Hartford was one of those New England ports whence ventures were shipped on sundry vessels to unforeseen and often strange destinations.

In conclusion I wish to pay brief tribute to one of the last old-time stencilers, Z. Willard Brooks, who was born in 1812, and, from 1840 until his death in 1906, was a resident of Hancock, New Hampshire. Not long since his decorating equipment was found tucked away under the the eaves of his farmhouse dwelling. Brooks was not a chairmaker. He purchased furniture, unfinished, from a local manufacturer in Peterboro or Jaffrey and adorned it according to his own fancy. This he did in 1835 in behalf of his new bride, Eliza Gordon. At the advanced age of eighty he was the only gilder in the locality who had the nerve to climb the spire of the village church to restore its shining glory. Some of the stencils that he cut with his own hands survive with his kit of tools; but the pattern according to which men of his kind were fashioned seems to have been irrevocably lost.

Returning for a moment to Lambert Hitchcock, I trust that my notes may assist in reaching a fair appraisal of the man and his work. Though he may have been surpassed by some, he was equaled by few. He made chairs that were pleasing to the eye, comfortable, honestly and enduringly constructed, and extremely reasonable in price. He gave employment to a small multitude of country folk. To that extent he was a public benefactor. And though he seems ever to have been hovering on the verge of bankruptcy, he never lost his valiant spirit. He worked hard, traveled widely in search of markets for his wares, and yet found time to serve his state as a member of its legislature. If only for reasons of pure sentiment we set special store upon examples of his work, we need not be ashamed of our weakness.

Notes on Shaker Furniture

BY EDWARD D. AND FAITH ANDREWS

OF THE MANY *communal sects that settled in this country, particularly in the nine-teenth century, the Shakers made the greatest contribution through their craftsmanship as well as through their religious philosophy. The first person to undertake a serious study of their craftsmanship was Edward Deming Andrews. He and his wife became acquainted with the surviving Shakers themselves, visited their communities, studied their history and philosophy, and discovered in their furniture the concrete expression of what they stood for. They also brought together an important collection of Shaker furniture before others had begun to recognize its charm. Their first article on the subject appeared in* ANTIQUES *for August 1928. It is reprinted here, condensed and combined with another article that they contributed to our April 1929 issue. In 1937 Mr. and Mrs. Andrews published their comprehensive study in book form,* Shaker Furniture. *Since then, many collectors have learned to admire these simple products for their integrity of workmanship and excellence of line. Today, in fact, Shaker furniture is appreciated not only by antiquarians but also by admirers of modern design, who find in it a manifestation of their own doctrine of functionalism.*

THE SHAKERS, properly known as the United Society of Believers in Christ's Second Appearing, were a sect founded by Ann Lee of Manchester, England, between 1760 and 1770. In 1774 the founder and a small group of followers emigrated to America, where they first settled near Albany, New York. Despite many early hardships, the sect prospered after the Revolution, and, by 1870, boasted some eighteen distinct communities, scattered through Connecticut, Kentucky, Maine, Massachusetts, New York, New Hampshire, and Ohio.

The products of Shaker industry were by no means restricted to utilization by members of the sect. Indeed, cloth from Shaker looms, garments wrought by Shaker fingers, and innumerable other articles of one kind and another, made in Shaker shops, were vigorously merchandised wherever there was prospect of a market.

The especial interest which attaches itself to the craftsmanship of the Shakers is due mainly to the fact that it was a direct expression of the life and thought of a whole group of people. Even though this craftsmanship was probably in the main adaptive in character, it represented a common feeling toward life markedly in contrast with the individualistic artistic exhibitions of the "world," from which these spiritually-minded but industrious people sought to escape.

FIG. 1 — SHAKER CHAIRS.

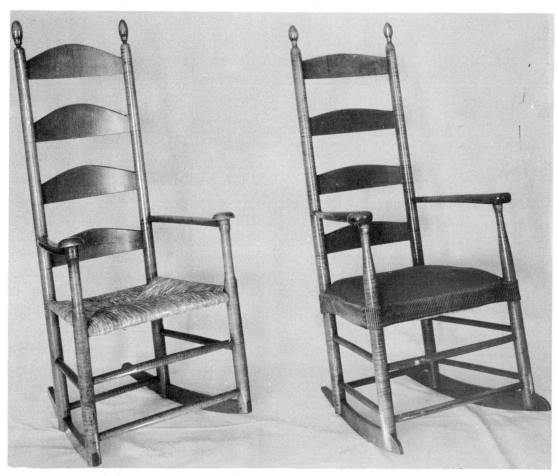

FIG. 2 — SHAKER ROCKING CHAIRS. Turnings of carefully selected curly maple. The age of such pieces is not determinable. The similarity to earlier colonial types is obvious.

Each community furnished its dwellings with appointments closely related in general design and purpose, whose variations never transgressed the laws of that innate simplicity which these people applied to their dress, their dwellings, and their mode of living. In the "world," fine furniture was made for those who appreciated it or could afford to buy it. The Shakers made furniture for themselves — it was a natural expression of a natural need.

Engrossed as these people were in the task of maintaining themselves in a world hostile or indifferent to their ideals, their early records speak chiefly of the great pulsating force in their lives — their religion. We read of their "hearts to prayer," but we cannot accurately trace the intricate origins of their program, "hands to work." No doubt they were required to construct household furniture on a fairly large scale soon after they came to this country in the latter part of the eighteenth century — 1774, to be exact. Converts to the sect often brought their personal effects into the order, but, sooner or later, the Shakers themselves had to supply their furnishings.

The infrequent references to the subject which one finds in Shaker literature indicate that among the earliest craftsmen, in some of the communities at least, cabinetmakers were included. When the Shirley, Massachusetts, settlement was bought by the state, Sister Josephine, in recalling the early history of that community, mentioned this occupation in her list of industries. J. R. MacLean, in his *Shakers of Ohio*, refers to the following vocations in Union Village, in 1819: blacksmithing, masonry, stonecutting, carpentry, tanning, fulling, clothing, cabinetmaking, tailoring, weaving, carding, and spinning. Clara Endicott Sears found among the Shaker journals at Harvard, Massachusetts, an account of chairs made there in 1843. By 1874 an illustrated catalogue of Shaker chairs, footbenches, floor mats, and so on, made at Mount Lebanon, New York, had been published, indicating that there the commercial possibilities of manufacturing furniture for outside consumers had been recognized.

Even though no distinct record exists, it is quite probable that, in the early days of the Society in America, every important permanent community to some extent constructed its own furniture. For instance — though a careful examination of the local history of Enfield, Connecticut, reveals no reference to such an industry — a great deal of furniture is known to have been made in the town. As time went on and the communities spread (and, later, as they decreased and concentrated), an interchange of supplies and workmen furnished aid in places where there had previously been little, if any, provision for making furniture.

In the last quarter of the nineteenth century, with the issuance of patents and the subsequent development of chairmaking for commercial purposes — especially at Mount Lebanon and Harvard — an inevitable standardization took place, resulting in a product quite distinctive and widely known. Popular interest in this community craftsmanship might soon have waned, however, if its authors had been hampered by unduly rigid, semi-ecclesiastic ideas of conformity. As a matter of fact, individual development was encouraged. The little groups were strengthened by assigning to each member the work that he or she was best fitted to perform, and then by permitting a free activity in the performance.

Many of the Shaker cabinetmakers were artists, for whom form rather than function held the larger meaning. For a prosperous half century or more after 1820, Shaker cabinetmakers, working freely and industriously at the task of adapting beauty to use, turned out an amazing assortment of "sprightly" pieces. Exceptional personalities, men of the skill of James Farnum, Gilbert Avery, John Lockwood, George Wickersham, Benjamin Youngs, Thomas Fisher, and Robert Wagan, attuned to the Shaker spirit of simplicity, designed and executed hundreds of unpretentious pieces. These, in turn, were copied by apprentices, or were altered to fit particular needs.

In the absence of available sources of information, the interesting problem of how just such and such styles were created must be answered indirectly. A study of the characteristic forms of Shaker furniture suggests the hypothesis that the early craftsmen adapted to their own designs existing colonial models before them. The Shaker chairs may well have been directly derived from colonial slat-backs; the trestle-board tables and light stands, from their early American prototypes. In like manner, the drop-leaf tables, chest of drawers, beds, and stools suggest an undeniable affinity to earlier forms.

Other evidences of adaptation may be adduced from the occasional light stands with drawers, the turnings of bedposts, the Windsor-type cross stretcher in stools, the "bread-board" feature of certain table tops, and the mushroom turning on the front posts of certain chair types. Plainly borrowed, also, is the general idea of the rare bureau-desks, as well as the broad features of Shaker slant-top desks, blanket chests, stretcher-base kitchen tables, candle-stands, and ironware.

It may be charged that the Shakers therefore originated no new designs and were not a creative people. In a sense this is true; but they were by no means mere copyists. In discarding all unnecessary embellishment and artifice, they reduced these earlier designs to their essentials of form and proportion, and, in so doing, achieved distinctly beautiful results.

Ready at hand were trees of plain and curly maple, birch, chestnut, butternut, and honey pine. These were sawed and planed and turned into elements which, finally, were as masterfully and conscientiously assembled, pegged and doweled together as ever joiner labored. The craftsmen were satisfied with none but the best tools and the best resultant quality. They constituted, in a sense, the first guild in America employed in manufacturing furniture on an extensive scale, and their ideals were those of the finest industrial societies of mediaeval days.

Anyone who has visited the Shaker settlements has probably noted the restraint and economy with which the furniture that came from their workshops has been disposed. The aspect of purity which invariably pervades the rooms of the spacious Shaker dwellings is not accidental. These people were wont to combine the appreciation of utility with a delightful sense of arrangement, which, added to what amounted to a passion for cleanliness, produced interiors of loveliness and refinement.

Moreover, necessity mothered many an invention within the isolated communities which sprang up in New York, Massachusetts, Connecticut, New Hampshire, Maine, Ohio, Kentucky, Indiana, and Florida. Chairs and tables were often adapted to special purposes.

FIG. 3 — SETTEE IN CHERRY. The ample proportions of this piece are in keeping with the spaciousness of Shaker rooms. Note the neatly turned knobs for holding the cording, and the massive dovetails of the frame.

FIG. 4 — SHAKER TRESTLE TABLE. Quite probably of the nineteenth century, but similar in many respects to very early American tables. The fiddle-shaped supports constitute one point of departure from early types. The high placement of the stretcher is another characteristic not common to early tables.

FIG. 5 — DUTCH-FOOT TABLE (*probably early*). An uncommon, possibly a unique example. Simple turning or tapering usually characterizes the legs of Shaker tables, though pieces were sometimes constructed with "button" feet.

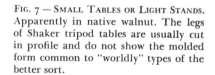
FIG. 6 — SHAKER TABLE. The top has been reduced in size. Original dimensions, 34 inches by 23 inches. Height of table, 24 inches.

FIG. 7 — SMALL TABLES OR LIGHT STANDS. Apparently in native walnut. The legs of Shaker tripod tables are usually cut in profile and do not show the molded form common to "worldly" types of the better sort.

FIG. 12 — TAILOR'S BENCH, FROM HANCOCK. A superior piece, all curly maple except the drop leaf. The chest was used by Shaker sisters for cutting out cloth for garments. Its movability is dependent on four small wooden casters fixed into the base of the frame. Within is a card with directions for removing the top of the bench. The instructions conclude: "This table was moved into the Elder Sisters' Room, June 22, 1843." Size, top, 72 by 32 inches; height, 33 inches.

FIG. 9 — DELICATELY CONCEIVED STANDS IN CHERRY. Note that the early, lipped drawer has given way to the later form. Native cherry, birch, butternut, pine, and maple were the woods most commonly used in Hancock and Mt. Lebanon.

FIG. 10 — WALL TABLE. This piece has a single leaf, and a drawer at each end. The form is an adaptation of a late eighteenth-century type. Wood, butternut and cherry.

FIG. 8 — DESK ON TRIPOD BASE AND SEWING STAND. As far as can be discovered, the desk is unique. The pedestal is curly maple, the desk itself, butternut. Whether the finely dovetailed drawers on the sewing stand are original or are later additions is undetermined. Several such stands exist, a fact which favors the first alternative. These pieces are apparently derivatives of colonial stands.

The back legs of Shaker side chairs, for instance, were often fitted at the base with an ingenious half ball of wood (sometimes of brass) joined in a socket by a thong, an arrangement which permitted the sitter to tip back easily or even to rock. Rockers were used early in the Shaker chair industry, an indication that austerity of belief did not imply undue asceticism in their manners and modes of living.

Because the Shakers placed chief emphasis on this utility of the products of their workshops, and because, therefore, their designs, once adopted, were perpetuated with high standards of excellence but with little subsequent artistic consciousness, their furniture has not received due appreciation. Yet there are many enthusiastic collectors of specimens of this interesting craft, who prize not only the things themselves, but also their associations with the modest folk whose spirit was transmitted to what they made.

FIG. 11 — SHAKER TALL CLOCK (*1806*). By Benjamin Youngs, a member of the early Watervliet settlement. He is said to have been the nephew of that Benjamin Youngs of wider note, co-author of *Christ's First and Second Appearing* (1808), who, at the time when this clock was made, was serving on the important mission which established Shaker societies in Ohio and Kentucky. The date, 1806, is probably correct, though crayoned later. Youngs also made wall clocks. The wood is cherry.

Victorian Art and Victorian Taste

BY FISKE KIMBALL

FISKE KIMBALL HAS *an international reputation as museum director, architect, writer, lecturer, art critic and historian. To* ANTIQUES *his major contribution has been a series of studies of Samuel McIntire of Salem and contemporary Salem cabinetmakers. The series is too long to reprint here, and fortunately its substance has now been incorporated in Mr. Kimball's scholarly book,* Mr. Samuel McIntire, Carver, The Architect of Salem *(1940). From his other writings in* ANTIQUES, *which cover such a diversity of subjects as sculpture, silver, and fabrics, we have selected this article, published in March 1933. It was written on the occasion of a special exhibition of Victorian arts at the Philadelphia Museum, of which Mr. Kimball is Director. We think it offers a stimulating approach, particularly for those who maintain that the decorative arts of the nineteenth century are of no academic or aesthetic interest.*

IT is a commonplace of the history of culture that each generation detests the art of its fathers, hesitantly tolerates that of its grandfathers, and takes to its bosom that of its great-grandfathers — which henceforth becomes part of the accepted canon of artistic propriety. In 1848, colonial houses were characterized by a Philadelphia "lady-historian," Mrs. Louisa Carolina Huggins Tuthill, as "hideous deformities to the eye of taste"; the churches were "wooden enormities." By the time of the Centennial celebration, in 1876, enthusiasm was rampant for everything made prior to the Revolution; but the Adam style and the classic revival were still banned. By 1920 these, too, had been admitted to admiration.

Such processes of rehabilitation begin by making specific exceptions. Prejudice against some period as a whole will persist, but is, in part, counteracted by amiable self-delusion. If we like a class of objects, we either put it back mentally into a previous, acceptable period, or else consider it as the bright harbinger of the better things of our own enlightened day. Even in France, people still curse the middle decades of the nineteenth century as the dark age of art. Yet Ingres, who painted until 1867, is properly absolved from complicity in its sins: he is thought of as a survivor of imperial classicism. Delacroix, who worked until 1863, is regarded as one of the "men of the '30's." The Impressionists, on the other hand, although their first exhibition was held in 1874, are viewed not as Victorians, but as moderns. Courbet and Manet were contemporary with Bouguereau. To stigmatize the latter as a "Vic-

FIG. 1 — PARLOR AT 28 EAST 20TH STREET, NEW YORK CITY (*1850-1875*). *American Rooms in Miniature by Mrs. James Ward Thorne, The Art Institute of Chicago.*

FIG. 2 — ROSEWOOD ARMCHAIR by John Jelliff & Co. Part of a parlor set used in New York City in the 1860's. *From the Newark Museum.*

torian," while admiring the other two, is arbitrarily to distort the period, which produced great as well as little men.

When the future scans its achievement in long perspective, the Victorian period will receive its due, and be allowed to count its great men as its own. But if, today, we continue to characterize as Victorians only those men of the period whom we do not admire, we are measurably justified by the fact that they were the very ones whom the Victorians most highly praised. What we really criticize is not *Victorian art,* but *Victorian taste.*

If we may venture to apply any single inclusive epithet to the art of the Victorian period, we may say it was the art of Romanticism. Ordinarily we date such Romanticism from the 'thirties, when Victoria ascended the throne. The art of Romanticism was largely an art of retrospection, with an interest in the old, the distant, the exotic. It was also an art of sentiment, in life and in literature. It worshiped nature and landscape. It reveled in admiration for the Middle Ages, their piety and chivalry as well as their naïveté and grotesqueness.

FIG. 3 — ROSEWOOD TABLE with white marble top, signed inside frame *J. H. Belter & Co.* Part of a large parlor set made for George Henry Bissell of New York. *Photograph courtesy Metropolitan Museum of Art.*

FIG. 4 — PAPIER-MACHE TABLE AND BELTER CHAIR (*Museum of the City of New York*); portrait of little girl (*collection of Mrs. Luke Vincent Lockwood*); with Victorian glass fruit dish, lorgnette, brooch, smelling salts bottle, and parasol. *Arranged by Mrs. J. Kearney Rice for New Jersey Garden Club display.*

Various aspects of this frame of mind became successively dominant. In England the first phase extended to about the mid-century. It was marked in architecture by the triumph of the Gothic Revival, in painting by the luminous naturalism of Turner, in furniture and decorative art by rever-sion to the rococo, not without consider-able originality of treatment. This was the time of rosewood furniture exhibiting an abundant curvature of outline and an ex-uberance of naturalistic fruit and flower carving.

The second phase may be said to begin

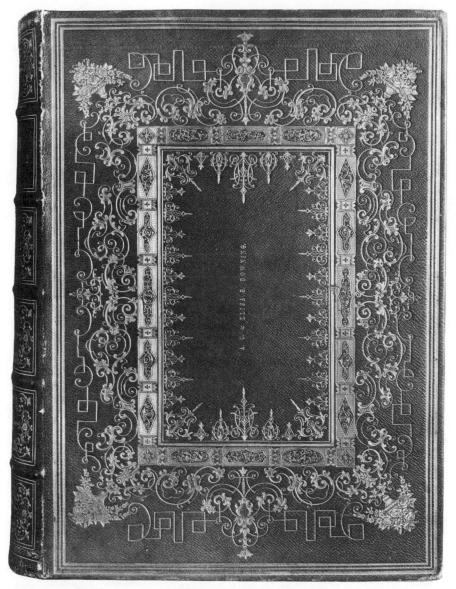

FIG. 5 — ILLUMINATED BIBLE, red morocco with ornate Victorian tooling, signed *E. Walker* on spine (*Harper & Bros., New York, 1846*). As expressive of one phase of nineteenth-century taste as the sentimental paintings and Rogers groups were of another. *Collection of Philip Hofer.*

with the great London International Exhibition of 1851, first of the world's fairs. By its very nature, this event emphasized the co-existence of varied sources of inspiration, among which artists or schools felt themselves free to choose one, or even many modes. It was the era, *par excellence,* of historical painting, fortified with a new historical knowledge of event and of *mise en scène.*

This historical attitude extended not only to the matter but also to the manner of painting. The Pre-Raphaelites sought to set the clock back to the time of Botticelli

FIG. 6 — CHECKERS UP AT THE FARM, group in plaster by John Rogers (*1829-1904*) published in 5,000 copies in 1877. *Society for the Preservation of New England Antiquities. Photograph courtesy Fogg Art Museum.*

and Mantegna. Their subject matter was drawn largely from the cycles admired and celebrated by the Victorian poets, of which Tennyson was soon the chief. In the arts of decoration, now thoroughly immersed in the "styles of historic ornament," a strong preference for the Renaissance was apparent. Furniture makers revived renaissance forms — in their characteristic material, walnut — with a liberty in adaptation that we, perhaps, think of rather as travesty.

In its third phase — established by the mid-'seventies — Victorian art reflected the ideas of Ruskin and of William Morris. These men realized, very rightly, that hitherto the art of the Middle Ages had been imitated in the letter rather than the spirit. Their effort was to effect a revival of the spirit of craftsmanship. Morris himself renewed, along mediæval lines, typography, tapestry weaving, and diverse related crafts. In architecture came the Queen Anne revival, based on suggestions from the simpler buildings of this monarch's time, and from the reigns of William and Mary, and King James. Charles Locke Eastlake led a related movement in the domain of furniture.

Victorian art is a term that may be thought to cover a multitude of sins. Victoria's reign was long — from 1837 to 1901; art, meanwhile, revealed an extraordinary diversity of manifestations. Many of them are still unsympathetic to us; but we are finding some of them at least endurable.

GLASS

Early American Glass

BY HELEN McKEARIN

To A VAST *army of glass collectors, American Glass by George S. and Helen McKearin
is a sort of bible. This monumental work, which appeared in 1941, is the most comprehensive treatment of the subject that exists. It incorporates the researches not only of
its authors but also of such students as Harry Hall White, Rhea Mansfield Knittle, and
Lura Woodside Watkins — many of which first appeared in ANTIQUES. Helen McKearin
herself has been a frequent contributor to ANTIQUES from its earliest days. While
her articles are all based on original research, some of them, like the one we have chosen
to reprint from the August 1941 issue, demonstrate especially well her ability to coordi-
nate and integrate the results of research so as to make them available to the layman. We
consider this article an extremely able summary of the whole subject of American glass,
expressed in language that anyone can understand.*

FOR most students and collectors "early American glass" is a comprehensive term indifferent to the factors of time and foreign influence. It bridges the widening stream of American glass manufacture from colonial days well through the mid-nineteenth century, covering all the various types and designs of glass which collectors have netted from that stream. While the term "early," as usually applied to a given piece of American glass, has its own peculiar variability, its implied time element is less general. It refers largely to the period when a given design, decorative technique, or method of manufacture joined the stream of American glass production. While patient students of the last two decades have pinned down many facts regarding these facets of American glass, the multitudinous problems they present are by no means completely solved.

Until the 1920's only two glassmaking centers had been the object of intensive research, that of South Jersey, then associated only with Caspar Wistar, and that of William Henry Stiegel at Elizabeth Furnace and Manheim, Pennsylvania. The researches of Hunter and Kerfoot in establishing the nature and characteristics of their output marked these two centers as the fountainheads of two distinct streams of tradition in glassblowing and decorative techniques in America. Subsequent studies have revealed the use of the same methods elsewhere, in the case of Stiegel before as well as after his ventures, and have emphasized the foreign roots of these traditions. In spite of these facts they are labeled Stiegel and South Jersey with the indelible ink of past error and common usage.

THE SOUTH JERSEY TRADITION

When we speak of the South Jersey tradition in glass we refer to individual off-hand pieces — by-products, not commercial wares — blown in the many bottle and window glasshouses of New Jersey, New York, and New England. In these houses the blowers habitually exercised their right to the fag end of the pot by blowing useful and ornamental objects for their own households and for friends. Since they were under no commercial compulsion to meet current fashion, they could form their pieces as fancy or taste dictated. The objects they created have the naïveté and peasant-like quality associated with folk art.

The general physical characteristics of these individual pieces are distinctive and unmistakable. They were blown mainly from window and bottle glass. Those from South Jersey were in shades of aquamarine, amber, green, sometimes blue, and also, in the 1880's, in such colors as opaque white and shades of rose and maroon; those from New York State usually in light greens or blue-aquamarine, occasionally shades of amber or olive green, and, rarely, blue; those from New England principally in various ambers and greens, less frequently aquamarine, and, rarely, blue and amethyst. Except for the very occasional use of the pattern mold in Jersey, all pieces were hand-blown. Decorative effects were obtained simply by color and shape or by a superimposed layer of glass tooled into a heavy swirl, swagging, or the so-called lily pad. Frequently an applied foot was crimped and the neck of a vessel threaded. Applied decoration, such as prunts and seals, quilling and rigaree, was also sometimes used on Jersey pieces. Later, decoration was achieved through the use of various color combinations in swirled and looped effects. No matter how delicate or graceful the shape and decorative treatment, the thickness of the metal invested the objects with a quality of sturdiness, rather than of fragility.

Many individual hand-blown pieces are found which are obviously in the South Jersey tradition, but are without definite identifying characteristics and unaccompanied by any history. Such articles are usually classified simply as South Jersey type.

Today few would have the temerity to attribute a piece of glass to Caspar Wistar's glasshouse established, in spite of England's ban on colonial manufacturers, near Allowaystown in 1739. Nevertheless, when he imported Continental glassworkers to man that factory, he probably was responsible for initiating an American glass tradition. Presumably it was carried about 1781 to the second Jersey factory, started at Glassboro by the Stanger brothers, former Wistar employees. Through the later migration of South Jersey blowers and the importation of other Continental glassmen it spread to the bottle and window glasshouses which gradually came into existence in the early 1800's in New Jersey, New York, and New England. Although there were a few eighteenth-century glasshouses in New York and New England, the majority were established after the turn of the century, as a spreading population and improving transportation created a wider market. Generally speaking, however, they were small houses producing bottles and window glass for a limited, virtually local, trade, and many were short-lived. The off-hand pieces — bowls, pitchers, and similar articles — blown by their workmen are to-

FIG. 1 — THE SOUTH JERSEY TRADITION. Expressed in an aquamarine pitcher made at Redford, New York. Threading of neck and lilypad decoration are typical characteristics.

FIG. 3 — "OHIO-STIEGEL." Small amethyst sugar bowl and cover; exemplifying eighteenth-century cover technique, with flange on cover which rests on rim of bowl. Body patterned in a sixteen-rib mold; applied petaled foot. Attributed to Mantua, Ohio. Height overall, 4⅞ inches.

FIG. 2 — STIEGEL "PERFUME" BOTTLES in *diamond-daisy variant, diamond-daisy,* and *diamond-above flute* pattern-molded designs; salt and "perfume" bottle in *checkered-diamond* pattern-molded design, possibly Amelung. *This and Figures 3 and 7 from the McKearin collection.*

FIG. 4 — BLOWN-THREE-MOLD GLASS PITCHER. Geometric type, combining sunburst, diamond diapering, and ribbing, patterned in a decanter mold. Applied handle.

day of comparative and often of extreme rarity. Some of the finest lily-pad pieces which have survived were blown at Stoddard, New Hampshire, and at houses in the northern and western sections of New York State.

The Stiegel Tradition

The Stiegel tradition in glass design and technique is the antithesis of the South Jersey. In general, it might be said to epitomize skills standardized to conform to the commercial requirements for table and decorative wares. Thus, it embraces a wide variety of types and decorative techniques.

The general physical features of the glass in the Stiegel tradition are as distinctive as those of the South Jersey. Both lead and non-lead glass were used. The colored metal, largely flint glass, was in shades of rich blues, purples, amethysts, and, rarely, emerald green. Shapes were expertly formed and rather sophisticated, faithfully following their English and Continental prototypes. Decoration was widely varied: wheel-cut, shallow stylized engraving, enameling, and expanded pattern-molded designs, such as paneling, ribbing, fluting, and variations of the "Venetian diamond," the latter sometimes in an all-over pattern and sometimes with small diamonds above long vertical flutes.

An aspect of "Baron" Stiegel's glass manufacturing which cannot be too often emphasized is that he brought to America skilled engravers and enamelers trained in Continental glasshouses, and blowers who had practiced the Venetian techniques in the English factories in the Bristol district. Consequently, the Stiegel glass not only had the design and decorative elements of the fine imported table and ornamental wares of the day, but also, as was intended, was so like them that it is frequently impossible to distinguish the domestic from the imported articles. However, it is probable the *diamond-daisy* and its variant, the *daisy-in-hexagon,* and the *diamond-above-flute* pattern-molded designs were originated at Manheim. No prototype of these has as yet been found in English or Continental glass. Nor so far as we know were these particular designs used in any other American glasshouse.

When students realized the extent of Stiegel's success in producing glass like that of his foreign competitors, and the fact that, after his bankruptcy, his craftsmen naturally continued to use the same techniques and designs in later factories where they found employment, the term "Stiegel type" was coined to designate pieces having the requisite "Stiegel" features but unaccompanied by any sort of indisputable evidence as to origin. It is quite possible that many of the plain and engraved flips so like Dutch glass were blown in early New York City glasshouses or in Philadelphia. It is probable that many of the wines and decanters attributed to Stiegel were made at the contemporary Philadelphia Glass Works which disputed Stiegel's claim of being the first flint-glass manufacturer in America. Pieces with engraved decoration once attributed to Manheim are now known to have been made in the New Bremen glass factory of John Frederick Amelung, in the Philadelphia-Baltimore area, in the Pittsburgh district, and some even in New England. It is known that some enameled decoration was used at New Bremen. Because of all these facts, "Stiegel" has become, with a few exceptions, a generic rather than a specific term.

During the years following the Revolution and in the early 1800's, the "Stiegel tradition" in pattern-molded glass was

FIG. 6 — PRESSED GLASS. Lamps of design attributed to Pittsburgh. Columnar candlesticks attributed to Sandwich because they correspond to fragments found on the site. *Photograph courtesy of Parke-Bernet Galleries.*

FIG. 5 — LACY GLASS. Deep dish made at Sandwich; clear glass. Diameter, 9¾ inches. *From the collection of Doctor Charles Green.*

FIG. 7 — PATTERNED GLASS DECANTER in *horn of plenty* pattern. A Sandwich pattern, copied in Pittsburgh; said to have been inspired by Halley's comet which appeared in 1835. The design is an adaptation of an old, almost universal, motif, found also in blown-three-mold and cut glass.

carried into the Ohio River and Pittsburgh districts by former craftsmen from Stiegel's and Amelung's glasshouses and by others trained either here or abroad in the same techniques. As the need for glass grew, so did the glasshouses. In a few of these early houses, a limited amount of tableware was undoubtedly blown for local trade, but their principal output consisted of window glass and bottles, the most essential articles in a newly opened country.

Although the old German post method of bottle blowing was practiced to some extent, the more common Stiegel method of using one gathering of glass blown in the dip mold (pattern mold) and expanded seems to have been preferred. The pattern-molded bottles and flasks and the household utensils blown in the same molds are now often called "Ohio-Stiegel." The pitchers, bowls, and similar articles in this group, which includes some of the finest and rarest pieces of American glass, were blown from fine-quality bottle glass, and, unlike most of the glass in the Stiegel tradition, have an individual quality. When flint-glass tableware was added to the regular products of existing factories and new ones were established for its manufacture, the Stiegel tradition in decorative techniques was perpetuated. But soon shapes and treatments were evolved which were distinctly midwestern and American. The advent of the pressing machine in the late 1820's revolutionized the industry in the midwest, as it did in the east.

Blown-Three-Mold Glass

Blown-Three-Mold is a milestone in the history of American glass manufacturing and design. So far as we now know, it was the first commercial tableware blown in full-size molds and was perhaps an independent American contribution to glass designs in molded tableware. This glass, blown in full-size three-piece molds, made its appearance about 1820, and was a distinctive American product for many years, probably until about 1835. To compete more successfully with the expensive and fashionable Irish and English blown glass with wheel-cut designs, ingenious glass manufacturers devised a means of simulating the cut glass by adapting its patterns to blown glass through the medium of the full-size mold. Though prompted by commercial expediency, Americans did not stop with mere imitation of a few simple designs; they created many of their own. Actually, a new type of glass was evolved.

The patterns in which Blown-Three-Mold occurs fall into three categories, according to their predominating motifs. Geometric, Arch, and Baroque. Designers made the most of the possibilities in combining the simple geometric motifs of vertical, diagonal, horizontal, chevron, and spiral ribbing with each other, and with diamond diapering and the sunburst motifs, of which there are at least nine. Consequently, the majority of the patterns fall into the Geometric group. Three or four of the simplest patterns are found on pieces blown in full-size two- or four-piece molds. Likewise, there are pieces blown in two- or four-piece molds in Baroque designs, which are included in the Blown-Three-Mold group because of their similarity in quality of metal and in design.

Comparatively few of the many patterns or various molds in which their variations were blown can be positively attributed to a specific factory. Excavations made by Harry Hall White have proved that a few patterns were used at Vernon, New York, for bottle- and flint-glass articles; and that bottle-glass pieces in one or two patterns were blown at Kent and at Mantua, Ohio, at Coventry, Connecticut, and at the Marlboro Street factory in Keene, New Hampshire. As my own studies have proved that the Keene molds were used for clear flint-glass pieces and the factory advertised flint glass, I believe that clear flint Blown-Three-Mold in certain patterns was made at Keene. The comparative rarity of articles in the patterns identified with these factories indicates that the production was not extensive. On the other hand, the number of patterns and of articles molded in them which have been identified as Sandwich indicate that Sandwich must have put out a large line of this ware. The majority of the patterns may have originated there.

While the full-size three-piece mold was used in other countries, evidently only the Irish used patterns similar to our American ones. According to Dudley Westropp, curator of the Dublin Museum, the types were probably introduced from America and production was very limited. The Irish designs were made up of the simplest motifs: ribbing, fluting, and diamond diapering.

PRESSED GLASS

If Blown-Three-Mold was the first independent American design in molded tableware, lacy glass was the second. Lacy glass was an entirely new type of American glass made possible by the development of the pressing machine in the late 1820's. And while the artistry passed from the glass-blowers to the mold designers and makers, the results in economical production and beauty of pattern justified the means. Many forms show originality, and the beautiful patterns in almost infinite variety were so designed as to enhance the metal's potentialities for brilliancy. Lacy glass may

have been inspired by the desire to out-shine cut glass but it was not, as is frequently intimated, an imitation of it. The intricacy and delicacy of most patterns could not possibly have been achieved by a cutting wheel.

For many years every piece of lacy, or other pressed glass, was automatically attributed to Sandwich. Unquestionably Sandwich produced quantities of it. Lura Woodside Watkins, Doctor and Mrs. Charles Green, and Ruth Webb Lee, studying the fragments excavated at Sandwich by Francis L. Wynn, identified a large number of patterns and articles. However, midwest and other eastern houses produced similar glass. And, it seems, *mechanical* pressing was initiated by Bakewell's of Pittsburgh, followed closely by the New England Glass Company, the Jersey Glass Works, Sandwich, and John L. Gilliland's Brooklyn Flint Glass Works. Gilliland's pressed glass received an award at the American Institute's 1829 fair. While I have found no design clues in the various advertisements of pressed glass in 1829 and the 1830's, I feel sure fashion would have dictated a similarity of pattern.

Of almost equal importance in American glass design are the fine lamps, candlesticks, and vases. While vase forms have been made for centuries, comparatively few lamps with closed fonts fitted with wick burners were made of glass before the advent of the pressing machine. This is true of candlesticks also. At first, the fonts of lamps and bowls of vases were hand-blown or blow in a mold and then attached to a pressed standard. Candle sockets were also sometimes blown. Moreover, the early pressed lighting devices and vases were not made in one section but of two or more parts made separately and joined by a thin wafer of glass. This method, which made possible an almost unlimited variety of combinations of standards (bases) and tops and also of contrasting colors, was both economical and ingenious. As in the case of lacy glass, undoubtedly all factories equipped to manufacture pressed glass on a large scale made lamps, candlesticks, and vases. We know that the New England Glass Company and the Boston and Sandwich Glass Company were important producers in the field, and even used some of the same designs. Some of the New England Glass Company lamps can be identified by the total absence of mold marks on the plain upper portion of their fonts. Lura Woodside Watkins in her researches found that Joseph Magoun, foreman of the pressing department at East Cambridge, obtained a patent in 1847 which made possible the pressing of fonts without mold marks. The patent ran for fourteen years. Consequently, the lamps with this important feature can safely be attributed to the New England Glass Company.

It was probably shortly after 1840 that the popularity of lacy glass with manufacturers and the buying public was eclipsed by pressed tablewares of a totally different type of design, one of simple dignity depending largely on form and geometric motifs for decorative effects. Some of the designs, such as the *Ashburton,* were probably made in the late 1830's. Lacy glass had been in vogue for several years and its molds were expensive to make; as the late 1830's were years of business depression, it is not unlikely that manufacturers found it necessary to economize on production costs. Moreover, the glass in the new patterns could be safely fire-polished, producing a surface simulating that of the fine glass which was blown and cut. Many fine patterns were produced in which eventually nearly complete table settings could be purchased. The simple designs composed largely of ovals, printies, and flutes were followed by fine ribbed designs, such as *bellflower* and *ivy.* Later came more elaborate patterns such as the floral, the *westward-ho* — by the 1880's their name was legion. They represent the triumph of mass-production methods.

Migrations of Early Glassworkers

BY HARRY HALL WHITE

THE FIRST PERSON *to approach the study of early American glass with the scientific method of the archaeologist was Harry Hall White. He excavated at the sites of early glasshouses in New England, New York, Pennsylvania, and Ohio, unearthed the foundations of the factories, and sifted the soil to locate fragments of their products. In this way he secured much incontrovertible evidence as to exactly what was made and where. The accounts of most of his excavations were published in several parts in* ANTIQUES, *and if we had been able without space limitations to choose the most representative of his writings, we should certainly have selected one of these articles. We think, however, that the one we have selected instead, directed to the neophyte collector, is particularly helpful in setting forth the main types of glass made in America, and the reasons why they were produced in certain regions at certain times. Since the article appeared in August 1937, this approach to the study of American glass has come to be followed more and more by students and collectors.*

THE vagrant tendencies of American glassworkers in early days have become almost proverbial. Evidence of how individual artisans and occasionally whole groups of them were seized by the migratory urge crops up constantly, though often briefly and in disconnected passages, throughout the historical source material on our native glassmaking.

Sometimes this evidence is no more than a casual statement regarding an individual. Sometimes it is a vague hint or a suggestion, leaving much — generally too much — to the imagination. Again, on the other hand, we meet with clear and circumstantial accounts of mass movements. We are, for example, aware of the romantic trek of Amelung men en route to Louisville,

and the persuasive diplomacy that halted the journey at Gallatin's venture in New Geneva, Pennsylvania. We have heard likewise of how crown-glassmakers were lured from Boston to Utica, New York, and of how men were shifted from Boston to the Union Flint Glass Works in Philadelphia. A less clearly documented record of these and other migrations has been left to us in the distinctive forms and modes of ornamentation on blown glass that the traveling workmen produced in the localities where they paused during their journeyings or came permanently to rest. By way of obvious illustration of this record, we find that the so-called lilypad ornament — though employed in New Jersey, certain parts of New England, and in several New

York factories — is not associated with Ohio. Conversely, the ribbed and swirled patterns of the midwest are not eloquent of eastern origin.

The whole territory from which comes most of the blown glass still surviving from early days lies north of Virginia and stretches westward from the Atlantic seaboard into the state of Ohio. During the period of our concern — roughly from a little before the Revolution until the mid-1800's — this far-flung domain harbored four different traditions of glassware forms and modes of ornamentation, each confined to a particular area and each revealing its specific peculiarities most clearly in such typical objects as bowls and pitchers. To be sure, we must not try to fix the boundaries of these areas with perfect exactitude. Within all of them we shall encounter overlapping and conflicting types, particularly in the New England-New York State section. Nevertheless, it is an indisputable fact that the experienced observer can almost unfailingly identify the area from which a piece of early glass has come.

Perhaps arbitrarily, yet not without reason, we have chosen Area 1 as the earliest stable source of American blown glass. It is shown on the accompanying map as comprising lower New York, all of New Jersey, much of Delaware, and a scrap of eastern Pennsylvania. Its presiding deity, first in the flesh and later in spirit, was Caspar Wistar. Yet it would be a mistake to discount the influence of men from the old glasshouses of Manhattan, of which we know both so much and so tantalizingly little. New York City must have been a veritable crossroads for artisan travel, and have contributed from its own overflow of imported Low Countries talent to the migratory streams that were moving north, south, and west.

AREA 1 is the source of bowls and pitchers in all the varying shades of green and amber. Later came the bicolored pieces and striated objects in the Nailsea fashion. The earlier pieces seem to occur in the deeper colors. Bowls and pitchers are found either plain or ornamented with dragged applications of glass in the so-called lily-pad design. They may exhibit a plain or crimped cast-on foot (Fig. 2.)

It is believed that the bicolored looped patterns in this blown glass are not so early as was originally surmised. They are probably a nineteenth-century product and in no wise associated with Wistar. Investigations thus far conducted at Wistarburg confirm this opinion. That the early, rather high, straight-sided bowls were a product of Area 1 is substantiated by fragments from my excavations at the Wistar site in South Jersey. Variants of this type are to be found in Areas 2 and 4. We are likewise aware that Area 1 was not a large producer of tripartite-mold-blown glass; though during the development of its large industrial centers from 1810 to 1840 it is certain to have made some glass of that type.

Glassworkers from Area 1, men versed in the so-called South Jersey technique, moved in considerable numbers northward to glasshouses in Connecticut, New Hampshire, and New York. Likewise the perennial westward urge carried some of the New Jersey glass forms to western Pennsylvania and Ohio, as will subsequently be noted.

IN AREA 2, which embraces a good deal of New York State and not a little of New England, we find the majority of what we term, as a broad designation, the "bottle houses." These factories were primarily

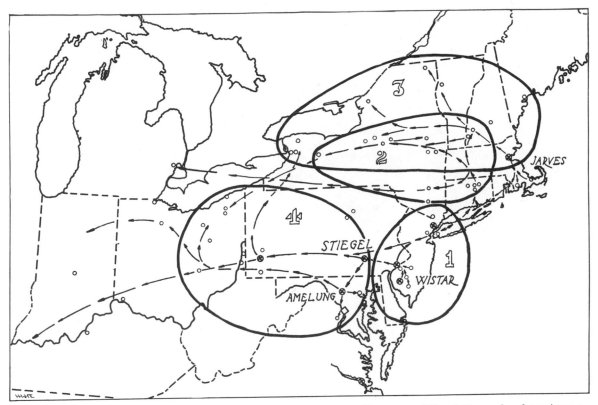

FIG. 1 — AREAS OF EARLY AMERICAN GLASSMAKING AND LINES OF WORKER MIGRATION. Offhand-blown glass from Areas 1, 2, and 3 frequently shows evidence of a common kinship in form and modes of decoration. The reason for this is in part revealed by the lines of worker migration indicated on the map by arrows. The migration lines in Area 4 are less confused for they mark the direct course followed mainly by former employees of Stiegel and Amelung, who thus bore westward a technique more delicate than that commanded by the New Jersey workmen.

FIG. 3 — TYPICAL VESSELS FROM AREA 2, NEW YORK AND SOUTHERN NEW ENGLAND.

a

b

c

d

FIG. 2 — TYPICAL VESSELS FROM AREA 1, SOUTH JERSEY FORMS. *a*, Deep bowl, and pitcher, the latter with threaded neck and slightly crimped foot. *From the George S. McKearin collection. b and c,* Pitchers in striated aquamarine and opaque-white glass, "Nailsea style." *d*, Blue pitcher on slightly flaring foot. In form allied with pitcher *a*.

concerned with bottles in the aqua, amber, and green metals. Prominent in New York State were Mount Vernon, Ellenville, Clyde, and possibly Lancaster and Lockport; while to the east in Connecticut, Manchester, Coventry, and Willington with Westford also contributed their quota of bottles and flasks. Of course, a few establishments in the area were chiefly occupied with window glass. Among these may be mentioned Utica, Vernon, Rockville, Woodstock, and Ontario at Geneva, New York.

The blown products of this area, other than bottles, are many and exhibit a wide range of color and ornament. Oddly enough, however, the supply of bowls has been ungenerous, though such as were made are quite specific in type, and hence easily recognized.

The colors of Area 2 glass are generally strong and the forms deep — an inheritance from Area 1. Pitchers from Keene exhibit the handsome lilypad motive more competently handled than is the case with the similar ornamentation in New Jersey. New York State bottle-house pitchers show a gradual departure from the ample lines derived from Area 1 toward the form of an inverted truncated cone. Area 2 turned out much tripartite-mold-blown glass in many colors and forms at Keene, Coventry, and Mount Vernon, but *not* at Stoddard, New Hampshire.

AREA 3 has been laid out on the map to include the approximate locations of the window-glass houses whose establishing marked the industrial rise following the Revolution and the War of 1812, up to, say, the centennial year of 1876. Here in bowl and pitcher forms we again recognize an inheritance from New Jersey-trained glassmen.

The area in question inevitably overlaps Area 2, since no natural geographical boundary separates bottle houses from window-glass houses. On the other hand, a very distinct line of demarcation is to be found in the color of the metal in their wares. Obviously bowls and pitchers from window-glass houses are in very light green, or in the nearest shade we have to the true aquamarine with its attractive bluish cast. This shade is frequently found in the glass of the Oneida Lake group: Cleveland, Canisota, Bernhard's Bay. The northern group, in which Redford and Redwood are prominent, made a richer shade of very light green — but it was window glass. The lilypad pieces from the last-named factories are, without question, the finest items of our later blown glass.

AREA 4 has yielded some of the most romantic and beautiful glass made in America. It is here that our glasshouse craftsmen most nearly achieved a national type of blown glass. Here, in so far as our American production is concerned, several types of ornamentation were originated. Occasional pieces of similar implication may have been made in houses outside this area, but not as a regular product.

Of the actual output of Stiegel and Amelung we have little reliable information other than that derived from the inventories and advertisements of these two unfortunate captains of industry. The collapse of their short-lived enterprises spilled their craftsmen into the ever-westward-flowing stream of emigration. Some of these wayfarers found lodgment in the newly founded glassworks of western Pennsylvania. Others fared onward to dimly perceived goals in Ohio. Wherever they congregated they produced a unique type of glassware, quite different in both form and ornament from glass made in Areas 1, 2, and 3, though here and there we occasionally recognize the influences of the older eastern forms — mostly in deep bowls. Pitchers and bowls from Area 4 may be plain or exhibit several modes of ornament, which, for lack of better designation, we may classify as *ribbed pattern, broken-rib pattern, swirled pattern,* and *diamond pattern.*

In addition to such patterns, Area 4 produced glass blown in tripartite molds. Just how much glass of this type and in what patterns the Pittsburgh district contributed we do not at present know. Our dig at Kent and Mantua permitted the identification of two molds used in these communities. To date they have been exemplified in the various shades of country glass.

On the other hand, patterned pieces in swirled, ribbed, broken-rib, and diamond pattern occur in many shades of green and amber; the green group leans more toward the amber than toward the olive. The amber group, on the other hand, is unmistakably of the golden variety, often with a very deep amber quality. Both a good strong green glass and a true aquamarine were blown in Area 4. Particularly from the Pittsburgh district do we find blown pieces in vibrant amethyst and sapphire.

To account for the extremely wide range of color found in Area 4 we must remember that within this territory lies Pittsburgh, the great glassmaking district, as well as the lesser towns of New Geneva, Wheeling, Zanesville, Ravenna, Kent, and Mantua. Here ancient traditional knowledge rubbed elbows with pioneering experiment, and at times the twain became intimate.

In conclusion, it seems evident from information now at hand that migrations occurred from the two glass labor centers of Area 1 — South Jersey, Philadelphia, and New York City — not only westward but northward through New England States and into New York State, that is to say, into Areas 2 and 3. From the two latter areas we may trace subsequent removals westward into Area 4, and even beyond into Michigan and Kentucky.

Due to the increasing industrial concentration at Pittsburgh, Area 4 drew heavily from the labor forces of the eastern glasshouses. But the Pittsburgh district, in turn, contributed largely to the manning of glasshouses in other places. Lancaster, New York, was started by Pittsburgh men. The Kentucky Glass Works at Louisville, Kentucky, was established by men whose names are similar to those which may be found in the city directories in Areas 1, 2, and 4.

Thus briefly I have drawn the bare outlines of that extraordinary American phenomenon of the late 1700's and the first half of the succeeding century — the migration of the glassworkers. Why was it that the men who cherished the New Jersey traditions of form and decoration favored a route that carried them northward into New England and thence by wide detour into New York State? Why was it, again, that the harsh highway across the Alleghenies beckoned so compellingly to the refugees from the disasters that overwhelmed Amelung and Stiegel? We may but guess at an answer. But quite as remarkable as the migrations themselves, perhaps even more so, was the tenacity with which each group of workmen clung to the craft traditions in which they had been trained and which they seem to have transmitted virtually intact to their apprentice successors.

FIG. 4A — TYPICAL VESSELS FROM AREA 3. New York State bowl and pitchers with threading and lilypad decoration.

FIG. 4B — AQUAMARINE NEW YORK STATE BOWL with lilypad decoration.

So it was that, as they passed from place to place to pause for a little or to remain, they marked their way with shining memorials of glass in which the student of today may find not only a rare loveliness, but a reflection, caught and fixed beyond erasure, of history and of romance.

FIG. 5 — TYPICAL VESSELS FROM AREA 4. *a*, Swirled and fluted Ohio sugar bowl and pitcher. *b*, Greenish-amber Ohio small bowl. *From the Harry Hall White collection. c*, Aquamarine broken-rib Ohio bowl. *From the Harry Hall White collection. d*, Diamond-pattern bowl, from Mantua, Ohio. *From the George E. Follansbee collection. e*, Stiegel-type creamer.

The Boston and Sandwich Glass Company

BY PRISCILLA C. CRANE

IN THE 1920's *apparently no one questioned that the Sandwich glass factory on Cape Cod was the source of all the lacy glass cup plates, dolphin candlesticks, and other varied objects in pressed glass, though little enough was known about it. One of the first articles to be published that gave any really sound history of the Sandwich glassworks was this one which appeared, in slightly longer form, in* ANTIQUES *for April 1925. It was based for the most part on information gleaned from a trip to Sandwich made by Miss Crane, at that time assistant editor of* ANTIQUES. *She inspected the site of the factory itself and had personal interviews with many of the men who had known it and worked in it, most of whom are now long dead. Not until nearly ten years after this article was written were the first excavations made on the site of the Boston and Sandwich Glass Company, and fragments of the Company's actual products unearthed. Only then was it possible to say definitely what were and what were not Sandwich pieces. The results of these studies were also published in* ANTIQUES, *but we have chosen this earlier article because it laid the foundation for the later research. Today it is still a classic work of reference, and a milestone in American glass history.*

THE Sandwich glass factory was started in 1825 by Deming Jarves (*1791-1869*), a resident of Boston who also had an interest in the New England Glass Company at Cambridge, Massachusetts. In his *Reminiscences of Glass Making*, published in 1865, Jarves thus described the founding of the factory:

"Ground was broken in April, dwellings for the workmen built, and manufactory completed, and on the 4th day of July, 1825, they commenced blowing glass, three months from first breaking ground. In the following year it was purchased of the proprietor, a company formed, and incorporated under the title of the Boston and Sandwich Glass Company."

According to the Act of Incorporation (Chapter 99, Acts of 1825, *Private and Special Statutes of the Commonwealth of Massachusetts*), the corporation was formed by Deming Jarves, Henry Rice, Andrew T. Hall, and Edmund Monroe, who were entitled to hold "real estate not exceeding $100,000 and personal estate not exceeding $200,000, as may be necessary and convenient for carrying on the manufacture of glass . . . As of February 22, 1826." Most of the invested capital seems to have come from Boston.

Sandwich was chosen as the location of the factory for two reasons. In the first place, there was an abundance of local fuel. At this time the New England glass facto-

[177]

ries burned wood, and easy access to timber was essential. Over 20,000 acres of forest land were owned by the Boston and Sandwich Glass Company. The wood was cut by farmers living in the hills back of Sandwich and brought to the village by ox team, a matter of six or seven miles.

Another advantage of the site was ease of transportation. The factory was built on the edge of a tidal creek, and this was later widened so that boats could come directly to the plant. The distance from Sandwich to Boston by water is approximately fifty miles.

There is no foundation for the statement that Jarves chose the site at Sandwich on account of the sand to be found in that neighborhood. In fact, the sand at Sandwich contains too much iron, and is too coarse for making fine glass. All of this product used at the factory was imported from Morris River, New Jersey, and from the Berkshires in western Massachusetts. It came at first by boat, and later by train.

The 1825 factory employed sixty or seventy hands and consisted of an eight-pot furnace, each pot holding 800 pounds. In 1849 a second house was built, and the two were known as the *upper* and the *lower* house. Each had a ten-pot furnace. Beginning in 1843 and continuing until 1867, the workmen were divided into four shifts, or "turns." The factory worked night and day for four days a week, and the men were free from Friday morning until the following Monday.

The Company looked after its workers in every way. The employees began to work while mere lads, and continued in service until they were old men. If they were unable to make good in one job, another would be found for them. The Company built workmen's houses and established a small village near the factory. The houses could be bought on the installment plan.

The earliest Sandwich products were tumblers, cruet stoppers, molded hats, toy decanters, twisted cruets, common salts, pint pocket bottles, ½-pint mold jugs, 5-inch mold patty pans, star and ball stoppers.

The first piece produced at the factory was blown July 4, 1825, by Charles W. Lapham. Chamber and "high blown stem lamps," "lamps on foot," and "peg lamps" were first made on July 30, 1825. "Six-inch round dishes, heavy plain ink, 5-inch molded patty pans, button stem short lamps, common pungeons, flint champaigns, molded salts for cutting, molded mustards, Liverpool lamp glasses, small and large rose foot lamps, oval molded, 9-inch dishes, fount inks, tulip lamp glasses, cylinder lamp glasses, flint licquieurs, cologne bottles, center dishes, 38-pound bowls, 21½-pound bowls and bird boxes" are among the entries of the first three months in the account book.

Glass was made for cutting in 1825, as indicated by several entries in the account book, but no statement occurs as to whether the cutting was done at Sandwich or elsewhere. Octagon dishes, sugar bowls, decanters, cruets, 10-inch oval dishes, 7, 8, and 9-inch octagon dishes, ship tumblers, etc., were common articles of manufacture, besides the ones already mentioned. Some of these were doubtless cut.

Familiar items appear in the records from an early date. On September 23, 1826, occurs the record of "310 Dolphin tall pungeants $18.10." On November 4, 1826, are first listed "34 Lafayette Chamber Cylinder Lamps $5.66" and "56 Lafayette lamps $14." Petticoat lamps are noted

FIG. 1 — VIEW OF SANDWICH GLASS WORKS. *From a woodcut owned by Mrs. P. W. Whittemore.*

FIG. 2 — THE FACTORY where Sandwich glass was made. *From an old photograph.*

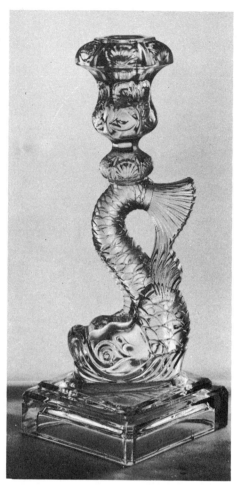

FIG. 3 — SANDWICH GLASS CANDLESTICKS. *Left,* early type with lacy bobèche and foot. *From the collection of Mrs. P. W. Whittemore. Right,* dolphin, in clear glass. *From the collection of Dr. Charles W. Green.*

FIG. 4 — LACY SANDWICH PLATES. *From the collection of Mrs. P. W. Whittemore.*

as first having been made on December 23, 1826: "211 petticoat lamps $25.22." On March 9, 1827, are listed "7 Lafayette Salts, $1.16." The first entry of cup plates is on April 27, 1827. Colored glass was produced as early as the thirties, but its great improvement and extension of manufacture did not occur until after the Civil War.

It has been claimed that the modern method of pressing glass was invented at the Sandwich works. Joseph D. Weeks wrote in 1880:

"The invention of the American press (for glass) is ascribed to a Massachusetts carpenter in the town of Sandwich about 1827 who, wanting an article of glassware made for some purpose, went to Mr. Deming Jarves and asked him if he could make the article desired. Mr. Jarves told him it would be impossible to make such an article. The carpenter asked if a machine could not be made to press glass into any shape. The idea was scouted at first, but, on second thought, Mr. Jarvis and the carpenter fashioned a rude press and made the experiment. This machine was intended to make tumblers, and when the hot molten glass was poured into the mold which was to determine whether glass could be pressed, the experiment was witnessed by many glassmakers of that time. They were nearly all of the opinion that the experiment would come to naught and were greatly amazed when the result demonstrated that it was possible to press glass. The first tumbler that was manufactured in the rough, improvised press remained in Mr. Jarves' possession for many years and then passed into the hands of John A. Dobson, a well-known glass dealer of Baltimore and was exhibited at the Centennial Exhibition by Hobbs, Brockunier & Co.,

where it was accidentally broken by Mr. John H. Hobbs."

Mrs. Williams, in *Sandwich Glass*, states that the pressing mold for glass was invented in 1827 at the New England Glass Company. In all of this the evidence is purely of the hearsay variety. The oldest surviving worker of the Sandwich plant gives credit for the pressing mold to the New England Glass Company. The date appears to have been earlier than 1827, however, since the process seems to have been known to Jarves previous to his establishing of the Sandwich factory.

Hiram Dillaway, an Englishman, was long the head moldmaker at the Sandwich factory, and designed most of its patterns. Without doubt, he and Jarves improved the process of pressing glass, which Jarves had perhaps known at the New England Glass Company. If such is the case, the story told by Weeks may be the correct one, with merely the change of location to Cambridge, and the date to before 1825. That Jarves was constantly interested in improving the process of pressing glass is without question. On May 28, 1830, for example, he took out a patent for an improvement in glassmakers' molds.

The molds employed for pressing glass were for the most part made of brass. For large articles the presses worked with a screw instead of a lever. The designs were cut on the plunger and pressed upside down and the article, while very hot, turned into a receiver of the same shape as the mold.

What is known as *lace* or *lacy* glass must have been turned out quite early in the history of the factory. *Snakeskin* glass is supposed to have been made about 1860; *hobnail* somewhere in the ten years following the Civil War; *cable* glass at the time of laying the French cable (1867); *opaque* after the Civil War. The *diamond* pattern was first cut by "Gaffer" Cook, who is said to have designed it. What is known as the *Grant* pattern, i.e., a pattern in which the diamonds are quite fine, was made at the time of Grant's candidacy for president (*1868*).

From 1825 to 1858 the factory output was "transported by boat to Boston in the sloop *Polly*, which was able at high tide to come up the creek almost to the doors of the factory." There seems to be no local record of this boat, and the evidence concerning the creek and the transportation of the glass is quite varied. I was told by one man that the creek was dredged and water gates were built, and that, when the boat had been loaded, these gates were opened so that the force of the water rushing out carried the boat through the creek. Entrance was only possible at high tide.

Another man told me that all the glass was loaded on flat-bottomed scows, and poled down the creek on high tide to the boats waiting outside. Supplies of coal, sand, etc., were brought up in the same way. He also said that there was a small railroad, or "bogey," built about 1827, to carry the glass across the marsh—approximately a mile—to the shore. This is said to have been one of the earliest railroads of its kind in America.

The merchants of the town had a sloop, the *Osceola*, which was used to carry freight and passengers to and from Boston, and no doubt it carried glass also. The creek now shows no signs of having once been dredged; at low tide it is merely a mud flat.

After the railroad came to Sandwich, in 1848, much of the factory's supplies and products was transported by rail. Several years after it had reached Sandwich, however, the Old Colony Railroad raised its rates, to the disgust of the Boston and Sandwich Glass Company. Accordingly, in 1853, the steamer *Acorn* was built. It was at this time that the channel was probably dredged to admit of her entrance.

For several years this vessel carried all supplies, and was also used as an excursion boat, the trip to Boston and back costing one dollar. The railroad soon came to terms with the Company, which then built a wharf at Cohasset Narrows, now Buzzards Bay, where coal, brought up the bay, was landed and was transported nine miles by rail to Sandwich, thus saving the long and hazardous trip around Cape Cod.

Much glass was exported to South America. Rio de Janeiro is a port which often appears on the books of the company.

In 1858 Deming Jarves resigned from the Boston and Sandwich Glass Company and built the Cape Cod Glass Company for his son, John, about half a mile from the old factory. It had all the modern improvements then known to glass manufacturing, and paid its workers ninepence more a day than its rival. It was never a commercial success. John Jarves was killed in the Civil War, and Deming Jarves died on April 15, 1869, after a long illness. The Cape Cod Glass Company was disposed of by the Jarves family, and completely abandoned after one or two experimental ventures.

Deming Jarves' place as manager of the Boston and Sandwich Glass Company was taken in 1858 by George Lafayette Fessenden, whose brother, Sewall H. Fessenden, was agent in Boston for many years. In 1870 the Company had offices in Boston, New York, Philadelphia, and Baltimore, but did little advertising and had few salesmen.

FIG. 5 — COVERED DISHES AND TRAYS in lacy Sandwich glass. *From the Green collection.*

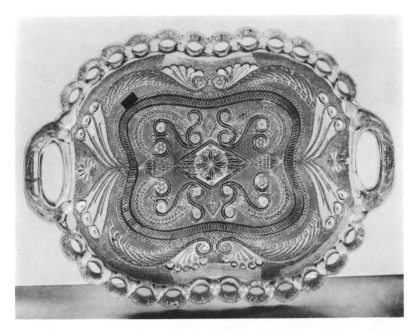

FIG. 6 — RARITIES IN LACY SANDWICH. Deep dish and covered oval dish. *From the Green collection.*

The Boston and Sandwich Glass Company was one of the best known houses in the country and its better products were much in demand. Most of its later work was in cut and etched glass, although it still continued to make cheaper pressed glass, together with lamps with metal bases, which last were imported from England. In the Philadelphia 1876 Exhibition the Company exhibited "Cut crystal chandeliers, rich cut glassware of every description, including the 'Daniel Webster Punch Bowl,'" according to the Official Catalogue.

In 1882, George Lafayette Fessenden was succeeded by Henry V. Spurr, who had long been head salesman in the Boston warehouse, and who had originally entered the Company's employ in 1849. The agent still continued to be Sewall H. Fessenden.

Competition in the glass industry became much keener after the Civil War, the western factories having the advantage over those in the east owing to their use of natural gas for fuel, and to their proximity to coal, sand, etc. The profits of the Boston and Sandwich Glass Company began to dwindle. For several years the works were run with no profit whatever. In 1887, however, a crisis occurred. The men had formed a union, at the instigation of a western "agitator." They presented demands for many new rules. The Company explained that it could not continue its business if these were put into force, and called attention to the good it had done and was doing for the inhabitants of Sandwich. Eventually it issued an ultimatum to the effect that, "If the fires are allowed to go out they will never be re-lighted."

The men, unable to believe that the Company meant what it said, struck. The furnaces were allowed to die. On January 2, 1888, the works were closed, never to re-open. The Company's charter was dissolved March 6, 1894, after the books had been destroyed. Cases of glass were dumped in heaps outside the factory, and many of the cheaper kinds of glass were sold to a chain of five-and-ten-cent stores. Then the population of Sandwich began to shrink. In 1857 it numbered 4800; today there are scarcely 1500.

It is said that, during the height of its prosperity, the Company cleared as much as fifty per cent a year for several years; and that, during the sixty-three years of its existence, it produced about $30,000,000 worth of glass.

After the closing in 1888, many attempts were made to start the old works again, but none were successful. Among others came Cardenio King, who bought the factory and remelted the *cullet,* or imperfect glass, producing a brown and unattractive output. This, too, proved a failure. Since then the factory buildings have fallen to pieces. What remained was torn down in 1920, except for one building used as a fish freezing plant, and a new building erected for a bark factory.

The ruins have been pretty well searched over for pieces of glass, some of which have been mounted into jewelry by a Sandwich woman. The town has no industry now, and the younger people are gone, leaving a sleepy Cape Cod village with but memories of the industry of the past.

Zanesville Glass

BY RHEA MANSFIELD KNITTLE

RHEA MANSFIELD KNITTLE *discovered Ohio for antiquarians. Disdaining the popular belief that the eastern seaboard was the birthplace of all American antiques, she brought the early products of the Western Reserve and the Ohio Valley to the notice of collectors, and demonstrated that they were worth collecting. While her original researches cover the fields of Ohio cabinetmaking, pewtering, pottery, and other crafts, her great specialty has always been glass. Her book,* Early American Glass *(1927), in the Century Library of American Antiques, was the first to consider the whole panorama of American glass and to record many of the factories that produced it in various parts of the country. It is hard to select from Mrs. Knittle's numerous articles in* ANTIQUES, *but we have chosen this one from the December 1932 issue because it links her two particular interests, and emphasizes her contribution in identifying the glass of Ohio.*

THE town of Zanesville, Ohio, was laid out in 1797. Favorably located for land and water transportation, it rapidly developed into a flourishing community. The vicinity abounded in the finest of clays and the best of sand — ingredients for glasshouse clay pots and for the metal itself.

In 1815, under the leadership of Isaac Van Horne, a glasshouse was erected, variously known as The White Glass Works, The Zanesville Glass Works, and Shepard & Company. First production was window glass and clear hollow ware; but in 1817 the capacity was enlarged, and colored bottles and colored hollow ware were added to the commercial output. This factory closed in 1851.

In 1816, another glass enterprise was started in Zanesville. Its trade names were The New Granite Glass Works and The Green Glass Manufactory. It was also known during a brief period as Taylor & Culbertson. Its output included window glass, hollow ware, and bottles. In 1848 the plant drew its fires. Thus in Zanesville, for over thirty years, two concerns were steadily manufacturing glass.

The similarity of certain Zanesville patterns to those produced earlier by "Baron" Stiegel at Manheim has puzzled students of early Ohio glass. Perhaps it is to be explained by the fact that General Van Horne, chief promoter of the Zanesville Glass Works, came from Bucks County, Pennsylvania, whence he may well have enlisted the services of glass blowers trained in the Stiegel tradition.

While the Zanesville origin of the examples here pictured is well authenticated, it must be remembered that contemporary Pittsburgh-district houses employed similar patterns. Hence it seems reasonable to use the terms *Zanesville-Stiegel* or *Ohio-Stiegel* to designate certain of these patterns. Other patterns might be referred to as of *Zanesville type,* just as we refer to *Stiegel* and *South Jersey types.*

Zanesville glass may be divided into five classes: *(1)* diamond-faceted patterns; *(2)* broken-swirl, or swirled and fluted patterns; *(3)* vertical-swirl patterns (really diagonal swirls); *(4)* perpendicularly fluted patterns; and (5) unpatterned pieces, no ornamentation but strapped handles, crimpings, or scallopings. These types are represented in the illustrations, which, except Figure 12, are from the Knittle collection.

Zanesville glass eventually covers a wide range of color. Green hollow ware was first produced in 1817, however, and it is very doubtful that any blue glass was either made commercially or blown offhand in Zanesville before 1855-60.

The examples illustrated bear witness to General Van Horne's determination that the Western country should have glass equal to that of the Eastern states from which its inhabitants had migrated. This spirit of enterprise characterized all the early development of Zanesville, which was quick to recognize the economic value of local industries. Within two decades after the first pioneers had "settled down" at the confluence of the Muskingum and Licking Rivers, Zanesville was ranking with the sizable older towns along the Ohio River, which had first attracted craftsmen, artists, and industrialists from the East.

NOTES ON THE ILLUSTRATIONS

Fig. 1 — Brilliant Sea-Green Cream Pitcher of Bottle Glass (*c. 1817-1830*). *Diamond-faceted type.*

Capacity: slightly more than ½ pint.

Similar in form to South Jersey type; in pattern, to Stiegel. Flaring body curves inward to wide neck; deep rim with slightly folded edge. Large handle deeply attached at top to rim and neck, and at base, with crimping and a small volute, to the body. Attributed to the Zanesville Glass Works by descendants of a worker in the factory, who owned it until 1929. Found in Muskingum County. Zanesville pitchers of this pattern seem not to have occurred in either blue or amethyst.

Fig. 2 — Amber Bowl or Pan, Made from the Finest Quality of Bottle Glass (*c. 1817-1835 to 1845*). *Diamond-faceted type.*

Diameter: about 6 inches.

Curves outward from small foot; folded edge. Found in the vicinity of Zanesville in 1930 and attributed to Zanesville by its former owners. Such shallow bowls are a distinctive and apparently exclusive Zanesville product. Specimens, in rich amber and green, range in diameter from about 4 to 8 or 9 inches. Very rarely found attached to a footed standard; in such cases the bowl is wider and shallower.

Fig. 3 — Deep-Amber Whiskey Flask (*c. 1817-1845*). *Diamond-facted type.*

Height: 5⅛ inches.

Known in glass collectors' vernacular as an *Ohio hip flask.* Chestnut shape. Slightly concave base. Pontil mark small and neat. Ridges form diamond shapes on upper half of bottle, which lengthen into ogival panels

Fig. 2

Fig. 1

Fig. 3

Fig. 4

Fig. 5

Fig. 6

toward the base. The half-pint sizes vary slightly in form and in proportionate length of diamond. Occurs in a wide variety of amber and green shades, and, rarely, in citron, yellowish-green, or clear glass. No authentic blue, amethyst, or emerald-green examples are known. Found throughout the midwestern glass district, and occasionally in other sections. Nevertheless, a well-autheticated Zanesville product.

Fig.　4 — Sea-Green Sugar Bowl *(c. 1817-1847). Swirled and fluted type.*

Height: about 6½ inches.

Squat body, curved in at neck and expanded abruptly into wide, flanged, saucer-like rim. High, domed lid drawn out into snapped-off finial. Found near Zanesville, and authenticated by technique and by a duplicate never out of original family until purchased in 1929.

Fig. 5 — Sea-Green Pitcher Made from Fine Grade of Bottle Glass *(c. 1817-1845). Swirled and fluted type.*

Height: 6½ inches.

Similar in form to Figure 1, though rim of neck flares less abruptly and spout is smaller. Handle beautifully strapped and ridged, crimped and folded at base. Found near Cincinnati, where considerable quantities of Zanesville glass were shipped and sold. Other pitchers of same shape, pattern, and color have been found in or near Zanesville and carry satisfactory attributions.

Fig. 6 — Yellowish-Green or Citron "Ohio Hip" Whiskey Flask of Superior Metal *(c. 1817-1845). Swirled and fluted type.*

Height: 7½ inches.

Almost egg-shaped; flattened sides and sloping curved ends; long neck, flaring a trifle; straight lip, cracked off and rubbed down. This example and one in grass-green found in and near Zanesville. Found in clear glass, rarely in green shades, citron, amber, and canary. Such flasks were probably made also in the Pittsburgh and Wheeling districts.

Fig. 7 — Citron-Colored "Globular Swirl" Whiskey Decanter with Long Neck *(1835-1865). Vertical-swirl type.*

Capacity: ½ gallon.

Mouth ringed; pontil mark deep. These *globular swirls,* as they are now known, are found in sizes ranging from miniature bottles holding not more than ⅛ of a pint to those of gallon size. Most common size is one quart. The swirls run sometimes left, sometimes right. Necks vary in length and width; some are collared, others are ringed. Colors vary from pale aquamarine to grass-green, from canary to citron, from Catanian amber to a dense near-black, and also include blue. These bottles are unusually impressive. They were probably made in Pittsburgh, Wheeling, and Louisville, as well as in Zanesville, where the majority were blown. They were used primarily as whiskey decanters; some still bear the original distiller's label.

Fig. 8 — Deep Green Salt Cup of Excellent Shape and Proportions *(c. 1817-1825). Vertical-swirl type.*

Height: 2⅜ inches.

Unusually early example, blown from rather coarse and bubbly metal. Urn-shaped bowl, with slightly flaring rim. Attached by buttonlike stem to the wide, heavy pad of green glass that forms sloping, circular foot. Found in Zanesville and attributed by owners to the Green Glass Manufactory. Vertical-swirl salts with Zanesville tradition or authentication have been found in clear, green, and amber glass, but never in blue.

Fig. 7

Fig. 8

Fig. 9

Fig. 10-

Fig. 11 -

Fig. 12

Fig. 13

Fig. 9 — BRILLIANT SEA-GREEN PITCHER (*c. 1817-1865*). *Vertical-swirl type.*

Capacity: 1 quart.

Somewhat stumpy in form. Handle well proportioned and fashioned, deeply reeded and crimped at lower end, terminating in a volute. Deep base and fairly large pontil mark, like those of the globular bottles. A sufficient number of these pitchers has come from Zanesville and surrounding territory to warrant attribution to the locality. So far as known, pitchers of this size and pattern occur only in shades of green and amber. This shape, pattern, and size are imitated today; but modern technique does not resemble the old, and handles cannot compare with their prototypes.

Fig. 10—BLOOD-AMBER, GLOBULAR, LONG-NECKED, "PUMPKIN" BOTTLE (*1830-1865*). *Perpendicularly fluted type.*

Capacity: 1 quart.

Extremely deep base, large pontil. The neck is ringed. Quality of metal excellent, as in nearly all globular examples. Color range includes the greens, from a very light aquamarine to grass-green; the citron shades; and honey, golden, blood, and dense amber. Although the *globulars* were manufactured primarily as whiskey containers, very old labels sometimes found on them indicate that they were probably also used for camphor.

Fig. 11 — SMALL PAN, OR BOWL, BLOWN FROM BRILLIANT, SEA-GREEN BOTTLE GLASS (*c. 1817-1865*). *Perpendicularly fluted type.*

Height: 2 inches; *diameter at top:* 5¼ inches.

Sides flare; edge is reamed or folded over its outer surface; base very deep, pontil wide, as in Figure 10. Found in Zanesville district and attributed to an early local factory.

Swirled, fluted, and other patterned bowls and pans of this shape were blown at various midwestern glasshouses. Some of them are extremely attractive. Quality of metal is generally good. Size varies from 4 to 12 inches in diameter, although no specimens are common. Like the bottles, these bowls, small and large, range in color through shades of green and amber.

Fig. 12 — GOLDEN-AMBER "GRAND-DADDY" FLASK, USED ORIGINALLY FOR WHISKEY (*c. 1825-1845*). *Perpendicularly fluted type.*

Capacity: 1 quart.

These so-called *Granddaddies* are exceptionally delightful specimens of early blown work. All are rare, and are found in a variety of swirled, fluted, and diapered patterns. The quality of metal is excellent. Colors occasionally include light sea- or grass-green, rarely citron or yellow-green; but shades of rich amber are most frequent. Since several examples carry indisputable authentication, the majority of flasks of this type may safely be attributed to Zanesville.—*From the Brooklyn Museum.*

Fig. 13 — BROWNISH-AMBER DISH ON STANDARD, OR COMPOTE (*1825-1855*). *Unpatterned type.*

Height: 3¾ inches.

Wide, shallow bowl with straight rim, supported by baluster or knopped stem on a broad, sloping, circular foot. Has been authenticated as a Zanesville example, although type was blown at other early American glasshouses.

Fig. 14 — BLOWN DEEP-AMBER SALT CUP ON FOOTED BASE *(c. 1817-1845). Unpatterned type.*

Height: 3½ inches.

Almost identical in form with Figure 8. Urn- or ogee-shaped cup, with gently flar- ing rim, is attached to a flat, buttonlike stem terminating in a circular foot. Found in Ohio; attributed to Zanesville because identical in form with authenticated Zanesville products.

Fig. 14

Rarities in Pattern Glass

BY RUTH WEBB LEE

RUTH WEBB LEE may be said to have put pattern glass on the map as a collectible. In the early 1930's, when the depression was curtailing the activities of antiques collectors, she focused attention on a whole new field of collecting possibilities, and gave people the information they needed for it. Today, due largely to her influence, pattern glass has become one of the major collectibles in this country. Some of it, in fact, has now become almost as rare as the older kinds of antiques. Mrs. Lee has contributed many articles to ANTIQUES on the history of specific glass patterns. Most of this information is now incorporated in her several books, the most recent of which is Price Guide to Pattern Glass. *We have chosen this article because it sets aims for the collector of pattern glass. It is reprinted from our March 1935 issue, brought up to date in the light of more recent discoveries.*

THE value of antiques is determined not by one but by several considerations. Beauty of design, quality of workmanship, choice of material, rarity, usefulness, historical associations, all tend to influence appraisal, though the order of their importance varies with the preferences of individual collectors. The appeal, necessarily, is always to a particular temperament. There can be no just quarrel with those who set design above rarity, or historical association above usefulness.

It must be admitted today that a greater number of American collectors are interested in pressed pattern glass than in any other type of antiques. In and out of depressions, the volume of sales and the range of prices of such glass have gone steadily up. Dealers frankly agree that in hard times the passion for pattern glass helped to keep alive the regard for antiques in general. It brought customers to the shops. The reason is self-evident: the desire to own antiques persisted, and collectors gratified it by purchasing pressed glass.

Research into the origin and age of various patterns, the establishment of an accepted nomenclature, the ascertaining of exactly how many forms are obtainable by those who desire to accumulate sets, all have helped. The reiterated objections of collectors who demand extreme age for their treasures — that pattern glass is not old enough to rank, for example, with Puritan furniture or colonial silver — has not checked the movement. As a matter of fact, there are pressed patterns collectible in sets that date back to the 1840's and possess, accordingly, a very respectable antiquity. Such glass harmonizes with still older furniture and surroundings. Great-grandmother was doubtless using just such glassware on a table that she inherited from *her* great-grandmother. And, by reason of its fragility, glass that belonged to grandmother is relatively more venerable than a Windsor chair, *circa* 1800.

The element of usefulness, another value-making factor of pressed glass, cannot be overlooked. Such glass is bought for practical as well as for sentimental reasons. It is enjoyed every day. It need not be enshrined in a cabinet. As an essentially American product, it "talks American" to lovers of American antiques. I have enjoyed exceptional facilities for noting the steady increase in the number of its collectors. Men, women, and children in all sections of the United States are today acquiring pressed glass. Even in Europe, the contagion is spreading.

The acquisitive yearning which is expressed in efforts to acquire a table service of *Ashburton, bellflower, comet,* or whatever the pattern may be need not subside with the completing of the set. Though scoffers may insist that the pattern lacks the element of rarity, there is a vast satisfaction in discovering the twelfth item of a sought-for dozen. And if this emotion is less intense than that experienced in unearthing an individual piece so unusual as to be almost unique, pressed glass still affords good hunting.

In many of the early patterns occur items apparently made in such limited quantity that very few specimens are obtainable today. The demand for these particular items may have been insufficient to justify continuing their manufacture, or the entire line may have been speedily discontinued for technical or commercial reasons, such as a too complicated mold, or too high production costs, or lack of appeal to the buying public. Again, some now desirable piece may have been made by a factory that did not remain long in business. Whatever the reason, all that collectors need realize is that pressed-glass rarities exist and that they are worth searching for and acquiring.

BELLFLOWER

The earliest mention of the *bellflower* pattern that I have found appears in a catalogue of M'Kee Brothers of Pittsburgh. This pattern goes back to the 1850's, and is listed as *R.L.,* presumably *ribbed leaf.* That some articles in this classification were made at a still earlier date is indisputable. The rarest *bellflower* piece I believe to be the cake plate on a standard. One is almost unobtainable today. In recent years I have heard of exactly one being sold and it had been mended. Next in order of rarity would probably be the octagonal sugar bowl, shown in Figure 1. Very few perfect specimens of this bowl are known and these have come to light in western states. We are justified in surmising that this exceptional sugar bowl was either an experiment on the part of a short-lived factory, or that the makers, finding that the round bowl of the type usually found today was more easily and cheaply produced, discarded the eight-sided mold. The octagonal base does not have a rim to hold a cover, thus the round lid does not fit well and slips about in a somewhat clumsy manner.

Next in order of rarity in the same early pattern are the colored specimens, such as the amber egg cup, the opal egg cup, the sapphire-blue spoonholder and syrup pitcher, the milk-white and opalescent syrup pitchers *(Fig. 11),* and other forms in color. The cologne bottles shown in

FIG. 1 — "BELLFLOWER" OCTAGONAL SUGAR BOWL. A more complicated form than most of this pattern. *Formerly in the collection of Mrs. C. C. Viall.*

FIG. 3 — "HORN OF PLENTY" RECTANGULAR COVERED HONEY DISH.

FIG. 2 — OPAQUE RIBBED COLOGNE BOTTLES, akin to "ribbed leaf," or "bellflower." "RIBBED IVY" CELERY VASE, apparently unique. *From the collection of George S. McKearin.*

FIG. 4 — "HORN OF PLENTY" OVAL COMPOTE AND ROUND COMPOTE, both on standards.

FIG. 5 — "THREE-FACE" HOLLOW-STEM CHAM-
PAGNE. *From the collection of Mrs. E. H. Bristol.*

Figure 2 are not the true *ribbed leaf*, though they come close to it. These bottles, marked as well as unmarked, are to be found in translucent white, opaque jade green, and rarely in a soft translucent lavender. The *ribbed ivy* celery vase shown in the same illustration is the only one I have seen.

HORN OF PLENTY

The *horn of plenty*, so much in demand by collectors today, has become one of the ten most popular patterns. In this design, the cake plate on a standard is again probably the most elusive item. To date I have seen three, in two sizes. The next rarest form would be the small rectangular covered honey dish (*Fig. 3*). A tray to match this dish was made, which fitted the base, but so far I have seen exactly one. This dish is undoubtedly one of the earliest pieces in this pattern. Few are known, particularly in perfect condition. Another noteworthy dish and one of the most popular is the butter dish of which the cover knob is a head of Washington, queue and all. One has been found in clear yellow. Look for its twin if you specialize in what is hard to find.

Horn of plenty claret glasses are so seldom found as to challenge the persistence of any collector. Tall and slender, with a delicate, graceful bowl, they are desirable for more reasons than their extreme rarity. Another extremely rare item is the oval compote on a standard (*Fig. 4*). Six-inch compotes on a high standard, covered or open, were usually listed in the early catalogues as "sweet-meat dishes." They are rare in any early pattern, and particularly so in *horn of plenty*. Spoonholders may be obtained in opaque white, in clear yellow, and one whiskey tumbler has been found in sapphire blue. In fact, one may always live in anticipation of an unusual piece in color in any of the early flint patterns, particularly those which were produced at Sandwich.

THREE FACE

There are many rarities in the later patterns, even in those of the Centennial period. Mrs. E. H. Bristol, of Foxboro, Massachusetts, formulated the largest known collection in the *three face* pattern, which is a product of the early 1870's. The rarest piece known is a lamp, made entirely in a brilliant amethyst. Next in rarity is the tall, ribbed biscuit jar. Few of these have been found but they are well worth years of patient searching. Among the most sought-after pieces are the hollow-stem champagnes (*Fig. 5*) as well as another form originally listed as the "saucer champagne."

Nearly all the glasses of the early pressed period that are five or five and a half inches in height are listed in the old company catalogues in my possession as "champagnes," and had solid glass stems. The pressed champagne glass with a hollow stem was apparently an innovation. If you have any doubts about the rarity of the hollow-stem type, just try to find them today! There are a number of reproductions on the market in this pattern now, including most of the stemware, so collectors need to be wary.

LION PATTERN

Of note in the *lion* pattern of the same period are the powder jar and cologne bottles (*Fig. 6*). They are so rare that I have not heard of more than two perfect sets. These are undoubtedly the most difficult pieces to find in this design. Other rarities include the oval salts (*Fig. 6*), cordials, covered cheese dish, milk pitcher (size between water pitcher and creamer),

FIG. 6 — "LION" RARITIES. Oval salts, one engraved. *From the collection of Joseph Makanna.* Matching cologne bottles. *From the collection of Donald Lannin.*

FIG. 7 — "MORNING GLORY" GOBLET, CHAMPAGNE, AND EGG CUP.

and bread plates in color. Look for them, if you seek that which is high in odds against you.

MORNING GLORY

Those who would accumulate a rare pattern obtainable in sets, and who have the necessary patience, persistence, and an unlimited purse, are advised to collect the *morning glory* pattern *(Fig. 7)*. To all appearances it is a product of the 1860's and was made only by the Boston & Sandwich Glass Company. Collectors in New England cherish a piece of it almost to the exclusion of anything else in the way of glass.

SPOONHOLDERS

There are a few collectors who have devoted themselves to accumulating what today are termed "spoonholders." These articles deserve the attention of rarity seekers. The examples shown in Figure 8 are early types. Many such vessels were originally made to match, in design, the bowls of whale-oil lamps. They were called "spillholders," and were dedicated to tapers or twisted paper spills which were used in lighting lamps, candles, and the wood in the fireplace at a time when matches were either expensive or unobtainable. Spillholders are of lead-flint glass, some quite brilliant and others rather dull, but all of them heavy and squat. In the 1840's many of them were made and advertised as holders for cigars. Later, when spoonholders came into general use, a gradual change in form occurred. The bowls became deeper and the stems longer. The opalescent specimen in Figure 9 is a good example of the transitional type. Some early ones are to be found in yellow, in clear with an amber band, and in translucent white. *Cable* has been found in varying fine shades of color, such as opaque powder blue, opaque green with panels of leaves in gilt, and in a soft opaque lemon yellow. Spoonholders are nice for short-stemmed flowers.

EGG CUPS

Some collectors have specialized in egg cups, both open and covered. One may gather a remarkably interesting collection of those small objects originally termed "egg glasses." They were made in practically all of the early flint patterns of tableware, as well as many of the later ones. After assembling such of these as may be had in patterns collectible in sets, Mrs. Harrison Hallett of Dennis, Cape Cod, turned her attention to exceptional specimens that sometimes are found not only in color but covered. Two of the latter, both in opaque white, are shown in Figure 10. As an old glassworker once informed me the covers were designed to keep the eggs warm as they were served. Covers were, however, gradually abandoned, perhaps because they broke so easily as to prove a liability instead of an asset. Thereafter egg cups came *sans* covers. Some enterprising perfumery house diverted the lovely colored egg cups to use as pomade jars. An opaque blue covered *diamond point* egg cup in my possession bears an original paper label lettered "Floral Perfumery" and part of the name of a New York importer is still legible, on the base. Some of the patterns in which these charming, rare covered egg cups may be found in color include *bull's eye; diamond point; cable; bull's eye and bar; fine rib; and sawtooth.*

OTHER EXCEPTIONAL PIECES

Many interesting items in milk white or opalescent, both early and late, are available to collectors who spurn easy finds. A pair of opal sweetmeat dishes in the

FIG. 8 — SPILLHOLDERS OF EARLY TYPES.

FIG. 9 — OPALESCENT RARITIES. *Left and right,* covered sweetmeats in *prism* pattern. *Center,* spoonholder of transitional type.

prism pattern, shown in Figure 9, dates back to the 1850's, and possibly to the 1840's. They were probably made by M'Kee Brothers of Pittsburgh. The *Liberty bell* mug in milk white with the serpent handle was produced on the grounds of the Centennial Exposition in Philadelphia in 1876, by Gillinder & Sons, in plain sight of the visitors *(Fig. 11)*. One of the most decorative of the dense white pieces of that period is the large swan dish with up-lifted wings, also pictured in Figure 11. Unfortunately the market has now been flooded with reproductions of this particu-

lar dish. Probably the rarest single item known today in milk-white glass is the *blackberry* water pitcher. Lately reproductions of a *blackberry* set have been advertised but it is not the true *blackberry* pattern, known to collectors by that name.

Limitations of space preclude the enumeration or description of all the rarities in a number of other interesting patterns. Nevertheless, enough are listed to convince collectors who complain of insufficient excitement in pressed-glass hunting that they are sadly mistaken.

FIG. 10 — COVERED EGG CUPS IN OPAQUE GLASS. *From the collection of Mrs. Harrison Hallett.*

FIG. 11 — RARITIES IN MILK GLASS. *Left, Libety bell* cup with serpent handle. *Center,* swan, an exceptionally fine piece of modeling. *Right,* syrup jug in *bellflower* pattern.

Except as noted, illustrations from the Ruth Webb Lee collection.

Old Glass Paperweights

BY MARY A. AND S. WELDON O'BRIEN

THERE IS SOMETHING *exotic about glass paperweights, enclosing flowers and lacework. Though not very ancient, they have a wide appeal. It is rather remarkable, since many of these paperweights were made within the memory of living man, that so much mystery has surrounded the question of how, when, and where they were made. The facts about their construction were recorded some years ago in* ANTIQUES, *and succeeding articles shed light on the factories that produced them. Nevertheless, a good many misconceptions are still widely held. This article, published in November 1949 by Mr. and Mrs. S. Weldon O'Brien, dispels some of the myths, and establishes some new facts. The illustrations are from the authors' own collection.*

PARADOXICALLY, the jewel-like glass paperweight encasing mille-fiori and filigree designs was first conceived by craftsmen of Italy when that country no longer held an important position in glassmaking, and was perfected and developed to include other decorative glass motifs by artisans of France, the last of the European countries to attain a fine "luxury glass."

At the Exhibition of French Industry held in Paris in 1839, Bontemps, director of the Choisy-le-Roi glasshouse, displayed examples of filigree glass of the old Venetian style; and millefiori and new specimens of filigree were shown at the following exhibition in 1844. Soon afterward, Saint Louis, Baccarat, and smaller factories started making filigree and millefiori glass. In 1845 the Paris Chamber of Commerce sent the learned chemist E. Péligot, then professor at the Conservatoire des Arts et Métiers, to the Exhibition of Austrian Industry in Vienna. His report on that exhibition devoted much space to a new "item of trade, the round shaped millefiori paper weights of transparent glass in which are inserted quantities of small tubes of all colors and forms assembled so as to look like a multitude of florets."

These millefiori glass paperweights which interested Péligot were exhibited by a Venetian named Bigaglia. Around 1838 he and a group of other Italian craftsmen, in an effort to regain supremacy in glass-making, attempted a revival of millefiori and filigree glass, which had occupied the attention of Venetian artisans throughout all periods. Bigaglia may have been inspired by the words of Sabellico, Venetian historian, who commented in a discussion of Italian glassmakers toward the end of the fifteenth century, "Consider to whom it did occur to include in a little ball all the sorts of flowers which clothe the meadows in spring.'"

FIG. 1 — VENETIAN MILLEFIORI PLAQUE dated on reverse *1846* with initials *G.B.F.*, probably those of the maker. Colors: blue, pink, turquoise, light green, and red. Decorative designs include a man-in-the-moon surrounded by stars (*upper left corner*), and a silhouetted gondola with gondolier (*center*).

FIG. 2 — CROWN-TYPE PAPERWEIGHT, attributed to Venice. Alternating opaque white and cobalt-blue ribbons. Central set-up containing silhouetted white monkey, surrounded by 7 set-ups of varying patterns and colors.

FIG. 3 — WHITE OVERLAY VASE WITH PAPERWEIGHT BASE, attributed to Venice. Designs in the weight include white lace filigree, white filigree surrounded by twisted colored threads, twisted opaque colored ribbons, and silhouette set-ups with figures of a dog, a leaping rabbit, and the same white monkey as in Figure 2.

FIG. 4 — SULPHIDE PAPERWEIGHT, attributed to Apsley Pellatt (*c. 1825*). The china-clay bust portrait of Lafayette appears silvery against a background of cobalt-blue glass.

FIG. 5 — LARGE BACCARAT FLORAL SPRAY PAPERWEIGHT. White pompon dahlia in center, with pink and white primrose and other flowers in blue and red, red and white, white and blue, each with matching bud; green leaves and stems.

FIG. 6 — SAINT LOUIS UPRIGHT BOUQUET PAPERWEIGHT, with filigree border. Elaborately faceted. Blue, yellow, pink, and white flowers with small serrated green leaves. Filigree border in exceedingly rare color combination, white with pure yellow.

FIG. 7 — FUCHSIA PAPERWEIGHT, attributed to Saint Louis. Crimson flower with blue center and stamens, large crimson bud, two small cherry-like buds, four green leaves, on orange-amber stem of woody appearance; all suspended over fine white *latticinio*, slightly depressed beneath spray.

FIG. 8 — CLICHY FLORAL SPRAY PAPERWEIGHT. Large pink Clichy rose and matching bud in center with blue and yellow viola and bud (*left*) and two green and purple thistles (*right*); green leaves of varying shapes, green crossed stems tied with pink ribbon.

Many weight collectors consider Venetian specimens of little importance except for their historical interest, but the millefiori plaque in Figure 1 exhibits a degree of technical perfection comparable to French millefiori at its best. This piece offers an interesting comparison with examples of mosaic and millefiori glass from the John Gellatly collection, now at the Smithsonian Institution. According to records there these were produced by Pietro Franchini the younger, a Venetian glassmaker of the mid-nineteenth century. One silhouette of a gondola is apparently identical to the center motif of Figure 1.

Authentic old paperweights containing millefiori set-ups of decidedly similar construction and colors are known, but so far their source is a controversial subject among collectors. The crown type, but solid glass, paperweight illustrated in Figure 2 is of this group. The crystal is of excellent quality, and although French examples are slightly heavier there is no question that this weight is old. The paperweight base of the white overlay vase of Figure 3 is obviously from the same source. These and similar weights have been variously attributed to France, America, Ireland, and — chiefly — England, but we believe that they were made by Italian artisans of the mid-nineteenth century.

Soon after Péligot's report of the "new" Venetian weight reached France, Saint Louis, always interested in creating unusual wares, produced the first French millefiori glass paperweight. A rare example of the type known as "full millefiori" dated 1845 is included in the factory museum collection, and at least one specimen signed and dated SL 1845 is in an American collection. Baccarat, then the outstanding French factory, usually waited for public reaction before adding anything new to its conservatively styled productions, but in this instance the lead of Saint Louis was followed almost immediately. Very rare Baccarat specimens contain the signature initial B and the date 1845. The young Clichy factory, founded at Sèvres in 1838 and transferred to Clichy around 1844, was probably the next French firm to take up the art, and Clichy productions soon rivaled in workmanship those of Baccarat and Saint Louis. Rare Clichy examples incorporate the initial C or the name CLICHY, but rumors of the inclusion of date canes have not been satisfactorily verified. Meanwhile, the popularity of paperweights led to their production by other factories on the Continent and in England, and soon also in America. Sandwich was probably first in America, starting around 1850. The figure 1825, first thought to be a date in certain Sandwich specimens, is now known to be an error caused by insertion of the wrong end of an 1852 date cane.

Paperweights were among the items of glassware presented in 1851 to the Conservatoire des Arts et Métiers by both the Baccarat and Saint Louis factories. Among these were "sulphides," "millefiori," "floral," and "butterfly" designs. These same factories have also preserved specimens of paperweights in their factory museums, and Saint Louis has some sketches of its designs. The archives of Clichy seem to have been destroyed, but much information about the products of this factory can be found in reports on the industrial exhibitions of the mid-nineteenth century. One of the two Clichy weights presented in 1849 to the Sèvres porcelain factory is now exhibited at the Musée des Arts Decoratifs in Paris.

Much useful information on French pa-

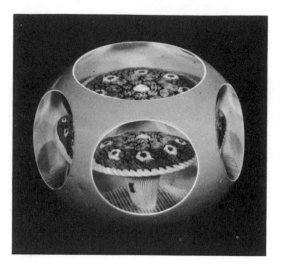

FIG. 9 — FRUIT PAPERWEIGHT, attributed to Saint Louis. Delicately striped yellow apple, one yellow-amber pear, four red cherries, on a bed of green leaves, all with amber-yellow stems and resting on a basket of white *latticinio*. The rather loose construction of the fruit, the deeply serrated, spiky, finely veined leaves, and the *latticinio* are Saint Louis characteristics.

FIG. 10 — RARE CLICHY PAPERWEIGHT. Large concave facets cut through the double overlay — Dubarry pink over white — disclose the mushroom bouquet formed of millefiori set-ups, including eleven pink Clichy roses and white tubular ribbons. *All illustrations from the authors' collection.*

FIG. 11 — SAINT LOUIS DOUBLE OVERLAY, with coiled salamander. Probably the most outstanding example of a very rare type. Constructed by blowing and the use of a four-part mold. Apple green (scarcest of overlay colors) cut to opaque white and then to crystal, with added gilt decoration. Dates at least from 1848, since in October of that year Launay alluded to an order for "lizard" weights of this type. (Enlarged.)

perweights is contained in *Les Presse-Papiers Français de Cristal* by R. Imbert and Y. Amic (Paris, 1948). Probably the biggest "news" lies in the attribution by Messrs. Imbert and Amic of certain specimens to the Saint Louis factory. They give many quotations from letters written to the director of Saint Louis between 1847 and 1851 by Launay of Launay, Hautin and Co. Throughout the period of finest paperweight production the output of Baccarat and Saint Louis was entrusted to this Paris firm for distribution, and Launay set down many observations not only about French weights but about those of other European countries. He indicated that German productions were cheap and of inferior quality. In 1849 he referred to the popularity of Clichy weights and the number of new customers which this factory had acquired, bearing out the theory that Clichy was successfully competing with the older factories before 1849.

There is some evidence that the "sulphide," embodying a bas-relief portrait of china clay in glass, may have been the first type of finely executed paperweight made. Ceramic cameos were invented in Bohemia in the mid-eighteenth century, but perfect encrustation in fine flint glass was not achieved until the first quarter of the nineteenth century, when this method of decoration was widely used by artisans of England, France, Germany, and Bohemia in glass objects such as jewel pendants, tumblers, vases, and flasks. By 1819 Apsley Pellatt, owner of the Falcon Glasshouse in Southwark, London, had introduced and patented his process of encrusting a porcelaneous cameo in glass. The application for this patent specifically mentioned the intended use of "Crystallo-ceramic" or sulphides in paperweights. The col-

lection of H M Queen Mary includes several fine sulphide weights considered by an English writer to be Pellatt's work between 1819 and 1825. Pellatt himself admitted that the technique of executing sulphides and enclosing them in glass was communicated to him by "a French gentleman," but no serious claim has been advanced that sulphide paperweights were made in France earlier than about 1845. Another English writer attributes the rare sulphide seen in Figure 4 to Pellatt and dates it about 1820. The remarkable silvery appearance, texture, fineness of detail, bright cobalt blue, and the placement of the entire ornament so near the base of the weight, together with the high crown, are Pellatt characteristics; a similar example in England is signed. According to one English collector, signed Pellatt examples are more numerous than generally supposed.

The products of individual French factories have certain characteristic peculiarities. Foliage, for instance, plays an important role in determining source. Baccarat leaves vary in shape but are mostly ovate with somewhat pointed tips. Occasionally two leaves of sword-like shape are placed opposite each other near the end of a thick stem that turns rather sharply; in large sprays, two such stems are usually crossed in an X *(Fig. 5)*. The Saint Louis craftsmen favored small spike-like leaves with deeply serrated edges and slender, slightly curving stems drawn gracefully down side by side into a delicate point *(Fig. 6)*. Certain Saint Louis specimens have a much thicker orange-amber stem and branch of woody appearance, with carelessly formed leaves *(Fig. 7)*. A plain dot or tendril-like bits of colored glass served as the center of many Saint Louis flowers. Clichy florals display long, tapering buds and many pointed, deeply serrated green leaves of somewhat broader shape than those of Saint Louis, as well as a much broader type of leaf in which five points are prominent *(Fig. 8)*. In these rare sprays, usually a gay colored ribbon holds crossed or extended stems together. Floral examples of Clichy display a remarkable quality of life and growth.

The decorative unit variously known as filigree border, filigree ring, cable border, cable ring, or filigree cable (used mostly in *upright bouquet* or *millefiori mushroom bouquet* weights) may also be indicative of the source. Baccarat generally used a filigree border consisting of a tubular rod composed of white spirally twisted threads, around which an opaque colored thread was wound. Saint Louis employed two different types of such borders; the one more frequently used consisted of a white twisted flat ribbon of filigree encircled by an opaque colored twisted thread, and the rarest type was a flat ribbon-like structure apparently made by collapsing a tube made up of alternate white and opaque colored threads *(Fig. 6)*. Clichy did not use these borders, but lengths of filigree were laid horizontally and parallel for the purpose of concealing the underside of lace backgrounds. In one example a Clichy craftsman used sixteen different styles of filigree in this manner.

Most French fruit paperweights have been attributed by American collectors to Baccarat, but Imbert and Amic give Saint Louis the credit for creating and specializing in these weights. They ascribe to Baccarat only the scarce *strawberry*, containing one or several berries in semi-high relief, and even this attribution is tentative. The type of weight shown in Figure 9, similar to one usually attributed to Baccarat, is illustrated in their book as a Saint Louis product. In 1850 Launay wrote regarding a shipment of fruit paperweights from Saint Louis.

A near counterpart of the *fuchsia* paperweight *(Fig. 7)* is reported to be in the Saint Louis factory museum, though the type is usually attributed to Baccarat. The Sandwich works produced a similar *fuchsia* of great beauty, and collectors will remember that Sandwich not only hired former craftsmen of Saint Louis but displayed a decided propensity to follow certain techniques and styles originally introduced by this factory.

On the basis of our extensive research and careful comparison of colors, designs, and techniques in many French weights, including signed ones, we agree with Imbert and Amic in attributing examples such as Figures 7 and 9, and other fruit paperweights, to Saint Louis.

In view of the number of technical skills required, the length of time and patience involved, and the indication of comparatively low retail prices at the time of manufacture, collectors may wonder how the production of paperweights was made commercially profitable. Execptionally skilled craftsmen probably made interchangeable units and intricate ornaments, which could be assembled by less proficient workmen in weights of more or less standard designs and color combinations. The most elaborate weights, however, must have been executed by outstanding artisans.

The guiding criteria for successful collecting are authenticity, craftsmanship, beauty, condition, and rarity.

SILVER

The Beginnings of American Silver

BY C. LOUISE AVERY

A SUBJECT TO *which The Magazine* ANTIQUES *has long devoted special attention is what we call the regional characteristics in American antiques — the points at which silver, furniture, and pewter of New England, for instance, differ from contemporary products of New York and Philadelphia. One of the first articles to bring out this theme in relation to silver was this one by Miss C. Louise Avery published in August 1930. That same year she published her book,* Early American Silver, *in the Century Library of American Antiques, developing the theme more fully. At that time Miss Avery's interest was primarily in American silver, but now her attention has shifted to the European decorative arts. As Associate Curator of Renaissance and Modern Art at the Metropolitan Museum she contributed an article to* ANTIQUES *in June 1949, on the subject of European porcelain based on an exhibition which she arranged at the museum.*

IF anyone is really eager to become acquainted with early American silver, let him choose a pleasant week in the autumn and drive from Boston to Philadelphia by way of New Haven and New York. By stopping successively at the Museum of Fine Arts in Boston, the Yale University, Metropolitan, and Philadelphia Museums, he may see nearly two thousand pieces (exclusive of flatware) made in America prior to 1800, probably at least half of them dating before 1750. They will be representative works of the several hundred different silversmiths who formerly lived throughout this region, and will thus acquaint the visitor with those little personal touches that reveal the individuality of the craftsman, and will familiarize him with the more general earmarks that distinguish the silver of one locality from that of another. But,

best of all, they will open his eyes to the beauty of old silver.

If one wishes to pursue minutely the study of Colonial silver, there is abundant material at hand, both in the silver itself and in documents relating to those who made it and those who used it. In earliest days, there were four principal centers of Colonial silversmithing — Boston, Newport, New York, and Philadelphia. As these developed at different periods and under different influences, it is worth while to look at them individually. The Southern colonies — Virginia, Maryland, and the Carolinas — because of their strong royalist sympathies and the agricultural character of their affairs, lagged in the development of native silversmithing until well into the eighteenth century.

Probably the earliest silver made in the

Colonies was produced by English crafts-men who had emigrated to Massachusetts, and by their local apprentices. Doubtless silver was made in Boston before 1650, al-though none is extant which may claim so early an origin. Between 1650 and 1700, however, silver was fashioned in quantity by Boston smiths; and this, together with the output of the early years of the eight-eenth century, is as fine in design and ex-ecution as any ever produced in America.

The colony of Massachusetts Bay was vigorous and resourceful, and soon devel-oped an active commerce besides many lo-cal industries and crafts. By virtue of the wealth thus acquired, it was able to patron-ize silversmiths, who, in their turn, became highly proficient. They were, as a group, men of integrity and strong personality, prominent in their communities and re-spected by their fellow-townsmen. Since the Colonists were chiefly of English extrac-tion, and endeavored to follow English cus-toms and foibles, the silver fashioned for them by the local artisans was, naturally, based upon contemporary English models. Colonial fashions changed with the Eng-lish, though not so quickly, because com-munication was slow and laborious. In-fluenced by the rigorous conditions of New England life and the Puritan dislike of os-tentation and extravagance, Massachusetts silver is patterned after only the simpler styles, and consists chiefly of utilitarian pieces.

Examples of early domestic silver are preserved for us, not only by descendants of old families, but also by the old churches, where, today, numbers of tank-ards, caudle cups, beakers, and mugs are to be found. Surprising as this may seem at first thought, it is readily explained by the fact that the Colonists were non-conform-ists, and were, therefore, content to use a miscellaneous assortment of domestic cups for their communion plate. In many in-stances, these cups had been used in the homes of the donors long before their pre-sentation to the church. Had the Puritans been more conventional in their choice of communion silver, we should now have far less evidence of domestic modes.

Of Boston silversmiths, the earliest with whose work we are now familiar were John Hull and his partner, Robert Sanderson. A number of finely modeled standing cups (*Fig. 1*) and caudle cups by these men still belong to New England churches; and a few more are in museum or private collec-tions (*Fig. 2*). The next great figure is Jere-miah Dummer, a prolific and powerful craftsman (*Fig. 3*).

Even more productive, and far more versatile, John Coney might well take first place in the ranks of American silver-smiths. Unquestionably, he is the peer of any other one might name. Many large and extremely handsome pieces bear his mark, such as the loving cup belonging to Har-vard University (*Fig. 6*), the sweetmeat box shown in Figure 4, the capacious punch-bowl belonging to Mrs. Henry Parish, and elaborately embossed caudle cups in vari-ous collections. They are noble specimens.

A contemporary of Coney's, who, how-ever, lived for many years longer, was Edward Winslow. The latter's admirers might, with a fair degree of justice, con-test Coney's claim to first place. One of Winslow's most charming pieces is a choco-late pot in the Clearwater collection, which bears the arms of the illustrious Hutchin-son family. It would make dull reading to list twenty more names, yet one would thus pay no more than a proper tribute to other able Boston craftsmen who worked in the

FIG. 1 — STANDING CUP. By Sandersen (*1608-1693*) and Hull (*1624-1683*), two of Boston's earliest and most prominent silversmiths. Its form was inspired by English cups of the first half of the seventeenth century; its shapeliness bears evidence to the taste and skill of its makers. Pricked with the initials *TBC* for The Boston Church (First Church), to which it was presented for use as a communion cup. *Height: 8 inches. Property of First Church, Boston.*

FIG. 2 — CAUDLE CUP. By Robbert Sandersen of Boston. Modeled after embossed English cups of the Charles II period. Most unusual in showing engraved turkey amid foliage. Caudle was a mixed drink of spiced wine or ale, generally served hot. *Height, with handles: 4 $^{15}/_{16}$ inches. From the collection of Henry F. du Pont. Photograph by courtesy of Metropolitan Museum of Art.*

FIG. 3 — BEAKER. By Jeremiah Dummer (*1645-1718*) of Boston. Given by Edward Boylston to the Brattle Street Church, Boston. *Height: 4⅜ inches. Boston Museum of Fine Arts.*

FIG. 4 — BOX FOR SWEETMEATS. By John Coney (*1655-1722*) of Boston. Inscribed, *The Gift of Grandmother Norton to Anna Quincy born 1719.* Presented by a descendant to the Boston Museum of Fine Arts. A particularly handsome example of a rare type of box. *Length: 8½ in.*

FIG. 5 — BEAKER. By Moody Russell (*1694-1761*) of Barnstable, Massachusetts. Inscribed, *The gift of Shearjashub Bourn, Esq. to the Church att Sandwich 1719.* Beakers were extensively used as communion cups. This represents the most common style in the first half of the eighteenth century. One of a pair now in the Metropolitan Museum of Art. *Height: 4 inches.*

FIG. 6 — LOVING CUP. By John Coney (*1655-1722*). One of the handsomest pieces of Colonial silver. Engraved with the Stoughton arms, and bequeathed by the Honorable William Stoughton, Lieutenant-Governor of Massachusetts, to Harvard College, 1701. *Height: 10¼ inches. Property of Harvard University. Photograph by courtesy of Boston Museum of Fine Arts.*

late seventeenth and early eighteenth centuries.

Newport, though less important than Boston, was nevertheless an active commercial town, serving the rest of Rhode Island and Connecticut as a place of export for agricultural and other produce, and of import for many of the manufactured commodities that were required. The city had her proficient silversmiths in the eighteenth century — Samuel Vernon, Arnold Collins, Daniel Russell, and Samuel Casey. But the greater prestige of the men in Boston, close at hand, must account for the general prevalence of the latter's handiwork in Rhode Island. Presumably, when a wealthy merchant contemplated ordering something really splendid, he considered Boston skill greater than home talent. As a commercial center, Newport eventually yielded precedence to Providence, but not until the Revolution had crippled her trade and seriously depleted her population.

New York silver is peculiarly interesting, because it represents a combination of Dutch and English influences. The earliest pieces were wrought by Dutch craftsmen, or by men of Dutch descent, and are definitely Dutch in design. Chief among them are the tall engraved beakers (*Fig. 8*), the sturdy baptismal basins, and the two-handled bowls with formal floral designs in panels round their sides (*Fig. 9*). As the New York silversmiths seem to have been an extremely conservative group, many Dutch characteristics persisted and mingled with later English fashions.

New York tankards afford an outstanding illustration of the blending of the two styles. Their shape was presumably derived from English tankards of the Restoration period, but they are modeled with a massiveness and vigor essentially Dutch. The majority of English and of New England tankards are plain; those made in New York are generally enriched with embossed, engraved, or cast ornaments inspired by Dutch design. Most characteristic are the cherub and other masks, foliate scrolls, birds, pendent festoons of fruit and flowers, and cyphers (*Fig. 10*). The New York engraving of coats of arms is especially flowing in line and beautiful in execution.

Early New York silversmiths of marked ability include Jacob and Hendrik Boelen, John and Koenraet Ten Eyck, Jacobus Van der Spiegel, Peter Van Dyck, Benjamin Wynkoop, Bartholomew Schaats, Simeon Soumain, and the Huguenots, Bartholomew, John, and Charles LeRoux.

In Philadelphia, the controlling element was English Quaker, which, in terms of silver, meant simple English forms. The earliest pieces date either from the very end of the seventeenth century or, more probably, from the beginning of the eighteenth. Chief among the early silversmiths are John de Nys and Cesar Ghiselin, probably both Huguenots; Francis and Joseph Richardson; William Vilant; and Philip Syng. Philadelphia silver of the first half of the eighteenth century is not markedly dissimilar to that of New England of the same period. It exhibits a preference for certain types, such as the tankard with domed lid and no finial (*Fig. 14*).

The early Philadelphia silversmiths were distinctly able, but their successors enjoyed greater patronage; for Philadelphia, during the middle and second half of the century, became the richest and most important city in the Colonies and the infant Republic. Renowned for her abundant hospitality, she counted among her silver many fine tea services, but as these are

FIG. 8 — EARLY NEW YORK BEAKER. By Jacob Boelen (c. 1654-1729). Engraved, like many Dutch communion beakers, with interlacing strapwork, foliate scrolls, and medallions enclosing figures symbolizing Faith, Hope, and Charity. Inscribed, in Dutch, *A token of love and truth to the church in Kingston, 1683. Height: 7¼ inches. From the Metropolitan Museum of Art.*

FIG. 10 — TYPICAL NEW YORK TANKARD. By Peter Van Dyck (*1684-1750*), illustrating the massive proportions, flat lid with engraved cypher, "corkscrew" thumbpiece, applied mask and flowers on the handle, and border of foliation at the base. *Height: 6⅞ inches. From the Mabel Brady Garvan collection, Yale University Art Gallery.*

FIG. 9 — NEW YORK BOWL. By Simeon Soumain (*1685-1750*). Two-handled bowls with panels, sometimes enclosing conventionalized flower forms, are found in Dutch, and also in New York, silver. *Height, with handles: 4¹⁵/₁₆ inches. From the collection of Miss Margaret S. Remsen; photograph courtesy The Museum of the City of New York.*

FIG. 7—PORRINGER. By Apollos Rivoire (*1702-1754*), father of the famous Paul Revere. Porringers were extremely useful in the early days. *Diameter, with handle: 7¾ inches. From the Metropolitan Museum of Art.*

FIG. 12 — TEAPOT. By John LeRoux (became freeman in New York, 1723; later worked in Albany). The majority of early New York teapots are of this style, and probably were used interchangeably for tea and coffee. *Height: 8 inches. From Garvan collection.*

FIG. 13 — CREAMER. By Adrian Bancker (*1703-1761*) of New York. *Height: 5 inches. From the Garvan collection.*

FIG. 14 — TANKARD. By Philip Syng (*1703-1789*), one of the most eminent of Philadelphia silversmiths. He made the inkstand used at the signing of the Declaration of Independence, and now in Independence Hall. *Height: 7¼ inches. From Metropolitan Museum of Art.*

FIG. 11 — SNUFFER STAND. By Cornelius Kierstede (*1674-1753*) of New York and New Haven. The ornamentation of his silver is distinctly individual and is generally quite ambitious, even though rather crude in rendering. Shows pronounced Dutch influence, frequently mingled with English. *Height of stand: 8¼ inches. From Metropolitan Museum of Art.*

chiefly of post-Revolutionary date, they are outside our immediate sphere of interest.

And now our traveler, who set forth so hopefully in the first paragraph of this article, returns home from his little pilgrimage. He has had a pleasant and enlightening trip, and he sits down to his dinner well pleased with the world. But then, for the first time, perhaps, his eye falls critically upon his own table appointments, and the full significance of the old silver he has been studying is literally brought home. He perceives that, in the final analysis, it is not rarity or antiquity that attracts us to the handiwork of our early silversmiths, but the intrinsic merit of something at once beautiful and useful.

The silver on his table is the result of our modern system of quantity production and mechanical uniformity, and he compares, in his mind's eye, the mellow luster of the old pieces with the harsh brilliance of his own possessions. He realizes that, whereas he can find on his neighbor's table the exact duplicate of his most prized teapot, the least significant piece of old hand-wrought plate is like none other of its fellows. Our modern ware goes through many hands, from its conception to its realization; but the old silversmith was designer as well as craftsman. He conceived and wrought his piece, taking pride in its fashioning and a personal interest in its destiny; for, almost always, each article was made to order, the customer himself frequently supplying the material in the form of coin. And the silversmith, with infinite skill, though he worked with simple tools and meagre equipment, brought out of the shapeless metal a cup, a bowl, or a tankard that today commands our highest admiration.

Jesse Kip, New York Goldsmith

BY JOHN MARSHALL PHILLIPS

JOHN MARSHALL PHILLIPS *is Professor of Art at Yale University, Director of the Yale University Art Gallery, and Curator of its Mabel Brady Garvan collections. In the course which he has been teaching at Yale since 1932 he has pioneered in interpreting the American background to college students. The course covers the development of American architecture, furniture, silver, glass, prints, painting, and sculpture from 1607 to 1900, in their historic, economic, and social setting. While his knowledge obviously covers a wide field, he is best known as the leading authority on early American silver, and it is on that subject that he has done most of his writing. He is the author of* Early Connecticut Silver 1700-1830, Masterpieces of New England Silver 1650-1800, *and* American Silver. *For* ANTIQUES *he has written, among others, a series of articles which was later reprinted in booklet form,* The Hundred Masterpieces of American Silver in Public Collections. *The present article, from our July 1943 issue, records one of Professor Phillips' important discoveries in the field of American silver.*

A NEW YORK land deed of 1704 in which a certain Jesse Kip was styled "Goldsmith" furnished the solution of one of the most baffling of the silversmith problems. This was the identity of the unknown smith whose work, characteristic of New York in the period 1685-1710, was signed *IK* in a rectangle.

Jesse Kip was baptized December 19, 1660, in the Dutch Church in New York, the fourth son of Jacob Hendrickzen Kip (*1631-1690*) and his wife Maria de la Montagne. She was the daughter of Doctor Johannes de la Montagne, Huguenot physician, member of the Governor's council, and sometime vice-director of Fort Orange. His godparents were his maternal uncle, Gysbert van Inburgh, Abraham Janszen, and his maternal aunt, Petronella de la

Montagne. Jesse's background was a balanced combination of Dutch and French Protestant ancestry, of which he was the third generation in New York. This heritage may account in some degree for his artistic temperament. Little is known of his early years; there is no record of his apprenticeship, which should have begun about 1674, at the time of the final surrender of the city to the English. Among the possible masters then in New York were Jeuriaen Blanck the elder, and Ahasuerus Hendricks. To be sure, Jacob Boelen and Cornelius van der Burg had just opened their shops. Under one of these, young Jesse must have served his time.

The earliest known record of Kip, following baptism, is as a witness June 6, 1695, along with his cousin Gysbert van In-

[219]

burgh, to the will of Benjamin Blagge, a mariner. A marriage bond was issued, September 30, 1695, to Jesse Kip and Maria Stevens, or Stevenson. She was the daughter of Thomas and Elizabeth Lawrence Stevenson of Long Island. The Kips lived in a house in the North Ward, which in 1699 was valued at £30. In accordance with the family tradition, Jesse accepted civic responsibility. His grandfather, Hendrik Kip, described by the poet Stedman as "Hendrik Kip of the haughty lip," was a member of the Council of Nine. His son Jacob, father of the silversmith, was Secretary of the Province and a member of the Council. We find that in 1697 Jesse was one of the assessors in the North Ward, in which his fellow silversmiths, Jacob Boelen and Ahasuerus Hendricks, were alderman and collector. In 1698 Jesse served in the same capacity, having as his co-worker another silversmith, Gerrit Onckelbag; Jacob Boelen continuing as alderman. In 1699 they were again chosen, with Jacob Boelen as examiner.

In 1696, in an indenture made between Bastian Congo, "a Free Negro man," and Abraham and Jesse Kip, Jesse is referred to as a merchant. The sole reference to him as a goldsmith occurs in the land deed mentioned. It is reproduced in facsimile in the *History of the Kip Family in America*, by Frederic E. Kip, and refers to land near Kip's Bay, which Jesse, his mother, brothers, and sisters deeded to their youngest brother, Samuel, in 1704.

Late in October 1720, an elder brother, Jacobus Kip, died at Newtown, Long Island, bequeathing the new house he was building, a water mill, and appurtenances, to his brothers and sisters. It is likely that he was one of the victims of the yellow fever which swept New York City in 1702,

and which shortly after carried off Jesse's younger brother and possible apprentice, Benjamin (*1678-1702*). The latter had received his freedom as a registered silversmith of New York City that May; his legacy in Jacobus' will of "so much money as for to by his Tuels," suggests that he was about to go into business for himself.

Eventually Jesse bought up the shares of his remaining brothers and sisters, possibly at the instigation of his pretty wife, for the fulling mill of Jacobus and the new house he was building were just across the creek from Stevens Point, the home of her father, and the site of a prosperous fulling mill which belonged to him and his brother Edward. In due time, Jesse purchased the other mill. His removal from New York to Newtown took place sometime after December 11, 1709, the date of his son Johannes' baptism in the Dutch Church of New York, and before either the purchase of the second mill, October 16, 1711, or May 15, 1712, when his son William was baptized in the First Reform Church at Jamaica. He died at Newtown in April 1722, survived by his widow and numerous children.

Of his silversmithing period, which extends roughly from 1682 to 1710, only nine pieces are known to have survived the melting pot. They are three tankards, a porringer, two bowls, a pierced strainer spoon, and two sucket forks. Of these, the sucket forks are the earliest, engraved on their shafts with the legend *Maria Van Renslaer* for Maria van Cortlandt van Rensselaer (*1645-1689*), the daughter of Oloff Stevense van Cortlandt and wife of Jeremias van Rensselaer, second lord of the manor. Suckets were a popular sweetmeat in the seventeenth century, and were of two varieties, wet and dry, hence the functional combina-

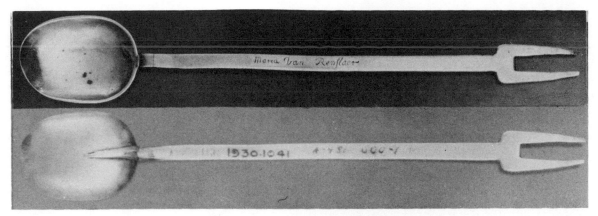

FIG. 1 — SUCKET FORK BY JESSE KIP (*New York, 1660-1722*) (*two views*). Engraved on the shaft *Maria Van Renslaer*. A similar fork, similarly engraved, is in the Museum of the City of New York. *From the Mabel Brady Garvan Collection, Yale University Art Gallery.*

FIG. 2 — THREE-PINT TANKARD BY JESSE KIP (*two views*). Engraved *P* over *IM/A°-1692*-within a plumed mantling. On the serrated edge of the cover is boldly engraved a fleur-de-lis. The earliest dated New York tankard. This and Figure 1 carry Kip's early stamp, the others his later one in which the letters were less crudely cut. Maker's mark shown below. *From the collection of Mrs. Walter M. Jeffords.*

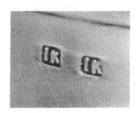

FIG. 3 — TANKARD BY JESSE KIP. Cover engraving of a man-of-war. Very like the Onckelbag-Shelley tankard of 1698 in the Clearwater collection at the Metropolitan Museum of Art. *Owned in Bermuda.*

FIG. 4 — TANKARD BY JESSE KIP (*c. 1700-1710*). Originally owned by Abraham de Peyster. *From the collection of the late Mrs. J. Amory Haskell.*

tion spoon-fork. One of these is in the Mabel Brady Garvan collection at the Yale University Art Gallery, the other at the Museum of the City of New York (*Fig. 1*). Next in point of time is the three-pint tankard shown in Figure 2. It is the largest of the seventeenth-century New York tankards and the earliest dated example. These three pieces bear the early stamp of Kip, in which the letters are more crudely cut than in the stamp appearing on the other pieces. More florid in decoration, with typical New York motif, such as the stamped foliated base band and corkscrew thumbpiece, is the tankard of Figure 3. Its cover is ornately engraved with a man-of-war remarkably like the one on a tankard fashioned in 1698 by Onckelbag for Giles Shelley (now in the Clearwater collection at the Metropolitan Museum). This similarity recalls in a striking fashion the close association of these two craftsmen as assessors in the North Ward in that year. The remaining tankard (*Fig. 4*), plainer in detail but of pleasing proportions, is one of the "seven tankards" mentioned in 1728 in the inventory of Colonel Abraham de Peyster, who, like Kip, was of Dutch and French Protestant stock.

For the Stuyvesant family Kip fashioned a porringer, the handle of which is delicately pierced with a lacelike design featuring a cross, heart, and diamond, distinctive of New York. It is still owned by the family.

The remaining pieces are the strainer spoon, now in my collection, and two drinking bowls of the delightful paneled type found only in New York. The larger of the two (*Fig. 5*) displays a mastery of hammerwork, casting, and engraving. Again the fleur-de-lis is displayed prominently in each of the six panels. The other

bowl (*Fig. 6*), similar in design but much smaller, is engraved with the initials *VD* over *IM* and the date *1699*. Family tradition, recorded by J. E. Stillwell in his *Historical and Genealogical Miscellany*, states that it was a racing trophy for a one-mile race on the King's Highway in Middletown, won by a colt raised, trained, and ridden by a slave of Jacob and Maria van Dorn. It is still owned by their descendants and, if the tradition is sound, is the second racing trophy of American make. It is interesting to note that the earlier, a racing piece of 1668, was refashioned into a porringer by Kip's cousin, Peter Van Inburgh (*1689-1740*). Its handle is similar to that of Kip's porringer. It is most likely that Peter was one of Jesse's apprentices, as his father Gysbert, a first cousin of Jesse's, was brought up in the Kip household, his parents being victims of the Indian massacre at Esopus. And although it is mere speculation, it is of interest that the probable year of Jesse's leaving New York, 1710, was the year when Peter Van Inburgh would have set up his own shop. Jesse's other silversmithing connections by blood or marriage were with Benjamin Wynkoop, who married Kip's first cousin Femmetie Vanderhuel, and with Cornelius Kierstede, whose aunt and uncle, Catharine and Lucas Kierstede, married respectively Johannis and Rachel Kip, brother and sister of the silversmith. In view of this close family connection, it is probable that Jesse was Kierstede's master, being fifteen years his senior. Perhaps it is significant that the only two New York silversmiths to receive their freedom in May 1702 were Jesse's probable apprentices, his younger brother Benjamin and Cornelius Kierstede.

The credit for the discovery of Jesse Kip in his rôle as artificer in the precious metals belongs to his descendants, Mrs. Olive Beaupré Miller and Mrs. Hazel Haring Beldon, who through the courtesy of AN-TIQUES consulted the author as to the extent of his work. This discovery gives added interest to those pieces fashioned by him, which have brought satisfaction and pride of ownership for the past two centuries.

FIG. 5 — PANELED DRINKING BOWL BY JESSE KIP. Distinctive New York form. Masterfully fashioned in every detail. Caryatid handles; thumb grip is a finely cast female head. Engraved *S* over *TA* in a plumed mantling. *From the Metropolitan Museum of Art.*

FIG. 6 — PANELED DRINKING BOWL BY JESSE KIP. Similar to Figure 5 but much smaller. Showing engraved and flat-chased ornament of base, and fleur-de-lis motif in panel decoration. Engraved *VD* over *IM, 1699.* Believed to have been racing trophy. *Privately owned.*

The Sanders-Garvan Beaker
by Cornelis VanderBurch

BY MRS. RUSSEL HASTINGS

THERE ARE MANY *avenues leading to antiquarian knowledge. Some people come to it through an initial interest in a specific collectible, some through esthetic appreciation and stylistic analysis, some through a local interest in some particular region. Mrs. Russel Hastings arrived at it through genealogy, which led her to important discoveries regarding early New York silver and painting. One of the most interesting and valuable of those which she recorded in* ANTIQUES *is this account, from the February 1935 issue, of the source of the designs engraved on a historic beaker by a New York silversmith.*

IN SOME respects the most impressive piece of early American silver in the Mabel Brady Garvan Collection at the Yale University Art Gallery is the so-called "ceremonial beaker," which, until its acquisition by Mr. Garvan, had been handed down through eight generations of the Sanders family of Albany and Schenectady (whose name has been shortened from the earlier Dutch form, Sandersen). This beaker is slightly taller than any of the other large beakers of New York origin or association that betray Dutch influence. Its workmanship is excellent. Its reputed history is plausible. The man now generally accepted as its maker was Cornelis VanderBurch (*c. 1653-1699*), the earliest native New York silversmith thus far recorded. The really arresting feature of this masterpiece, however, is the series of cryp-tic decorations that adorn its surface.

In ANTIQUES for May 1929 was published an interesting article concerning the Sanders beaker and the alluring patina of tradition which it had accumulated during its long sojourn with the descendants of the original owner. Yet, though interesting, the account is not altogether satisfying. In the minds of the curious it prompts more questions than it answers. So it came about that I was drawn into a deeper study of the piece, particularly of its engraved decorations, and of the smith who stamped his mark upon the finished work. The results of the search have been dramatic in the extreme. To be sure, they have all but completely eliminated the overlay of tradition which enshrouded the piece; but the facts now revealed are far more captivating than the legend.

[225]

Tradition vs. History

According to the article in ANTIQUES, the beaker in question was presented to Robbert Sandersen in 1685 by Indian tribesmen, in token of gratitude for services rendered by the recipient as interpreter and intermediary during sundry negotiations between the savages and their white neighbors. The story is an attractive one. But is it true? Is it even likely?

Sandersen was well liked by the Indians and enjoyed their confidence. Had this not been the case, he could hardly have brought his diplomatic undertakings to a successful conclusion. We may further credit some of the tradition of Sandersen's popularity to the fact that later generations may have confused him with another ancestor, the well-known Major Glen of Schenectady County, whose wife was beloved by the savages because she "had been kind to French prisoners," and whose home and family were, in consequence, spared in the Schenectady fire and massacre of 1690. But without indubitable evidence to support the tradition, are we justified in believing that the silent children of the forest would have sent to Manhattan and ordered a silver beaker for bestowal upon their paleface friend? Such a performance, in 1685 or in 1935, would seem singularly at variance with Indian character and conceptions of propriety. Since, as a matter of fact, not an atom of evidence in its favor is available, let us examine a more plausible theory as to the beaker's reason for being.

It is a matter of record that, on August 10, 1685, a deed conveying certain lands from the Indians to the ownership of that canny Scot, Robert Livingston, was duly signed. Livingston was long Commissioner of Indian affairs and used the opportunities afforded by his office to obtain from the natives part of the domain constituting Livingston Manor. The tract affected by the deed of 1685 consisted of the six hundred acres, known as Tachkanick (modernly Taconic), lying east of the present Germantown-on-the-Hudson. It is to be particularly observed that the document referred to names Robbert Sandersen as "interpreter," a rather ingenuous title for the diplomat who beguiled the Indians into exchanging their territory for what today seems a scanty mess of pottage. In later years it was testified that Livingston, in accumulating the acreage of his manor, "was at great charge, trouble and expense in purchasing the same from the native Indians, and particularly that part thereof which is contiguous and adjoining to the colony of the Massachusetts Bay, called and known by the name of Tackanack."

The outcome of the bargain between Livingston and the Indians, with Sandersen acting as interpreter, was a small principality for the Scot and a handful of miscellaneous loot for the savage parties to the contract. If a special donation to memorialize the *coup* was in order, the obligation for its bestowal clearly rested upon the new potentate. That under the circumstances the gift should take the form of a handsome silver beaker would be quite in keeping. Livingston was in a position to obtain such an object and to ensure its correct inscribing. The Indians were not.

So, briefly presented, the historical likelihoods confront the figments of tradition. In default of demonstrable proof one way or another, the reader is at liberty to take his stand on whichever side he prefers.

The Beaker's Engraved Medallions

The Sanders beaker is elaborately engraved. Its lip is bordered by strapwork panels enclosing floral scrolls. Below, at each of three equally spaced points on the cylindrical sides, occurs a wreath-enframed medallion: one portraying a spray of blossoms in a vase; another, an apparently dead or sleeping animal surrounded by a low earthwork; another, a group of feeding geese. Between the medallions, and rising above the scalloped ornamentation about the base, we descry the engraved figure of a lizard pursuing a spider and, in turn, being devoured by a stork whose leg is entwined by the coils of a serpent; a figure of death mounted on a crocodile; and a representation of an eagle, with a tortoise in its talons, flying above a sharp upheaval of rock.

Obviously symbolic in meaning, these curious designs have been variously interpreted. But the correct elucidation of their source and intent has waited upon a discovery made only after long and diligent search. It may now perhaps be best approached by a somewhat circuitous detour.

One of the lights of learning in seventeenth-century Holland was Jacobus Cats, who was born in Brouwershaven, Zeeland, November 10, 1577, and, after a long and active life, died not far from the Hague in September of 1660. Educated in Leyden, Orleans, and Paris, by profession a lawyer, twice an emissary to England, where he was knighted by King Charles I, Cats is chiefly remembered as a didactic poet. His profuse writings consisted of allegories, moral dissertations, idyls, and what not else.

Cats' allegories, which appeared in the form of short aphoristic fables and reflections, presented variously in Dutch, French, German, Greek, Latin, Italian, Spanish, or English, as befitted the author's wide scholarship and his somewhat poly-

FIG. 1 — THE SANDERS-GARVAN SILVER BEAKER (1685). Originally a gift to Robbert Sandersen, and for generations owned by his descendants, who shortened the name to Sanders. First published in ANTIQUES for May 1929, where its making was credited to Carol Van Brugh of New York. It is now ascribed to Cornelis VanderBurch, more usually spelled Cornelius Vanderburgh. Height, 8 inches, Weight, 18 ounces. *Mabel Brady Garvan Collection, Yale University.*

FIG. 2 — VASE OF FLOWERS ON THE SANDERS-GARVAN BEAKER. Of this design no exact prototype has been discovered, though the general motive is frequently encountered in seventeenth- and eighteenth-century books of engravings.

FIG. 4 — CYPHER ON THE BASE OF THE BEAKER. Below this cryptic symbol occurs the silversmith's mark of Cornelius Vanderburgh (originally Cornelis Luycasse Vanderburch), the initials *C.V.B.* in a heart.

FIG. 3 — THE ERMINE AND THE RING OF MUD (*Integrity*). Showing the original illustration for Veldt-Teycken in the Jacobus **Cats** folio volume of 1658 and the derivative silver engraving on the Sanders-Garvan beaker. Abstract of the accompanying poem: The ermine, when surrounded by mud, prefers death to soiling his precious coat, so starves to death, rather than venture forth. Joseph, hero of the poem, flees from a beautiful woman who offers him not only love but riches and power. Some persons laugh at the Josephs of the world, but he who in his youth thus conquers the flesh is indeed blessed. *This and other Cats engravings courtesy Folger Shakespeare Library, Washington, D. C.*

glot audience, were once the most popular secular literature in Holland, second only to the Bible. Usually illustrated with engravings after designs by the artist Adriaen vander Venne *(1589-1662)*, the poems were first issued, at irregular intervals, in slender volumes. Calculated to appeal to old and young alike, these little books found their way into the homes of all classes in Holland, where their author came to be affectionately spoken of as "Father Cats." We have knowledge of the fascination which these books held for young folk. As a boy, Sir Joshua Reynolds owned a copy of *Proteus,* Cats' early work of Emblem Book form. It had made its appearance in 1618, and had been brought to England by Joshua's Dutch great-grandmother. Its weird illustrations enthralled the future Royal Academician, who spent many hours in making drawings from them. To this exercise, indeed, has been ascribed the artist's subsequent occasional excursions into the horrible.

In 1655 the printer and publisher Jan Jacobus Schipper of Amsterdam conceived the ambitious plan of issuing the collected works of Cats in one volume with text and illustrations complete. Pessimists assured the foolhardly printer that the cost of the undertaking would land him in bankruptcy. Nevertheless he persevered, and was rewarded for his enterprise by sales that presently exhausted the first printing of the book and within three years justified the issuance of a second edition in a thick Royal Folio.

These collections are known today as the "Second Bible of the Dutch," and examples of them were almost certainly carried across the ocean to New Amsterdam by emigrants from Holland. Here they were doubtless even more eagerly thumbed than they had been in the homeland and became familiar sources of manifold inspiration. Two copies, at least, of the amazing 1658 volume are today preserved in the United States, one in the Folger Shakespeare Library in Washington, the other in the New York Public Library. To the copy in the Shakespeare Library must go the credit for solving the riddle of the engravings on the Sanders beaker, and thus happily terminating a long and arduous quest. For it was during an examination of this ponderous tome that, one after another, Vander Venne's illustrations for Cats' effusions were revealed as the unmistakable source whence he who ornamented the beaker directly borrowed not only his symbolic ideas but the forms in which to clothe them.

It might, of course, be contended that the New York silversmith Cornelis Vander-Burch probably copied both the shape and the decoration of his masterpiece from an earlier beaker brought from Holland or the east coast of England, where Dutch styles in silver were prevalent. Such an hypothesis seems far-fetched. It is more reasonable to believe that, with a copy of Father Cats at hand, the craftsman made his own selection from the book's rich store of poetry and picture. Whether he was furnished the volume by his client, or owned a copy himself, or borrowed one from his rascally, scholarly stepfather (who had come out from Holland in 1669, presumably with a library of sorts) is of no particular moment. Some fellow craftsman may have executed the engravings on the beaker, but conjecture in that direction is futile. Perhaps the volume from which these careful transcripts were made may turn up with annotations that will settle the question.

FIG. 5 — LAZY FOX AND FEEDING GEESE (*Industry*). Original illustration and derivative silver engraving. Abstract of accompanying poem: It has been decreed by Adam that those who would eat must work. The lazy fox keeps his feet dry and therefore must endure an empty belly. Those who will not labor may not count on sympathy . . . The silver version omits the fox and arranges the geese in a more compact composition. From Spiegel van den Voorleden.

FIG. 6 — THE STRONG AND THE WEAK (*Magnanimity*). Original illustration and derivative engraving. Abstract of accompanying poem: The spider eats the fly, the lizard eats the spider and is seized by the stork, which, even before it can fly aloft with its prey, is seized by the serpent. Likewise the dragon gobbles up the snake and the peasant slays the dragon. Thus, no matter how powerful a man may be, there is always someone of still greater power. Remember that whatsoever you do to the weak will be visited upon you by those stronger than yourself. The law of the woods holds also for the world outside. From Spiegel van den Voorleden.

We may now return to a more detailed consideration of the designs on the beaker of our concern. These are here reproduced side by side with the pictures from which they were taken. Since an accompanying caption explains the implication of each symbol, it is not necessary to repeat that information in the present text. The representation of Death astride a crocodile occurs in the Emblem Book *Proteus*. In the earlier editions of this work the crocodile proceeds from right to left; in later appearances he reverses his direction — testimony to reëngraving of the subject. The other symbols are to be found in the *Spiegel* (Mirror of the Past and Present) and the *Self-Strijt* (Inner Strife, or Self-Discipline). The sixth design, a plant flowering from an urn, does not occur in the Cats folio; but, in sundry variations, it is frequently encountered in Emblem Books, particularly those of the German botanist, Doctor Joachim Camerarius. The beaker version of the motive may well be an improvisation on the part of the engraver.

The Sanders Device

The device on the bottom of the Sanders beaker lets down the bars to yet another succulent pasture. From time to time marks based on the Latin cross, particularly that form which, by the addition of an hypotenuse to either upper angle, becomes a "4" or its reverse, have appeared in the America of the seventeenth and eighteenth centuries. Such mysterious figures have been vaguely known as "merchants' marks," "house marks," and so on. A small collection of leaden bale seals thus impressed is preserved in the Numismatic Society's rooms in New York City. The *Bulletin* of the New York Historical Society for January 1931 prints an article by William L. Calver on similar bale seals

found among Revolutionary relics. Other examples have, from time to time, been recorded in the *New York Genealogical and Biographical Record*. Pieces of glass exhibiting like mysterious devices have been unearthed by excavators during the restoration of Williamsburg, Virginia, and have likewise been found on old Virginia tobacco casks. Wilberforce Eames, that seasoned and inspiring antiquarian, when shown a photograph of the cipher on the base of the Sanders beaker, suggested its possible kinship with the printers' marks of the Renaissance. Following this hint, search has revealed hundreds of examples of the Latin cross thus used in a diversity of forms from the Renaissance onward for some three centuries. Harold Bayley, in his recently published volume, *New Light on the Renaissance as displayed in Contemporary Emblems*, propounds the theory that these printers' marks and watermarks on paper, particularly those employing the sacred numeral "4," were a means of secret communication between heretical printers who were trying to outwit the Church and its restrictions. No doubt the germ of ancient magic abides in these curious symbols, though its particular potency may have been forgotten even when the symbols themselves were in common use. The cipher on the beaker of our interest may justly be viewed as a personal mark, and there seems little doubt that it was the "merchant's mark" of Robbert Sandersen.

Emblem Books

Concerning the books of the kind that afforded models for the pictorial engravings on the Sanders beaker, a separate essay might be written. Particularly interesting is the vast subject of Emblem Books, to which Shakespeare was deeply indebted.

Fig. 7 — Death and the Crocodile (*Faithfulness*). Original illustration and engraved derivative. Abstract of accompanying poem: The crocodile continues to increase in size so long as he lives. Even when Death bears down upon him, he continues to expand. So it is with true love. Those who cherish ambition or greed in their hearts never find the greatest happiness. *From the Proteus.*

Fig. 8 — The Eagle and the Tortoise (*Humility*). Original illustration and engraved derivative. Abstract of accompanying poem: The eagle, bearing the tortoise in his talons, soars to dizzy heights to show his passenger the world. The tortoise thinks himself an honored cosmopolite; but he is mistaken. Presently he is dropped upon a sharp rock and his hard shell broken into fragments, so that he may the more easily be devoured by the eagle. How many at court suffer a like fate! He who climbs too high with too many airs is a candidate for destruction. *From Spiegel van den Voorleden.*

They were collections of short, illustrated moral poems, and were prevalent on the Continent though but little known to English readers of today. Study of their countless illustrations could not but assist us in determining the provenance of our early designs in architecture, gardens, costume, furniture, and household implements. No better depiction of the varied activities, social and commercial, of olden times may be found than is spread before us in these delightful volumes. The Cats folio gives a more than photographically vivid portrayal of Dutch life in the seventeenth century. In consequence, it brings us likewise into closer touch with the time and temper of New Amsterdam than any surviving record made on this side of the water.

Old Sheffield Plate

BY FREDERICK BRADBURY, F. S. A.

THE NAME OF Frederick Bradbury, F. S. A., is associated with old Sheffield plate in more ways than one. He was, first of all, of an old Sheffield family long associated with the making of rolled plate as developed in that English city in the eighteenth century. Then he was the recognized authority on the subject, author of the definitive History of Old Sheffield Plate, *issued in 1912. For* ANTIQUES *he wrote a two-part article which provides an excellent summary of the whole subject. Originally published in July and August 1931, it is here presented in somewhat condensed form.*

SHEFFIELD plate is the term applied to articles made from copper and coated with silver by the process of fusion. Sometime toward the middle of the eighteenth century, Thomas Boulsover, a Sheffield cutler, while undertaking repairs to the haft of a knife, observed that silver and copper became fused when heated to a given temperature, and that when subjected to hammering the two metals could be dealt with as one. This caused him to experiment, so that eventually he produced buttons and boxes apparently made entirely of silver, although actually they had a copper foundation coated with the more precious metal. Joseph Hancock, who served his apprenticeship with a relative of the inventor, realized the wider possibilities of the discovery, and was the first to apply the process to the making of saucepans, coffeepots, candlesticks, and other large articles for domestic service, which closely resembled in their detail hallmarked silver specimens.

These pioneers were soon followed by more cutlers, who added the production of Sheffield plate to their other activities. The more prominent among them were Thomas Law, Nathaniel Smith, Matthew Fenton, John Hoyland, Jacob and Samuel Roberts, Richard Morton, and John Winter. Two factors were necessary for the complete success of the new invention — capital and skilled labor. The money required was readily obtained from local sources, but the highly trained assistance of London silversmiths was also essential. Ultimately, when their services were enlisted, the success of the undertaking was assured.

Thus it will be seen that old Sheffield plate as a craft had a very small beginning, was entirely the result of a fortuitous circumstance, and for some years was confined to the making of insignificant articles only. It is a curious corollary that the manufacture of plated buttons by the original process is still an active industry, whereas all

FIG. 1 — BUTTON SHOWING CREST OF SCOT-
LAND — CROWNED LION HOLDING SCEPTRE
AND SWORD.

FIG. 2 — BOX IN HIGH RELIEF DEPICTING
BUST OF THE YOUNG PRETENDER, SURMOUNTED
BY RISING SUN (c. 1740-1745). *Diameter:*
2½ inches.

FIG. 4 — COFFEEPOT BEARING THE INITIALS OF H.
TUDOR (c. 1758). *Capacity: 4 gills.*

FIG. 3 — PAIR OF CANDELABRA, SHELL PATTERN, BY T. & J. CRESWICK (1812).

the subsequent productions of the craft for household use, covering the rococo, Adam, regency, and Victorian periods of design, have passed away never again to be resuscitated.

The first articles of importance to be made by the new method were boxes. That shown in Figure 2 is of peculiar interest as recording the earliest date that can be accurately assigned to old Sheffield plate snuffboxes. This box was a specialty that was manufactured in Sheffield by Wilson (formerly in partnership with Boulsover), and commemorative of the Scottish rebellion of 1745. Collectors would do well to acquire some of the interesting mid-eighteenth-century snuffboxes before they disappear entirely. (A sequence of illustrated specimens will be found in my *History of Old Sheffield Plate*, pages 21 and 22.)

Presuming the invention of fused plated silver to have occurred *circa* 1740, and Boulsover's connection therewith to have ceased (except for the production of metal sheets) about the year 1750, we are brought to the date when Joseph Hancock first visualized the ultimate development of the process as a possible serious rival to the art of the silversmith. Illustrated here *(Fig. 4)* will be found one of the contemporary forms of coffeepots of the George II style, constructed from the new plated metal by one of the London silversmiths whose services were requisitioned in the early days of the industry.

The importation of these workmen to Sheffield greatly stimulated the craft, because of the close resemblance between their new plated ware and the articles they had formerly made in solid silver from designs with which the public had become familiar. This plate is highly prized by collectors as representing the earliest period of Sheffield manufacture; and, if in sound condition, it is still capable of fulfilling its original function.

The Argyle or jacketed gravy holder with space for hot water *(Fig. 5)* was much in demand at this period. The original invention is attributed to John, the fifth Duke of Argyll *(1723-1790)*. There is today a constant demand for this useful article of old Sheffield plate, and good specimens are extremely scarce. The jacketing method of heating is at times found to have been applied to both teapots and sauce tureens. The contents of coffeepots and tea urns were heated with spirit lamps, and of entrée and cheese dishes by removable hot-water plates.

Candlesticks occupied the earliest attention of the old Sheffield platers. At the commencement of the industry there was a greater demand for articles providing light than for any other of the household furnishings procurable in the new medium. Consequently, the production in fused plated ware of chamber candlesticks, taper sticks, bougie boxes, and taper winders soon became a specialty. Candelabra, both silver and plated, came into prominence very late in the eighteenth century; consequently both old Sheffield plate and silver specimens in pairs, of an earlier date, command exceedingly high prices by comparison.

A candlestick with shell pattern was one of the first to be made in Sheffield plate. It is singular that with very slight variation this design continued in popularity throughout the life of the industry. Figure 3 illustrates one pair of candelabra so ornamented, and made in 1812. Specimens were turned out by the old process as late as 1850. Hence the task of dating old Sheffield candlesticks of this variety is rendered

FIG. 5 — ARGYLE OR GRAVY WARMER BY RICHARD MORTON (*1768*) *Capacity: ½ pint.*

FIG. 6 — COFFEEPOT BY J. HOYLAND, MARKED WITH HIS
INITIALS (*c. 1765*). *Capacity: 4 gills.*

FIG. 7 — COFFEE SERVICE AND TRAY BY ROBERT GAINSFORD (*1818*). *Length of tray: 24 inches.*

somewhat difficult, when collectors, by allocating specimens to the pre-1830 period, seek to import them into the United States free of charge.

Candlesticks about 1750 to 1765, previous to the period of Adam influence, are usually of columnar form. The early examples are somewhat scarce, and as museum specimens they are of great interest. Candlesticks are sought today in sets of four, and as such prove most attractive possessions to a modern household. The prices of groups of four, if found in good condition, are relatively much greater than are those of odd pairs.

There are great varieties of the designs of the pre-Adam period, both in silver and old Sheffield plate. Obviously the originators had in mind the five orders of architecture and at times took considerable liberties with adaptations therefrom, combining rococo ornament with the fluted column. Such candlesticks are usually to be found in first-class preservation on account of the thickness of silver deposit in use at the period.

As the influence of the brothers Adam in production of old Sheffield plate developed, the demand for candlesticks based on the five orders gradually subsided, and, between the years 1770 and 1790, the desire for tableware in character with the new architectural interiors became entirely the vogue.

John Winter, master cutler of Sheffield in 1771 and maker of the finest silver and plated Adam candlesticks, seems to have led the field in adapting the extravagant design that preceded the Adam influence, which dominated every form of architecture towards the end of the eighteenth century. From about 1785 to the early nineteenth century, the desire for unrestrained decoration in silver and plated ware was succeeded by an artistic and subdued style. Both shapes and designs in Sheffield plate, not only of candlesticks, but of every article throughout the household, displayed traces of the volute and other Greek ornaments.

The old Sheffield platers had now exhausted all the hitherto known sources of decoration for candlesticks, and were at a loss to know where to look for original conceptions. That the attention of early nineteenth-century designers was occasionally drawn to recent discoveries in Egypt is proved by a candlestick *(Fig. 9)* combining sphinx, lotus, and acanthus ornamentation. For the most part, however, the tendency in this period of old Sheffield plate was towards severe plainness. John Parsons, who, in 1783, had succeeded his uncle in the management of the business of John Winter & Co., set the fashion in the new style, at least so far as candlesticks were concerned.

Solid silver hall-marked candlesticks with fused plated Sheffield-made branches are much sought by collectors. These candelabra usually carry three lights, but sometimes they have two lights and an urn center. As adjuncts to a Chippendale dining table or Sheraton sideboard they are both useful and ornamental.

Waiters, or, as they are more commonly called in England, salvers, must be considered among the articles formerly in daily use. They are still plentiful, though the majority show distinct signs of wear. They may be divided into three classes.

The first were made *circa* 1750-1780, with a double stamping to a hollow back *(Fig. 19)*. An extra heavy deposit of silver was added to the front surface that engraving might not expose the copper. Swages and mount were conjoint, and feet usually

FIG. 8—CANDLESTICK BY J. PARSONS (*1798*). Oval base and one of the innumerable variants of lotus decoration. *Height: 12 inches.*

FIG. 9 — CANDLESTICK BY JOHN ROBERTS (*1806*). Sphinx head and lotus decoration. Round base. *Height: 13½ inches.*

FIG. 11 — TAPER STICK, ADAM DESIGN, BY JOHN WINTER (*1775*). *Height: 6¼ inches.*

FIG. 10 — CANDELABRUM BY JOHN GREEN & CO. (*1799*). One of a pair having three sockets, fluted decoration on pillar and base, and silver candlesticks. *Height: 17½ inches.*

Fig. 12 — Chamber Candlestick by Roberts Cadman & Co. (*1802*). *Height: 6¼ inches.*

Fig. 15 — Egg Stand and Salt by Richard Morton (*1799*).

Fig. 14 — Bougie Box by John Love (*1789*). One of many small accessories concerned with illumination. *Height: 2⅜ inches.*

Fig. 13 — Taper Winder by Samuel Roberts (*1795*).

Fig. 16 — Tea Service. Silver teapot (*1802*); fused plated sugar and creamer by George Ashforth & Co. *Capacity of teapot: 4 gills.*

FIG. 17 — OVAL SAUCE TUREEN AND COVER BY J. T. YOUNG & CO. (*1795*). *Length: 11¼ inches; width: 7½ inches.*

FIG. 18 — TEAPOT BY NATHANIEL SMITH (*1796*). *Capacity: 3 gills.*

FIG. 19 — SALVER BY GEORGE ASHFORTH (*c. 1760*). Shaped gadroon border and hollow back. Mount and swage struck conjointly; claw-and-ball feet stamped in sections. Front surface heavily plated. *Diameter: 16 inches.*

FIG. 20 — SALVER MADE BY RICHARD MORTON (*c. 1785*). Straight gadroon mount made from decorated drawn wire and attached separately; extra heavily plated shield soldered in centre; volute feet. *Diameter: 14 inches.*

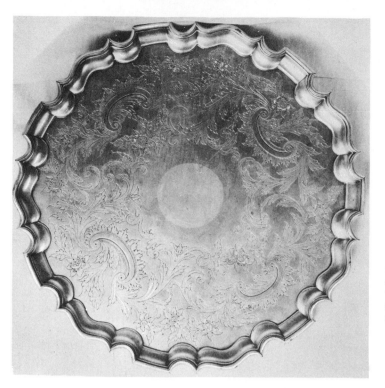

FIG. 21 — SALVER BY T. WATSON & T. BRADBURY (*c. 1815*). Flat chased decoration and Chippendale border; mounts struck from thin silver, filled with solder, and attached separately; feet in form of reversed scrolls stamped in two halves and solder-filled. *Diameter: 23 inches.*

FIG. 22 — TWO-BOTTLE INKSTAND BY T. J. & N. CRESWICK (*1812*). Gadroon and scroll silver mounts; scroll-and-claw feet; center taper stick covering sand box. *Length: 9½ inches.*

FIG. 23 — OLD SHEFFIELD PLATE OF DECORATIVE PERIOD (*early nineteenth century*). *Left to right: Upper row,* wine cooler by John Watson (*1812*); montieth wine cooler by Roberts & Smith (*1828*). *Lower row,* cake basket by Younge & Deakin (*1813*); epergne with acanthus decoration and crystals from Whittington Glass House, by T. Creswick (*1820*); cake basket with claw feet, by Daniel Holy (*1805*).

of the claw-and-ball variety.

The second *(1780-1810)* were similarly made but had a heavily plated silver shield soldered to the center plate, for engraving *(Fig. 20)*. The designs, as was the case with the earlier group, were more or less confined to those on the orthodox silver models — shell, gadroon, and bead. There was a variation in the feet from claw-and-ball to volute.

The third group, illustrated by Figure 21, embraces the invention of silver edges and the rubbing in of silver shields. Hence appeared specimens more serviceable, more closely akin to the silver originals, and more varied in design.

The making of inkstands *(Fig. 22)* puzzled the earliest platers. Not until the advent of the London silversmiths were these articles equal in artistic merit to other productions, like candlesticks and hollow ware in general.

The demand for plainness in design lasted until about 1805, when decorative ornament began once more to assert itself. In the coffee service and tray of Figure 7 it will be observed that the plain gadroon designs of the previous ten years are being gradually eliminated. Only the coffeepot displays the full gadrooned mount. Creamer, sugar bowl, and teapot are almost wholly decorated with leaves and flowers. On the mount of the tray the running gadroon has almost entirely disappeared.

By 1820, there came into fashion what might almost be termed a revival of the rococo in both silver and Sheffield plate. Whether the riot of design that heralded the accession of William IV can be attributed to the Sheffield platers or to the London silversmiths cannot here be considered. It is sufficient, however, that, between 1830 and 1850, the Sheffield plate manufacturers excelled not only in the vastness of their output but also in the intricacies of their designs. To such an extent had they, by that time, dominated the fashions in silver and plated ware that the London silversmiths resorted to making purchases from them, which they then struck with their own punches and sent to the London Goldsmiths' Hall for assaying.

The Sheffield craftsmen had now become so clever that silver and old Sheffield plate were almost indistinguishable. Figure 23 includes specimens, dated from 1805 to 1828, whose workmanship has never been surpassed. There is consequently an ever-increasing demand for such items, when they can be procured in a perfect state.

The death knell of the old Sheffield plate trade was struck soon after the accession of George IV, by the gradual substitution of Argentine metal for copper as a foundation, and by the advent of the process of electrodeposition. The craft, however, lingered on until the great exhibition of 1851. Yet even then, as is indicated by the reports of the jurors, it was inconceivable that the older process was to be entirely supplanted by the industry today described as electroplating. Soon the term *Sheffield plate* was no longer in use, and it is now familiar only with the word "old" as a prefix. But in that phrase we offer today tardy recognition of the intrinsic merit of an art associated with the skillful workmanship of the late eighteenth and early nineteenth-century craftsmen. It is an art not to be confused with the more imitative and mechanical processes utilized in the present era.

PEWTER

The American Pewter Porringer

BY LEDLIE I. LAUGHLIN

TODAY THE NAME *of Ledlie I. Laughlin is virtually synonymous with early American pewter, because his monumental book,* Pewter in America, *published in 1940, is the standard reference on the subject. That two-volume work was the result of many years of patient research and collecting. It superseded the pioneer book on the subject, J. B. Kerfoot's* American Pewter *(1924), and the less comprehensive book by L. G. Myers,* Some Notes on American Pewterers *(1926), and incorporated much material first recorded by Mr. Laughlin and others in The Magazine* ANTIQUES. *His own first contribution to* ANTIQUES *was this article in May 1930 on the American pewter porringer, in which he emphasized the distinctive characteristics of this form. The illustrations here are reproduced from his book by special permission.*

SO alluring has the collector of American pewter found the search for rare touch marks that, in many cases, he has failed to make due note of the forms on which these touches are impressed. Some shapes are so definitely American, in fact so definitely the work of specific pewterers, that they may be identified without need for examining the touches upon them. It is merely a matter of comparing their characteristics with those of examples already classified on the basis of their marks. Of all forms made by American pewterers, the porringer, with its exceptional diversity of handle designs, lends itself most readily to such a study, and best repays it.

Porringers were used by the earliest English settlers in America, and were, with little doubt, made by our first pewterers. The form became virtually obsolete in England soon after the middle of the eighteenth century — certainly by 1775 —

though for another quarter-century porringers continued to be made in Bristol for export to this country. Most of the surviving American specimens, however, were produced after 1800. In Philadelphia and the South there was, apparently, little demand for these vessels after the Revolution; and existing New York specimens, all of them made prior to 1800, are rare. But, in New England, porringers were turned out generously until about 1825. For a few years longer their manufacture continued in Connecticut and Rhode Island, though on a declining scale; and then, about 1830, abruptly ceased, not to be resumed.

The porringer was ordinarily cast in two parts, the bowl and the handle. We shall not tarry long over the former. Its function was purely utilitarian — to hold food — and, after a vessel had been evolved satisfactorily to serve that purpose, succeeding makers deviated but little from a standard form. We find, in general, but two shapes of porringer bowl: first, the normal container with bulging sides, contracted at top and bottom, surmounted by a narrow perpendicular lip, the bottom consisting of a flat circular gutter with domed center; second, the basin with handle, which is, in reality, not a porringer at all, but a porringer-basin. The latter type of bowl is usually found only in the larger porringers, with a diameter of 5½ to 6 inches, and in diminutive tasters or doll-size basins.

But, whereas the shape of the bowl invited little experimentation, the handle was a feature well adapted to individual decorative treatment. It afforded such endless opportunity for diversification of pattern under favorable circumstances that each pewterer might easily have devised a design peculiar to his own product. Unfortunately, however, molds were very costly in early days. A fledgling pewterer, on completing his apprenticeship, usually started out with an old set of molds, either inherited or purchased, and these in turn he passed on to his successor; so that the same molds were forced to serve one generation after another. And, even when the young pewterer had to buy an entire new equipment, custom and the conservatism of his trade led him to select shapes to which the public was accustomed. Consequently, instead of hundreds of different designs in porringer handles, we have, thus far, found less than two dozen varieties impressed with the touches of American pewterers.

Even at that we may congratulate ourselves, for no such multiplicity is known in England; and it is probably greater than can be matched among surviving porringers of any Continental country. The reason is perhaps discoverable in the fact that our pewterers were men of diverse nationalities, catering to buyers who naturally preferred the styles to which they had been accustomed in their respective homelands. Hence the American output embodied English forms, Continental forms, and variations upon, or combinations of, the two.

We may roughly divide all porringer handles into two distinct classes: first, the solid type; and, second, the pierced, or openwork, type. The former was an inheritance from the continent of Europe. Howard H. Cotterell, the foremost authority on British pewter, told me that he had never seen an English porringer with a solid handle. It is the pierced handle which is characteristic of British porringers. To be sure, this latter form is found also on some Continental pieces; but, generally speaking, the British handle is perforated, the Continental, solid. In this country we find both forms, with the perforated decidedly in the majority and evidently the favorite.

Before taking up the American shapes, it seems wise to call attention to a few of the styles favored by the pewterers of England. Mr. Cotterell very kindly sketched for me, in silhouette, four generic types of English porringer handle *(Fig. 1)*. There were, of course, many others, but few of them have survived to the present day.

Contrary to usual opinion, I am satisfied that the earliest form of American handle was pierced rather than solid; for the majority of our early settlers, and the earliest American pewterers on record, were Englishmen, who would naturally have followed English custom. But in the districts where Continental influence was strong we might reasonably expect to encounter solid handles; and in those very sections they come to light.

In the country districts of Pennsylvania,

FIG. 1 — A GROUP OF ENGLISH PORRINGER HANDLES. *a*, 1674 to *c*. 1730 or 1735; *b*, 1675 to *c*. 1717; *c*, 1695 to *c*. 1760; *d*, *c*. 1730 in England. This last shape has also been found with the touches of Dutch pewterers. Especially drawn by Howard H. Cotterell, F. R. Hist. S., and printed by his permission.

FIG. 2 — TYPES OF HANDLE MOST FREQUENT ON SURVIVING AMERICAN PORRINGERS. Over ninety per cent of marked American porringers fall into one of these three classifications: *a*, Rhode Island handle; only form used by Providence makers; found also on some Newport pieces. Except for one example by the Boardmans of Hartford, never reported on any porringers made outside of Rhode Island. Period, 1771 to *c*. 1825. This specimen by Gershom Jones of Providence (*1774-1809*). *b*, New York and New England (except Rhode Island). Period, 1770, or earlier, to *c*. 1825. This specimen by unidentified maker (*1775-1800*). Initials *W. N.* cast in relief on reverse of handle. *c*, New York and New England (except Rhode Island). Period, 1770, and probably much earlier, to *c*. 1820. Same design in silver of seventeenth and eighteenth centuries. Compare English handle (*Fig. 1b*). This specimen by Thomas Danforth, 3d, of Rocky Hill, Connecticut (*1777-1790*). Some pewterers had molds for both *b* and *c*. *Author's collection.*

FIG. 3 — AN EARLY DESIGN. Used in both Great Britain and the Colonies. Period in England, *c*. 1690 to 1720. Probably obsolete in this country before 1770. Rare in both countries. This specimen bears the initials *I. W.* (possibly John Will of New York) on reverse of handle. It is, with little doubt, American, *c*. 1760 or earlier. *Diameter: 5 inches. From the collection of Mrs. J. H. Krom.*

FIG. 4 — FOUND IN BOTH AMERICA AND ENGLAND. Exceedingly rare in this country. Period in England, c. 1725. This specimen by John Danforth of Norwich, Connecticut (c. 1772-1792). *Diameter: 4½ inches.* As Danforth inherited his molds from his father, Thomas, working as early as 1733, we may assume that the mold for this handle dates from c. 1733. Probably not used after c. 1780. *From the author's collection.*

FIG. 6 — PERHAPS UNIQUE. A four-inch porringer by Joseph Belcher of Newport, Rhode Island (c. 1780). Similar in outline to French solid-handle porringers of the same period. During the Revolution a large French expeditionary force was quartered at Newport, and Belcher probably mended foreign examples, which inspired his model. *From the collection of Mrs. J. Insley Blair.*

FIG. 7 — TASTER WITH FOUR HANDLES. Single-handle specimens, otherwise identical, also exist. All these pieces bear the name *R. Lee* cast in relief on handle support. Date probably c. 1790. Crude and frail. More interesting for oddity than for beauty or usefulness. *Diameter: 4 inches. Formerly in the collection of W. C. Staples.*

FIG. 5 — PORRINGER BASINS. *a,* Found only with Richard Lee touches. Period, c. 1788 to c. 1805 (northwestern New England). No counterpart in English pewter. The elder Lee spent his early years in and near Rhode Island. Hence his reminiscence of the normal Rhode Island handle (*Fig. 2, left*). Though handsome in outline, the handle was probably too frail for the hard service to which these vessels were put. Rare. *Diameter: 5⅞ inches. b,* Dolphin handle of John Danforth (Norwich, Connecticut). Cf. Figure 1*d.* Although not so graceful as its English prototype, doubtless more serviceable; much more ambitious in design than any other American handle. Probable date, 1733-1780. See comment in Figure 4. *Diameter: 5⅝ inches. Author's collection.*

FIG. 8 — AMERICAN TASTERS. Tiny vessels of this type were in use in vine growing countries of Europe, but, it is believed, were never made in England. Except for *b*, which has a slightly domed base, all five are merely diminutive basins with handles. *a* is a form — not a very successful one — used by Thomas D. Boardman of Hartford, *c.* 1810. The apparent intention of the designer to produce a handle resembling a crown in outline suggests that the mold was made for some pewterer first working when the Colonies were still under British dominion. *Diameter: 3¾ inches. b, c,* and *d* (measuring 3¼, 2¾, and 2¼ inches respectively) bear Richard Lee touches (Springfield, Vermont, *c. 1800-1820).* As far as now known, these shapes were used by no other maker. *b* is a very substantial vessel of considerable merit. Others extremely fragile. One can conceive of no use to which they could have been put other than as toys. *e* measures just 2⅛ inches in diameter; the smallest of marked American porringers. The letters *I.C.L. & Co.* are cast in relief on the reverse side of handle; attributed to Isaac C. Lewis of Meriden, Connecticut, in the 1840's. Poorly made; interesting chiefly on account of size. *Author's collection.*

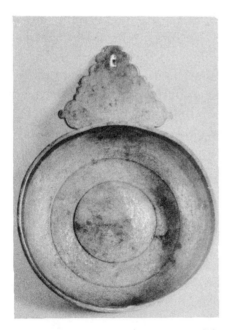

FIG. 9 — SOLID HANDLE. Rare and possibly earliest form of American solid handle. No known counterpart in English or Continental pewter. *Diameter: 5½ inches.* Maker unknown. Similar in outline to the pierced handle of Figure 3. *Mabel Brady Garvan collection, Yale University.*

FIG. 10 — THE NEWPORT HANDLE (*c. 1770-1800*). On porringers by the Belchers and Melvilles. This example bears the touch of David Melville (*1775-1794*). *Diameter: 5½ inches.* Melville's inventory includes two types of porringer handles, "solid" (as here) and "flower'd" (see example, *Fig. 2a*). With the notable exception of the one known Philadelphia porringer, all handles of this solid type are of Newport origin. *From the collection of Dwight Blaney.*

FIG. 11 — PORRINGER BASIN. Type found only in country districts of Pennsylvania where German population was large. Made by Elisha Kirk of York (*c. 1780-1790*). *From the author's collection.*

largely settled by Germans and Swiss, solid-handle porringers were the normal form. Likewise the only Philadelphia porringer thus far identified has a solid handle. It is probable, however, that Philadelphia pewterers of English birth or extraction made porringers with openwork handles. But that matter can be determined only if, and when, other Philadelphia porringers are identified.

In only one other section of the Colonies do we find the solid handle; and there apparently it did not supplant the pierced form, but was manufactured in competition with the latter. Newport, in 1770, was the most cosmopolitan town in New England, with a foreign trade greater than that of New York. It is, therefore, not surprising that the solid handle should have obtained recognition among the pewterers of the Rhode Island city.

In time, we may possibly learn that early pewterers of Dutch lineage in New York or Albany employed the solid handle; but it would be, to say the least, inexplicable were we to find such a form bearing the touch of a pewterer of Massachusetts, Maryland, or any of the southern Colonies, where the great majority of settlers were of English extraction.

An examination of the accompanying illustrations will give an acquaintance with the forms most frequently found in England and America. They will also enable the reader to distinguish between the solid handles of Newport and those of Pennsylvania; the pierced handles of Rhode Island and the shapes made in other Colonies; and, in some instances, to determine, by pattern alone, the handiwork of individual pewterers.

It must not be inferred that this brief survey covers every known variety of American porringer handle. Several designs which differ but slightly from one or another of those illustrated have purposely been omitted. It is, furthermore, certain that other patterns are hidden away in collections which I have not had the good fortune to examine. These, we may be sure, will gradually come to light. The interest in pewter awakened by the late Mr. Kerfoot has set many other collectors to studying the craftsmanship of the early pewterers, and to searching for documents concerning these men.

It is to be hoped, however, that the different forms here presented will afford collectors a reasonably comprehensive view of the scope of porringers; and will enable them to determine a little more readily than heretofore the date and source of examples which come under their inspection.

For the embryo collector casting about for some form of his forefathers' handiwork on which he may concentrate his attention with the maximum of interest, I recommend the American pewter porringer. Once a household article on the tables of rich and poor alike, today the vessel is obsolete. The alloy in which it was made has passed from daily use; and the name itself, reminiscent of another age, is meaningless to many of this generation. A perfect symbol of all that we, in this machine-made day, have lost, the porringer has not only beauty, simplicity, and distinction, but the glamour that surrounds any art form of an era that has forever gone.

ARCHITECTURE

The Houses of the First Settlers in New England

BY GEORGE FRANCIS DOW

GEORGE FRANCIS DOW *was one of the first in the country to exert an influence toward the appreciation of our early architecture and its conscientious restoration. He restored many important early houses in New England, and was a pioneer in approaching such work from a truly scholarly point of view, with respect for the integrity of old buildings. For many years he was also managing editor of* Old-Time New England, *the quarterly publication of the Society for the Preservation of New England Antiquities. In this article from* ANTIQUES *for August 1930 he dispelled the old myth that our earliest American houses were log cabins. Dr. Henry C. Mercer, one of the ablest antiquarians, had already published in 1927 in* Old-Time New England *a careful study of the origin of log houses in the United States. This article of Mr. Dow's nevertheless antedated by ten years the book by Harold R. Shurtleff called* The Log Cabin Myth, *which created quite a stir when it appeared.*

WHEN the English settlers first landed in New England, their imperative need was shelter for their families. For a time, their wives and children could remain on board the vessels in the harbor; but not for long. When the *Mayflower* dropped anchor off what is now the town of Plymouth, the wind blew very hard for two days; and on the third day, Saturday, December 23, 1620, as many as could do so went ashore and "felled and carried timber, to provide themselves stuff for building." The following Monday, they "went on shore, some to fell timber, some to saw, some to rise, and some to carry; so no man rested all that day." *(Mourt's Relation, Boston, 1841.*

Bradford writes that "they builte a forte with good timber." Isaac de Rasieres, in 1627, described the structure as "a large square house, made of thick sawn planks, stayed with oak beams." Some of the planks and frame of this fort were afterwards used in the construction of the Howland house, which is still standing in Plymouth.

The oldest existing houses in the Plymouth Colony were built in the same manner; and some half dozen or more seventeenth-century plank houses may yet be seen north of Boston. Moreover, when the ship *Fortune* sailed from Plymouth, in the summer of 1621, bound for England, part of her lading consisted of "clapboards and wainscott," showing clearly that the Colonists, soon after landing, had dug saw pits in the English manner and had begun to produce boards in quantity suitable for the construction of their own houses and for

FIG. 1 — PARSON CAPEN HOUSE, TOPSFIELD, MASSACHUSETTS
(*built 1683*). Restored in 1913, under direction of George
Francis Dow. Considered one of the finest existing examples
of seventeenth-century domestic architecture in New England. The kitchen in this house is reproduced in the American Wing of the Metropolitan Museum of Art, New York.
The restored front door, shown at the right, is a copy of
that of the "Indian House" at Deerfield, Massachusetts,
preserved in the Deerfield Museum. *Owned and occupied
by Topsfield Historical Society.*

exportation.

In the summer of 1623, Bradford mentions the "building of great houses in pleasant situations." When a fire broke out in November of the following year, it began in "a shed yt was joyned to ye end of ye storehouse, which was wattled up with bowes." It will be seen that this shed was not crudely built of logs or slabs, but that its walls were wattled, and, perhaps, also daubed with clay, in precisely the same manner with which the Colonists were familiar in their former homes across the sea. An original outer wall of the Fairbanks house, built in Dedham, Massachusetts, in 1636, and probably the oldest house standing in New England, still has its "wattle and daub" preserved in a gable end.

There is a widespread misconception that the Colonists, on reaching New England, proceeded immediately to build log houses. Historians have described these dwellings as chinked with moss and clay, and as having earth floors — precisely the type of house erected on the frontier and in the logging camps at a much later period. A well-known, but entirely fanciful, picture of Leyden Street, at Plymouth, shows, reaching up the hillside, a double row of log houses, which the Pilgrims are supposed to have constructed. In point of fact, no contemporary evidence has been found to support this present-day tradition. The early accounts of what took place following the settlement of the coastal villages are full of interesting details relating to day by day happenings; but nowhere do we find allusion to a log house such as many modern historians assume existed at that time. And what can be more natural and humanly probable to expect than that English housewrights, who had learned their trade overseas, should come ashore and build houses and outbuildings in the very manner they had learned through a long apprenticeship in their former homes? Can we of today assume that, upon the spur of the moment, these workmen invented a new type of building, the log house — a construction such as they had never seen in England, and a kind unknown also to the Indians?

What sort of shelters did the Indians build for themselves? Reverend John Higginson, the first minister at Salem, Massachusetts, writing in 1629, described the houses of the Indians as "verie little and homely, being made with small poles pricked into the ground, and so bended and fastened at the tops, and on the side they are matted with Boughes and covered with Sedge and old mats." (*New England's Plantation*, London, 1630.) These were called "wigwams," and, as they were easily constructed and the materials were readily at hand, many of the poorer Colonists built similar rude huts for their own use.

Governor Winthrop records in his *Journal,* in September, 1630, that one Fitch of Watertown had his wigwam burnt down with all his goods; and, two months later, John Firman, also of Watertown, lost his English wigwam by fire. In the following February, he writes, "The poorer sort of people (who lay long in tents, etc.) were much afflicted with the scurvy, and many died, especially at Boston and Charlestown." On March 16, he notes that "about noon the chimney of Mr. Sharp's house in Boston took fire (the splinters being not clayed at the top), and taking the thatch burnt it down."

The printer of the *Boston News-Letter,* the first regular newspaper printed in Boston, was Bartholomew Green. He died in

Fig. 2 — The Spencer-Pierce House, Newbury, Massachusetts (*built c. 1651*). The kitchen ell, at the rear, gives the structure a cruciform shape. Note the porch, with its porch chamber, typical of the better seventeenth-century Massachusetts house, and also the niche over the door, in which a statuette might have been placed. The original windows were fitted with casement sashes with leaded glass frames. The wooden addition at the left is of later date.

Fig. 3 — Jackson House, Christian Shore, Portsmouth, New Hampshire (*built c. 1664*). Supposed to be the oldest house in Portsmouth. The lean-to at the back and the addition at the end were built later. The house contains much original interior finish. This, like other early dwellings, has suffered many alterations. Until 1710, or thereabouts, all New England houses had casement sashes. After that period, the sliding sash was gradually introduced. *Owned by Society for the Preservation of New England Antiquities.*

FIG. 4 — JOHN WARD HOUSE, SA-
LEM, MASSACHUSETTS (*built in
1684*). Now located on the grounds
at the rear of the Essex Institute.
Restored by George Francis Dow
in 1914. Note the overhang at
front and end, lean-to at back,
and two gables in the front roof.
The windows reproduce the early
treatment. Now furnished in the
seventeenth - century manner.
Shops in the lean-to show later
period.

FIG. 5 — ELEAZER ARNOLD HOUSE,
LINCOLN, RHODE ISLAND (*built c.
1687*). Typical Rhode Island
stone-end house, having the finest pilastered stone chimney now
remaining in Rhode Island. The
stone fireplace in the hall is ten
feet, nine inches wide. Front door
and windows represent later improvements. *Owned by Society
for the Preservation of New England Antiquities.*

1732, and, in the next issue of the paper, appeared an extended obituary wherein we find the statement that when, in 1630, Bartholomew's father, then a lad of fifteen, arrived at Boston ". . . upon their coming ashore, both he and several others were for some time glad to lodge in empty casks to shelter them from the weather, for want of Housing."

Thomas Dudley, writing to the Countess of Lincoln, in March, 1631, relates that "divers houses have been burned since our arrival (the fire always beginning in the wooden chimneys), and some English wigwams which have taken fire in the roofes with thatch or boughs." (*Force's Tracts,* Washington, 1838.) Dudley's own house was wainscoted with clapboards nailed to the walls. John Goyt settled at Marblehead in 1637, and "first built a wigwam and lived thar till he got a house." (*Essex County Court Records,* Vol. VI, p. 363.) The town clerk of Woburn, Edward Johnson, writing in 1652, mentions the rude shelters of the first settlers. "Yet, in these poor wigwams, they sing Psalms, pray and praise their God, till they can provide them homes, which ordinarily was not wont to be with many till the Earth, by the Lord's blessing, brought forth bread to feed them, their wives and little ones." (*Wonder Working Providence,* London, 1654.)

The only log houses that were erected in New England until toward the end of the seventeenth century were garrison houses, built of carefully squared timber dovetailed at the corners, according to European methods of military construction. An excellent example is the Damme Garrison, preserved at Dover, New Hampshire, a one-story building, erected after 1665 and before 1698.

The log house built of round logs, notched at the ends and overlapping at the corners, chinked with clay, moss, grass, or other materials — the log house of the frontier and the lumberman — was probably introduced by the Swedes when they came to the Delaware River in 1638.

The houses built by the first settlers in New England — exclusive of the temporary makeshift structures of the early years — were modeled after traditional English forms, and, so far as material and labor permitted, reproduced the homes that had been left in Old England. The overhanging second story, the gables in the roof, the casement sash, the large boards, the porch and porch chamber, the ornamental brackets and drops, the molded wainscot, and the hardware—like the furniture and utensils within the dwelling — were all copies of remembered forms at home. They reflected years of past apprenticeship and a deep-seated tradition that was only gradually modified by the changed conditions of life in a new land.

Venetian Blinds in the Eighteenth Century

BY HELEN COMSTOCK

VISITORS TO RESTORED *eighteenth-century houses are frequently surprised to see the windows equipped with what they take to be modern Venetian blinds. That such blinds were actually in use in the 1700's has long been recognized, but little documentary information on the subject has been available. This article, from* ANTIQUES *for February 1948, is the first which has brought together the eighteenth-century references to Venetian blinds in France, England, and America. Helen Comstock, Gallery Editor of* ANTIQUES, *has been American Editor of the* Connoisseur *since 1931. In her writings on the decorative arts she has covered authoritatively most subjects that interest collectors, making a special study of English and American furniture. She has contributed a number of articles on American furniture to* ANTIQUES, *including* Transitional Features in American Chairs, American and English Chairs, *and* Federal Furniture.

THE antiquity of the Venetian blind is undisputed but its early history is obscure. Not the least mysterious fact about it is that only in English is it called Venetian blind. In Italy the term is *persiana*, in French *jalousie*, or more specifically, *jalousie à la persienne*, which, like the Italian, indicates an association with Persia. Whether the introduction into Italy of some form of oriental blind was due to Marco Polo or to Venetian traffic with the East in general is not clear. Havard, in his *Dictionnaire de l'ameublement et de la décoration*, cites a definition from the earlier *Dictionnaire abrégé de peinture et d'architecture* (Paris, 1746) which indicates that the *jalousie* had not yet acquired in 1746 those mobile features which distinguish it today. It was still the blind formed of strips of wood set diagonally

which permitted a view without being seen, a louvered window which was known in many European countries in the seventeenth century and without doubt earlier.

Havard says that it is not known who invented the mechanism which controls the opening and shutting of the parellel laths at any desired position, but an advertisement in *Annonces, affiches et avis divers*, 24 Août, 1757, No. 34, p. 135, indicates that they were being made in that year by one Lebeuf near Saint-Germain-des-Prés below the Saint Benoît gate. He informed the public that his *jalousies* could be raised or lowered to any desired extent, which made them different from those formerly in use. In 1769, one Labadie of the rue Phélipeau substituted iron for wood and made *jalousies* "more convenient and cheaper than those made of wood."

These, which were worked on chains, were approved by the Académie Royale d'Architecture. In 1782 there is an advertisement of *jalousies de la Chine en canne*, "which are very strong and yet a child of six or seven years can move them," as announced in the *Journal Général de France*, 7 Août, 1782, which seems to indicate that the oriental inspiration had been strengthened by further contact with the Far East. However, the more common term was *à la persienne*, as in an advertisement of the year 1768: "for sale, of Mme. Lépine, midwife, rue de la Mortellerie, two pairs of oak jalousies *à la persienne* . . ." Many other advertisements mentioning them as *persiennes* are similarly noted by Havard as appearing in the eighteenth century.

In England Venetian blinds were undoubtedly used about the same time although the *New English Dictionary*, which as a rule may be trusted to give very early mention of terms, does not offer any example of their use. However, Sheraton's reference to them in the *Cabinet Dictionary* (1803) indicates they were well known. It is generally agreed, nevertheless, that their use was not so common in England as in America.

Sheraton writes: "Venetian blinds are for the same purpose [as the plain rolling blind] but draws up by pullies fixed in a lath one inch thick, the same as a festoon window curtain . . ." Later he mentions "Venetian blinds with brass chains, instead of the usual way of hanging the laths in green tape," which is all that he contributes to our knowledge of their construction, although he says that "these last mentioned have been introduced by Mr. Stubbs," whose shop was in Oxford Street. He remarks that these "bid fair for answering the intended purpose as external window blinds. The Venetian part is closed under a cornice when drawn up, and in letting down, is guarded by a frame, so that the wind cannot blow them aside." Sheraton's most interesting suggestion is that they may have been used as outside blinds.

The origin of the term Venetian blind is still a mystery. Perhaps the louvered window was introduced to England by Italian builders and other craftsmen who were present in great numbers in the seventeenth century, and when the French invention was made in the eighteenth the term continued in use.

In America it is of interest to note that the Declaration of Independence was signed in a room having Venetian blinds. Some ten years later the Congress Chamber was serving as the studio of Robert Edge Pine, who painted his *Congress Voting Independence* in the room in which the event took place. Pine died in 1788 and his painting, now in the Historical Society of Pennsylvania, was finished by Savage, who also engraved it. The painting does not show the blinds, but they are clearly seen in the unfinished trial proof, a detail of which is illustrated here. When the Chamber was restored, Pine's work was referred to for details of the interior (Charles Henry Hart, *Pennsylvania Magazine of History*, January 1905).

At Williamsburg, Venetian blinds were used in the Governor's Palace and are mentioned in the inventory of Lord Botetourt, who died in 1770. There is documentary evidence that they were used at the Raleigh Tavern and in private houses. Joshua Kendall, house-carpenter and joiner, advertised them in the *Virginia Gazette*, January 1770. Jefferson's diary includes a note that he paid $2.66 as a surcharge for Venetian

FIG. 1 — DETAIL of unfinished
trial proof of engraving by
Edward Savage of *Congress
Voting Independence*, by Rob-
ert Edge Pine and Edward
Savage. *From The Old Print
Shop, Harry Shaw Newman.*

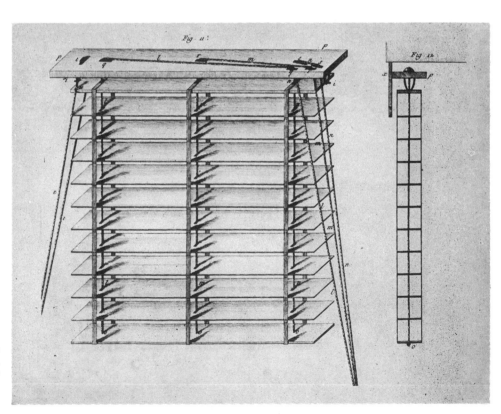

FIG. 2 — ROUBO, *L'art du menuisier* (Paris, 1769). Plate 29,
*Les jalousies connues sous le
nom de Persiennes.*

blinds purchased abroad, and the corres-
pondence of Washington to his nephew,
George Augustine Washington, mentions
them under date of June 10, 1787. Washington, then in Philadelphia, asks for exact
dimensions of the windows in the dining
room, "that I may get a Venetian blind,
such as draws up and closes, and expands,
made here, that others may be made by it,
at home." Ten years later others were supplied for him from Philadelphia, as shown
by an entry in the Presidential Household
Account Book, February 15, 1797, and
these are probably the ones which were
shipped to Mount Vernon on March 17,
when he departed for home.

An advertisement of 1765 offered Venetian curtains, and this may be the earliest
advertisement of Venetian blinds in this
country — though the term may possibly
refer to something quite different. It occurs
in the announcement of John Mason, an
upholsterer who had opened a shop in
King Street, Charleston, as published in
the *South Carolina Gazette*, February 2,
1765 (Prime, *Arts and Crafts in Philadelphia, Maryland and South Carolina*).

Except for Mason's ambiguous notice,
the earliest advertisement we have found
appeared in 1767, when John Webster, an
upholsterer from London, "at the house occupied by Mr. William Rush," in Philadelphia, announced ". . . the newest invented
Venetian sun blinds for windows, on the
best principles, stained to any color, moves
to any position, so as to give different lights,
screens from the scorching rays of the sun,
draws a cool air in hot weather, draws up
as a curtain, and prevents from being overlooked, and is the greatest preserver of
furniture of anything of the kind ever invented." (*Pennsylvania Journal*, August
20, 1767.)

The advertisement of Charles Allen, a
maker of Venetian blinds, appearing in the
Pennsylvania Journal, October 3, 1771, is
interesting because he learned his trade in
two capitals, "having worked for the two
most celebrated men in that occupation,
viz, Mr. Bradshaw in London and Mons.
Fleuri in Paris." Apparently London and
Paris, not Venice, set the style in Venetian
blinds.

A workman from another quarter was
George Richey, "upholsterer and tent-
maker from Edinburgh," advertising Venetian blinds in the *Pennsylvania Gazette*,
October 17, 1771; while Abraham Mad-
docks, "upholsterer from Dublin," advertised them in the *South Carolina Gazette*,
January 28, 1773.

It is conspicuous that Charleston and
Philadelphia had the greater number of
makers of Venetian blinds. Among them
are John Blott, 1771, and John Linton,
1774, Charleston; Hyns Taylor, Philadelphia, 1776; George Haughton, Philadelphia, 1775; M. Alken, Charleston, 1785;
Bradford & Clements, Charleston, 1792;
Samuel Benge in Philadelphia, who advertised only as an upholsterer in 1789, but in
1793 as "upholsterer and Venetian blind
maker." He was succeeded by Richard We-
vill, who "has taken stock in trade of the
late Samuel Benge's opposite Congress Hall
in Chestnut Street . . . having conducted
the above (upholstery) business in two of
the principal houses in that line in London
for near twenty years."

In Baltimore, Smith & Co., carvers and
gilders, advertised in the *Baltimore Tele-
graph* in 1789: "Those ladies and gentlemen who mean to favour them with orders
for Venetian blinds against the approaching season are requested to be as early as
possible in their application."

Traveling northward makers become fewer. In New York an anonymous maker of Venetian blinds advertised under *Position Wanted* in the *New-York Gazette and the Weekly Mercury,* August 8, 1774: "A young man, an upholsterer lately from London," who made "window curtains of all sorts, Venetian window blinds . . ." (Gottesman, *Arts and Crafts in New York*). Toward the end of the century, when there were numerous makers in Philadelphia and Charleston, there was in New York apparently only Andrew S. Norwood, at 127 William Street, who advertised "Venetian and other blinds" in the *New-York Gazette,* July 20, 1798. In New England they seem not to have been made.

Venetian blinds have been used in many restorations of historic houses, such as Mount Vernon, the Hammond-Harwood house at Annapolis, the Governor's Palace and Raleigh Tavern at Williamsburg, Woodford and Strawberry in Fairmount Park, Philadelphia. So far as we know, however, there are no actual blinds still in existence which can be clearly proved to have survived from the eighteenth century.

From the working designs illustrated by Roubo in his *L'Art du Menuisier,* Paris 1769, Plate 29, entitled *Les Jalousies connues sous le nom de Persiennes,* it is apparent that technical construction in the eighteenth century made the blind virtually the same as ours.

PRINTS

The Greatest Show on Earth

BY HARRY T. PETERS

HARRY T. PETERS *used to call himself "the grand old man of Currier & Ives." He was one of the first to begin collecting the lithographs of this firm, and before he died had built the largest collection in existence. He had also assembled a great amount of information about them, and published books which are the standard references in the field:* Currier & Ives, Printmakers to the American People; America on Stone; *and* California on Stone. *This article, written for the July 1940 issue of* ANTIQUES, *conveys his enthusiasm and sense of humor as well as his vast knowledge of a topic which, while not very antique, represents an important phase of our development in the nineteenth century.*

THE Fourth of July, and Christmas, and the day when the circus comes to town — these remain red-letter days to millions of Americans, young and old. Who of the past generation did not thrill to the inimitable notes of the calliope, to the heavy tread of elephants, to the roar of caged beasts, the golden Roman chariots, the antics of clowns, and all the other sights and sounds of that great annual event, the circus parade down Main Street or Broadway! Strange peoples, strange animals, strange smells, all combined to offer escape from daily life. And even today, when "ponderous pachyderms" and the "blood-sweating Behemoth of Holy Writ" are almost as familiar as bread and butter, the Greatest Show on Earth still packs them in at Madison Square Garden. Nowhere on earth do people love the super-colossal, the bizarre, the eccentric, the startling, as do Americans; the circus is the supreme expression of an essentially American trait.

Besides providing incomparable entertainment, the circus paved the way for the giant industry of modern American advertising. From the first crude woodcut broadside to the gay lithographed poster of today, the graphic material advertising the circus provides a fascinating field for the collector. Circus posters have had a wide appeal for Americans of all ages from the very beginning — and their influence persists in the posters of today that advertise not only plays and movies, but toothpaste, cigarettes, and soup. Yet few have been preserved. Made for the moment, they were torn down and burned after the circus had moved on to the next town.

As in all other Americana, the material itself varies from very good to extremely bad. The art of crude, garish lithography lent itself naturally to the circus poster, whose purpose was to attract attention at whatever cost. But even the most atrocious of these pictures have a certain interest; if nothing else, they are amusing, and eloquent of bygone days. Difficult as it is to obtain good examples, in good condition, of lithographic circus posters, their predecessors offer an even more enticing field to the collector. Such prints as the little woodcut of Figure 1 represent the beginnings of the circus poster, and help to untangle the story of the development of the circus itself.

In early America, among a people absorbed in conquering the wilderness and building a nation, wandering entertainers first started putting on small shows at communication centers or in tavern yards where the coaches met. No entrance fees — just give the show and pass the hat! Some of the early woodblock scraps which have been assembled in collections are really the first American circus posters. One of the most interesting of these dates probably just at the beginning of the last century: "An extraordinary Calf. It has two heads, two ears, four eyes, two bodies, eight legs and two tails — Come and see it." This sounds surprisingly like Ripley's "Believe it or not." So does another which urged the curious to see the Russian "Pygarg," which combined the features of a camel, bear, bullock, horse, ass, rabbit, and heifer — but turned out to be a quite tame American moose.

The circus poster, however, like the circus itself, had its real origin in ancient Rome. Mural artists painted flamboyant pictures on the walls of the Roman arenas, where people were sometimes entertained and thrilled for as many as seven days and seven nights. What we now know as the circus came to us under the title of "Caravan." The word comes from the Turkish *Kara-wana*, which means, literally, an ambulatory show. The caravan was formed by a menagerie and a group of curiosities; these curiosities formed groups which eventually became known as museums — precursors of the museum of today.

It was not until the acrobatic equestrians arrived that we were on our way to the modern circus. Our circus is a descendant of the traveling minstrel or the man with the performing bear, and of the somewhat later menagerie man who had assembled several bears and other animals. To these were gradually added the gymnastic equestrians, the side show, and the pageantry — and behold, the modern circus!

The group of curiosities became a side show known as "the freaks," with the eternal fat man, bearded lady, dog-faced boy, human skeleton, snake charmer, tattooed man, and all the rest of that strange and wonderful world.

The mainstay of the circus has always been the wild animals. The first lion was brought to Boston by a sea captain in 1716, the first camel in 1721, the first polar bear in 1733, the first orang-outang in 1789. But of all animals, most important to the circus is the elephant. In 1796 the ship *America* sailed into New York harbor, from Bengal, with our first elephant aboard. Ever since, in America as in the days of the Roman circus, the show has been measured by its elephant herd. Circuses were known as a one-elephant, two-elephant, or three-elephant show, until the great era of Barnum & Bailey (and subsequently Ringling), whose herd amounted to sixty-eight elephants, sixty-eight — count them!

One of the threads that we can follow in the graphic art of the circus is the recurrence of what Darwin called our common ancestor. The simian made his first public appearance in New York in May 1789, billed as *The Orang Outang, or Wild Man of the Woods (Fig. 2).* Compare this early American woodcut with the broadsides of

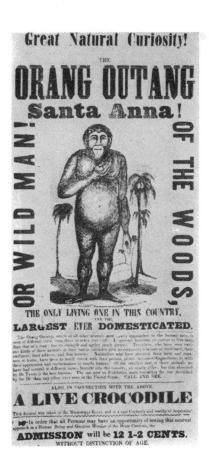

FIG. 1 — THE FORERUNNERS OF THE CIRCUS. Rare early woodcut from *Hawkers and Walkers in Early America*, by Richardson Wright. The woodcut was the precursor of the lithographic circus poster, as the wandering entertainer whom it advertised was the forerunner of the circus itself. *Reproduced by courtesy of J. B. Lippincott Company.*

FIG. 2 — GARGANTUA OF 1789. The first "wild man" exhibited in America. This early woodcut represented the popular conception of the human ancestor according to Darwin.

FIG. 3 — THE MAIN ATTRACTION OF THE CIRCUS (*1834-1835*). Largest known early woodcut of its type, and very scarce.

FIG. 4 — JACOB BATES, FIRST EQUESTRIAN. He performed in New York in 1773 after a successful European tour. From an engraving by Nusbiegel (*1766*).

"Gargantua," the central attraction of the current World's Greatest Show, and with the "most marvelous creature living" shown in Figure 9. Similar comparison of early appearance and late survival could be made through the entire menagerie as well as the side show.

Jacob Bates, famous English horse rider, appeared at the Bowery Theatre, New York, in 1773; and with him entered that perennial favorite of advertising phrases, "having appeared before all the crowned heads of Europe." Bates had performed before the Emperor of Germany, Empress Catherine of Russia, George III, Ferdinand the Great, and a long list of potentates. He seems to have been the first great trouper, and to have set the fashion for the foreign touch that has been followed here for more than a century. His best portrayal is by Nusbiegel, engraved at Nuremberg in 1766 (*Fig. 4*). Another English equestrian by the name of Poole was here about the same time, but he was not so colorful a character as Bates.

The mention of equestrians recalls the real father of the American circus, John Bill Ricketts of Philadelphia, who built our first permanent auditorium there in 1795. He proudly boasted of his friendship with George Washington. He sat for Gilbert Stuart, who painted a very fine though unfinished portrait of him in a composition including his horse's head.

To a Hudson River boy, Isaac A. Van Amburgh, go the honors for being the first of the modern lion-tamers. He achieved fame not only here but in Europe. An early lithograph shows him in the thrilling act which fascinated good Queen Victoria (*Fig. 5*). Sir Edwin Landseer, famous for his paintings of wild animals, had for some years been painting less sensational sub-

jects; he was now commissioned to paint Van Amburgh dominating a cageful of snarling beasts. In the foreground of the painting, just outside the bars, appears a bunch of violets, which was understood to show that the American tamer of the king of beasts had received the gracious patronage of the Queen-Empress. Van Amburgh has had many modern successors, such as Clyde Beatty and the tamers publicized by the Bostocks. Indeed, the main act of the Ringling show this year stems from his performance.

Don Rice was America's first and greatest clown. Extraordinarily beloved by the American people, he was an intimate friend of Abraham Lincoln, Robert E. Lee, William C. Bryant, Edwin Forrest, and most of the other prominent men of his day. During the Civil War he passed from the north to the south and back with his show. He invented many of the acts that are still current. It was he who introduced the trained mule so popular in circuses and rodeos today (*Fig. 6*).

Forever linked with the circus is the name of P. T. Barnum, about whom at least a dozen books have been written. The great promoter started at the age of twenty-one by hippodroming Joyce Heath, the "168-year-old nurse of George Washington." He ended by having our first Madison Square Garden built for him. He was the final manager of the Crystal Palace, America's first World's Fair. Between times he established and promoted museums and really organized the modern circus. Two of his best-known creations, if that is the word, were Tom Thumb, the most famous diminutive human being of all times, whose marriage in fashionable Grace Church Barnum arranged (*Fig. 7*) — and Jumbo, the great elephant, whose importa-

FIG. 5 — ISAAC A. VAN AMBURGH, FIRST MODERN LION-TAMER. This poster marks the first appearance of a circus menagerie with Barnum and Van Amburgh in association.

FIG. 6 — DAN RICE AND HIS TRAINED MULES. There is only one known copy extant of this lithograph advertising a famous clown.

FIG. 9 — MAN OR MONKEY? One of a series of "Darwinian" posters, and No. 12 of Barnum's *Gallery of Wonders*. The original was a gentle old negro valet when not impersonating the "missing link".

FIG. 7 — TOM THUMB'S MARRIAGE. Memorializing one of Barnum's greatest publicity stunts, perpetrated in 1863.

tion from England created an international furor (*Fig. 8*).

Barnum's *Gallery of Wonders (Fig. 9)*, produced by Currier & Ives, is one of the most fascinating groups of prints to collect. After thirty years of search I have not been able to complete it. It assumes an extremely important place, not only in a circus collection, but also as basic material in the history of advertising.

Collecting in the field of circus material

is still in its infancy. As in any branch of Americana, the earlier items are the more desirable. The early woodblock prints are rare. So, too, are certain of the lithographs, though the lithographic circus poster is still in full swing today. The accompanying illustrations, which cover a span of over a century, are but a sample of the graphic art of the circus awaiting the appreciative collector.

Fig. 8 — Jumbo in England. This famed elephant and Tom Thumb symbolized the largest and smallest of living things.

Except as noted, illustrations from the collection of the author.

FOLK ART

Schimmel the Woodcarver

BY MILTON E. FLOWER

ALONG WITH THE INTEREST in American primitive painting that has developed in the past generation a corresponding interest in what is called folk carving has grown up. While it may or may not be correct to classify some of the old ship fireheads, cigar-store Indians, and weathervanes as folk carvings, it is generally agreed that the Pennsylvania German products belong in this category. The best-known of all the Pennsylvania carvers is Wilhelm Schimmel, whose distinctive wood carvings, particularly of eagles, have been much admired for many years. Until the appearance of this article in October 1943, however, virtually nothing was known about the man himself. Who Schimmel was remained to be recorded by Milton E. Flower, a native of the Pennsylvania district where Schimmel lived and worked.

SCHIMMEL was the last of the primitive woodcarvers. Though dead for fifty years, he is vividly remembered as a somewhat terrifying old man who sat by the roadside cutting blocks of wood into what seemed useless, if fascinating, objects. No one who had ever seen Schimmel forgot him.

Exact details find little place in such memories. Incredible to old country folk is the thought that their "Old Schimmel" is regarded today as a noteworthy folk artist, whose carvings find a place in every important collection of Americana from the Metropolitan Museum to Greenfield Village.

Wilhelm Schimmel came into the Cumberland Valley near Carlisle, Pennsylvania, shortly after the Civil War. No one knows why this "big, raw-boned, ugly man" settled here. His rough voice, often unin-

telligible German speech, and peculiarities of manner encouraged many rumors — that he had fled his homeland because he had killed a man, because he was heartbroken at the death of his wife, or because he wished to escape military service — all pure suppositions. No one knew. From the late sixties until 1890 he shuttled from house to house up and down the valley, filling homes hospitable to him with the birds and animals he carved on his way.

When he came into Carlisle with a basket of his birds, he traded handiwork for meals, pennies, or drink. Frequently he passed a splendid carving across the bar in exchange for a pint of whiskey. At one time every tavern, restaurant, and barroom in that town boasted a Schimmel-carved eagle which it displayed conspicuously, often flanked by lesser works. After a few days in town, Schimmel would retrace his

[277]

way to the countryside he called home, often staggering up the street and roaring like a lion — a condition that terrified timid townspeople.

Greider's Mill, along the winding Conodoguinet Creek some six miles west of Carlisle, was home to Schimmel. John Greider, a miller and farmer, was the friend who trusted Schimmel implicitly, gave him lodging in the loft of his wash house, and recommended him kindly to relatives throughout the valley. Here, by the side of a covered bridge, Schimmel sat for hours on end, intently carving, as he sang loudly in German. The Greiders understood him and often placed their children in his care. And the children of the neighborhood, while fearing his temper, formed an appreciative audience when old Schimmel held up to their view what he called his "Fogels." They alone did not consider him queer.

Frequently he wandered across the valley to the home of the Waggoner family who lived at the foot of the mountain gap named for them. There, too, he was assured of meals and lodging in return for a helping hand with farm chores. Or again he would follow the western road along the mountain. His favorite tramps were within a twenty-mile area, from Carlisle to Newburg, and from the Conodoguinet Creek to the North Mountain. It was a region as fertile to Schimmel in sales as it has subsequently been to collectors of his work. On occasion he went into adjoining counties — Perry and Franklin, and sometimes as far east as Lancaster — but never for long. He soon returned to Greiders'. That family and their neighbors were the ones he knew best, although he said of an old woman in Newburg, "She makes my shirts, I cut her wood." In Carlisle he found acquaintances and understanding among certain German families, usually of a humble sort. To them he went when the Greiders' home was broken up. It was the Pennsylvania-German element of the valley, rather than the earlier-settled Scotch-Irish, with whom he lived and who knew him most intimately. They cooked meals for him when he was "on tour" and were his best customers, paying him the ten and twenty-five cents he asked for his work. A purposeful wanderer, he was never considered a bum.

Any barn's hayloft was a welcome place at night, and in town the cellar of a German friend, the loft of a livery stable, or customary free lodging in the county jail sufficed. But his violent temper and his German curses made townsmen wary and countryfolk circumspect in his presence. The latter made sure not to "tant" him, it has been said. Schimmel was always on hand at a barn raising. He could help, and he could reap a big reward in the blocks of wood that remained after the timbers had been cut. Also desirable were the heavy railway ties.

A similar fondness drew him to the place of Samuel Bloser whose farm on Possum Hill had a workshop. Bloser was a local undertaker and cabinetmaker. Such a profession with its good food made Schimmel call this house his second home. "Don't pick the blocks so close," Bloser would say peevishly, but the carver unheeding would shoulder his bag laden with every available piece. There was easy tolerance in all that region. They laughed at him, feared him, thought him dirty, and dangerous in anger, yet they admired him and fed him. The very aspects which today give his work its characteristic force were the things which made certain contemporaries disdain his

FIG. 1 — EAGLE CARVED BY SCHIMMEL.
From collection of Miss Ellen Penrose.

FIG. 2 — THE GARDEN OF EDEN. Carved in pine by Schimmel, each figure separately. Painted in
polychrome with heavy oil colors. *From the collection of T. C. Geesey. Water color rendering from
Index of American Design.*

FIG. 3 — TOY ANIMALS AND BIRDS CARVED BY SCHIMMEL.
From Earl F. Robacker and Barbara Lesher.

FIG. 4 — CARVED AND PAINTED WOODEN DOG. Probably by
Schimmel. *From the Metropolitan Museum of Art.*

carvings as crude. The other cutters of the black-walnut era were precisionists, working with geometrics, while Schimmel's carving was ever individual and full of feeling.

Schimmel carved all manner of birds and animals. Pine was his favorite medium. His only tool was a common pocket-knife which he sharpened assiduously. He made few mistakes. So sure was his eye that every stroke was made to count, a fact reiterated by those who remember watching him whittle. Only when he wished a smooth surface did he use bits of glass to eradicate his knife marks. After carving his bird or beast, Schimmel covered his work with gesso, a plaster wash, to prepare the surface for the final paint coat he always liked to use to brighten his carving.

Most treasured as well as most handsome were Schimmel's eagles, the largest of which had a wing spread of three feet from tip to tip. Smaller ones were regarded as mantel or whatnot ornaments; the larger ones were usually put on top of a pole to ornament the garden. Certain ones were displayed in schoolhouse yards, before a Bloserville boarding house, and in Carlisle on victory poles at election time. Large specimens as well as small had wings carved as if poised for flight. Best examples, such as the one illustrated here, present the salient characteristics of all Schimmel eagles. The wings of these birds are gouged out to show each individual feather, and the joint is at a sharp angle. No block was large enough for the largest of these birds, so wings were cut separately and dovetailed into the body, held by a single pin. Bird bodies were carved in saw-tooth fashion, as were the backs of the wings, from the head to the claws which grasp a woodblock base. Here again, in the strong, rough work found on the claws we recognize another Schimmel

trait, for by observation identity can best be established.

Schimmel eagles had a beak and head often confusingly similar to the small parrots which the carver also made. These latter birds were small and likewise perched on a block. Note, too, that the eagles were more Hapsburgian than of the American bald-eagle genus. Roosters, a favorite subject, were never carved about the wings but had smooth bodies and well-carved tail feathers. In size they varied from a naturalistic, foot-tall fowl to a miniature specimen two inches high. Squirrels had most carving centered on a curving tail lying over the animal's back, while lambs and dogs frequently had on some part the peculiar markings characteristic of good Schimmel work, notably, the sawtooth incising. One who remembers Schimmel working reports than on occasion he experimented by pasting sheep wool or fur on a finished animal. At times he tried his knife in fashioning stranger beasts, particularly lions, of which a few examples exist.

Schimmel's European background is evident also in the Biblical scenes he fashioned. Particularly impressive was his depiction of Adam and Eve in a realistic garden surrrounded by a picket-like fence. The tree was there with its red apples, the snake, and an enticing Eve. This was the counterpart of what the Bavarian peasants had carved for generations. This model the neighborhood wholeheartedly approved. At least three of these groups were carved by him. Schimmel exhibited one at the Cumberland County Fair in the 1880's. He hurled German curses at the judges who failed to award him a ribbon, despite acclaim from the people who knew him well. In his last months Schimmel carved a miniature of this garden scene and a very small portrayal of the crucifixion. But his fame rests largely on his eagles and animals.

There is a legend that Schimmel was a veteran of the Mexican or Civil War, or of the Franco-Prussian War. No one who remembers Schimmel believes that he ever bore arms for his adopted land. In light of the recollection of those who knew him no foundation for this rumor exists, any more than for the statement that he was affluent enough ever to have possessed better means of transportation than his own feet. The many who remember doubt that he ever turned a hand to "honest work," except for the Greider and Waggoner families.

Schimmel always painted his own carvings, using whatever paints he could acquire. Black, brown, red, and yellow ochre were favorite colors. His large birds were often drab, yet enlivened by red and yellow accents on wings and claws. His roosters were yellow ochre with black stippling over the bodies, but with careful brushwork on tails and on the smooth sides where he failed to carve wings. Such strokes were often impressionistic daubs. Another characteristic Schimmel addition was the insertion of leaf or bud-like pieces in the base of his eagles and parrots. These additions, designated "nests," were brightly colored and, to a trained eye, are a detracting feature of his work. But for the most part the virile strength of his rude, if forceful, production is both exciting and satisfying. To many, Schimmel's products have more appeal than the neat and realistic work of trained craftsmen such as Samuel McIntire. Schimmel's work exhibits the fundamentals of creative art, and, as with all folk art, "is the expression of the common people, not that of a cultured class." Easily recognizable and related one to the other, each carving has its own merits and demerits, making it individual and good art.

In life Wilhelm Schimmel was known less as a person than as a carver of birds and animals, of ornaments and toys. Suffering from an incurable ailment, he came to Carlisle after the breaking up of the Greider home. In a short time German friends found it necessary to take the sick man to the almshouse. He went, under protest, in mid-May 1890. He died the same year, August 3, aged 73, and was buried in the potter's field. Of three Carlisle newspapers only one made any note of his passing:

" 'Old Schimmel' the German who for many years tramped through this and adjoining counties, making his headquarters in jails and almshouses, died at the Almshouse on Sunday. His only occupation was carving heads of animals out of soft Pine wood. These he would sell for a few pennies each. He was apparently a man of a very surly disposition."

The weekly edition of the same paper remarked that "Schimmel was known to almost everyone in the country." His creative ability is more truly evaluated in this day than in his own; his work is sought and prized for its inherent artistry.

TEXTILES

The Fishing Lady and Boston Common

BY NANCY GRAVES CABOT

THE SUBJECT OF *American textiles has been less thoroughly studied than, for instance, American furniture or American glass, but important work has nevertheless been done. A specialized aspect of the subject is a group of eighteenth-century New England embroideries, known from their central motif as the Fishing Lady needle pictures. The existence of this group was first noted in* ANTIQUES *in August 1923 by Helen Bowen. In July 1941, Mrs. Samuel Cabot presented the following most valuable account, greatly extending the number of reported examples. In December 1941 she continued her discussion of the Fishing Lady group, tracing elements of the design to old prints, though the source of the Fishing Lady herself remains undiscovered. The collection of photographs of Fishing Lady embroideries mentioned at the end of this article as a permanent record to be deposited with the Museum of Fine Arts, Boston, has been still further increased. The number of recorded examples now stands at sixty-five.*

AN article by Helen Bowen entitled *The Fishing Lady and Boston Common* in ANTIQUES for August 1923 first noted a repetition of patterns which she had recognized in eight fine eighteenth-century needlepoint pictures of New England provenance. The motif of a lady fishing in seven of them, and the tradition that two of them had always been known as Boston Common pictures, provided the title for Miss Bowen's article. ANTIQUES subsequently illustrated four more pictures of the same designs, with editorial comment on the interesting problem of relationship that the subject presented. Exhibitions of old embroidery held in Boston in 1934 and 1937 produced five more, bringing the number of so-called "Fishing Lady" pictures to seventeen.

The embroideries were of such exceptional interest and beauty, representing as they did the finest type of American eighteenth-century needlework, and their relationship in design was so fascinating, that it seemed worth while to make a collection of photographs of these seventeen pictures for comparison, and as a charming record of the skill and taste in a lovely craft of the young ladies of early New England.

A search for further examples has yielded many more pieces, including samplers and crewelwork, until the "Fishing Lady" group of related embroideries now numbers fifty-eight. In spite of giving her name to the series, the Fishing Lady herself appears in but twelve. A "Reclining Shepherdess," as the central figure in eleven others, is a close rival in popularity.

[285]

Thirty-six are framed pictures in varying sizes, from small panels measuring ten by twelve inches to ambitious three to five foot panoramas, with patterns of figures disporting themselves in gay and elaborate pastoral settings. Two of these are wrought throughout in oriental stitch, the other thirty-four in tent stitch, with occasional French knots, on fine handwoven canvas in many colored crewels, with touches of silk and metal threads. There are ten pictorial samplers of few figures and animals in simpler scenes, with lovely floral borders, worked largely in satin stitch on fine linen with silks of glowing colors. The crewel embroideries on linen consist of eight chair seats and two petticoat borders, with animal and landscape motifs only.

Most important of the series are the large and very ornamental "chimney pieces," of which three, happily, still have their original and similar frames of mellow brown walnut with carved, dull gold molding. The frames are finely proportioned, their design inspired by their architectural purpose as overmantels, with gracefully swelling contours at the base to provide spaces for candle sconces.

The pattern of each of the "chimney pieces" has been skillfully planned with three separated groups of figures representing the occupations of the months or seasons, united by a lavish sprinkling of birds and animals, flowers and trees, which enliven the background and leave no spot without its interest. The knowing designer has left no monotonous area to deaden the energy of youthful fingers.

In all the smaller embroideries, motifs appear which are repeated in one or the other of the large "chimney pieces," thereby identifying them with the series. The units of design recur again and again

in fresh combinations to suit each worker. The individuality of these arrangements combined with the unequal skill of the young needlewomen gives charm to each piece.

The names of twenty-six of the embroideresses are known, and nineteen. of the embroideries are heirlooms still treasured in the families of the girls who made them. In three of the needlepoint pictures, names and dates are incorporated in the design. The earliest dated piece carries the legend, *Priscilla Allen daughter of Mr. Benjamin Allen and M . . . Elisbeth Allen Boston July the 20 1746.* Mary Avery and Sarah Warren have recorded their names and the year 1748 in their work. A fine chimney piece in the collection of Henry F. du Pont has the date 1748, but no name, above a cottage door. Six of the samplers have names and dates: Sarah Lewis 1767, Abigail Mears 1772, Mary Withington 1774, Grace Welsh 1774, and Peggy Parker 1774. In the 1784 sampler of Mary Russell and in a small silk picture by Polly Ellis, 1791, with which the series ends, the Fishing Lady motifs have dwindled to an incidental few, after a span of forty-five years.

When it has been possible to trace their history the work of the needlepoint pictures has usually been found to be the proud accomplishment of young ladies in their late 'teens and early twenties, daughters of prosperous and distinguished families of eighteenth-century New England, frequently connected. by ties of blood and friendship. The pictures may well have been the climax of female education at a Boston finishing school. This is a reasonable conclusion, since the girls' homes were too widely separated to allow for neighborly exchange of patterns, and Priscilla Allen, hailing from as far north as Falmouth,

FIG. 1 — "CHIMNEY PIECE." Wrought by Sarah Warren (*1730-1797*) of Barnstable. It resembles the Bourne heirloom with the Boston Common tradition, owned by the Boston Museum of Fine Arts, closely enough to serve for a fair comparison with Hannah Otis' actual view of the Common in Figure 2. In original brown and gold frame with brass candle sconces in lower corners. Size, 45½ x 20½ inches. *From the collection of Mrs. Archer O'Reilly.*

FIG. 2 — NEEDLEWORK PICTURE. Showing the Hancock House and Boston Common in the middle of the eighteenth century. Made at boarding school in Boston by Hannah Otis (*1732-1773*) of Barnstable. Sister of James Otis, "The Patriot." Size, 53 by 24 inches. *Privately owned.*

Maine, included *Boston* in the legend of her name and date.

From Maine also came the Reclining Shepherdess *wrought in 1757* by Martha Fry Hewes of Gardiner. The chimney piece formerly owned by Francis H. Bigelow was bought in Portland. From the neighborhood of Boston we have two made by girls of Charlestown, a Reclining Shepherdess by Mary Snelling Atkins, who was born in 1725, and a Bringing in the May by Johanna Ball, born in 1732. Two other Reclining Shepherdesses were made by Brookline girls, Susannah Heath and Hannah Goddard (*Fig. 3*). The fact that they were near neighbors, and later sisters-in-law, probably accounts for the only instance of almost exact resemblance of pattern in the series.

Salem is the background for two chimney pieces, the one dated 1748, belonging to Henry F. du Pont, and the frequently illustrated work by a member of the famous Derby family, in which the painted faces were once credited to Copley. Phebe Hobart, born in 1760, also of Salem, did her fine piece probably not earlier than 1778, at "Mistress Dean's," according to a yellowed legend found beneath her picture's modern backing. This is too late in the century to serve as a clue to the original source of the Fishing Lady patterns, but reveals the name of a later school where one of the designs had survived.

From North Andover there is a small picture by Hannah Phillips, born in 1742, daughter of Samuel Phillips, founder of Andover Academy.

It is interesting that the largest number of known embroideresses were near neighbors on Cape Cod. Desire Dillingham, daughter of John Dillingham of Harwich, was born in 1729, and married Benjamin Bangs of Harwich in 1749. Mary Avery, who dated her piece 1748, when she was but thirteen, was the daughter of John Avery of Truro, and later became the wife of Governor John Collins of Rhode Island. She traced her line from Richard Warren of Plymouth, passenger on the *Mayflower*, as did also Sarah Warren, whose chimney piece (*Fig. 1*) might be called the finest of the whole group. Sarah, daughter of James Warren of Barnstable, was born in 1730 and was eighteen years of age when she affixed her name and the date 1748 in large bold letters in the center foreground of her masterpiece. In 1755 she married her first cousin, the Honorable William Sever of Kingston, where she and her picture went to live in the beautiful Sever homestead — still standing and still beautiful. For nearly two hundred years the picture has been prized in the Sever family and until quite recently it had always hung over the mantel in the pine-paneled living room at Kingston.

It is beautifully wrought in tent stitch throughout on fine canvas with silk and wool thread. Though the colors in one hundred and ninety-three years have lost some of their original brilliance, the fading has been uniform, and the general tone of soft blues, reds, and browns is particularly pleasing. The sheen and highlights from a rich use of silk thread for costumes and flowers give it sparkle, and the vivaciousness of the design, with its Arcadian happiness, gives as much pleasure today as when Sarah brought it home to adorn the family mantel.

The Fishing Lady, lending half an ear to her persuasive swain, occupies the center of the composition, one of her twelve appearances on this pastoral stage. On the right, Corydon gathers pears for Phillida,

Fig. 3 — "Reclining Shepherdess." Embroidered by Hannah Goddard (*1758-1786*) of Brookline, Massachusetts. There are eleven variations of this scene in the Fishing Lady series. *From the collection of Mrs. George H. Wright.*

Fig. 4 — Needlework Picture. In pictorial embroidery ripe cherries and pears are not inconsistent with "Bringing in the May." *From the collection of Mrs. Lombard Williams.*

though the larger cherries in the next tree would seem to be more tempting. On the left the prim lady — a spinner in three of the other pictures— has laid aside her distaff, and, manifestly struggling with a New England conscience, waits for the perfume of a single flower to lure her to dalliance. Across the foreground sweeps a stag hunt of a scale that art school canons would have placed on the distant hills. Certainly to enjoy early pictorial embroidery it is best at the outset to forget the conventions of perspective, else one will lose the piquancy of surprise at flowers, butterflies, and houses of equal size, and the charm of much irrelevant detail.

Sarah lived among expert needlewomen in Barnstable. Her sister-in-law, Mercy Otis Warren, wife of her eldest brother James, though better known for letters and politics, has left testimony to great skill and industry in an embroidered card-table top, now at Pilgrim Hall, Plymouth. There was Eunice Bourne, two years her junior, maker of the chimney piece in the Boston Museum of Fine Arts, known as the Bourne heirloom with the Boston Common tradition.

And of the same age as Eunice Bourne was Hannah Otis, Mercy's younger sister, whose ambitious handiwork actually represents with sufficient fidelity for recognition the Boston Common of her day *(Fig. 2)*. This is another picture that has passed down in one family for nearly two hundred years. Hannah's nephew, Harrison Gray Otis, mayor of Boston in 1829, possessed it during his lifetime, and has left the following description:

"A view of the Hancock House, and appendages, and of the Common, and its vicinity, as they were in 1755-60. It was the boarding school lesson of Hannah Otis, daughter of the Hon. James Otis of Barnstable, educated in Boston. It was considered a chez-d'ouvre, and made a great noise at the time. The science of perspective was not worthy of Claude Lorraine, but perhaps not behind that of some who since then have had the care of the Common."

Two points in this account are of special interest: that Hannah had done her panel at boarding school in Boston, and that the embroidery had caused a stir in her own day.

It is to this renown that I attribute the Boston Common tradition which in our time clings to three of the Fishing Lady pictures, and to yet another of quite different pattern that is owned on Cape Cod. Certainly the fanciful Fishing Lady backgrounds do not represent Boston Common, as naïvely but realistically depicted by Hannah.

Helen Bowen discovered their lack of verisimilitude from maps and prints of the bare cow pasture and training field that was the Common in the middle of the eighteenth century. She sought to connect the pictures with historic textile activities that took place on the Common, and offered for consideration two possibilities: that they might have been worked there, as an adjunct to the short-lived fad for competitive spinning and weaving which took place on the Common after the arrival of the Dublin weavers about 1720; or that they might have been shown as an attraction at the Grand Exhibition held on the Common in 1753, fostered by "the Society for Encouraging industry and employing the Poor."

Since the task of embroidering a picture of such proportions and fineness requires months if not a year or more, the former

FIG. 6 — A SAMPLER VERSION OF THE "RECLINING SHEPHERDESS." Also
showing the running huntsman with vaulting pole. By Mary Withington, 1774. *From the estate of D. L. Pickman.*

FIG. 7 — PETTICOAT BORDER. Crewel embroidery of many colors on a fine linen ground. The stag chased by dogs, the trees, and
various floral motifs can be found in the needlework pictures illustrated. *From the Museum of Fine Arts, Boston.*

theory seems scarcely tenable. Moreover, the period of 1720 is not consistent with the Fishing Lady dates of 1746 and 1748.

The Boston *Evening Post* of 1753 gives a graphic description of the Grand Exhibition. It was a one-day affair on the occasion of the annual meeting of the worthy society, when about three hundred spinners and many weavers demonstrated their crafts, "and the Spectators were so numerous that they were compared by many to one of Mr. Whitefield's Auditories, when he formerly preached here on the Common." It is hard to visualize an *al fresco* display of embroidered pictures in that milling crowd.

On the other hand, here we have an actual landscape picture in needlepoint of Boston Common, made in the middle of the eighteenth century by the daughter of a Barnstable family, prominent in the small and intimate society of colonial New England. Furthermore, dating from the same period we have the landscape pictures of the Fishing Lady group also made by girls of Barnstable and neighboring Cape towns, which likewise have been handed down from generation to generation, but with meager historical data. May not the simple solution of the Boston Common tradition be that the mantle of fame of Hannah's *chez-d'oeuvre* has drawn into its folds these equally meritorious pastoral scenes?

Hannah was born in 1732 in the family mansion at Great Marshes, now West Barnstable on Cape Cod, and died there unmarried in 1773. Hers was a family prominently identified with public affairs in the colony of Massachusetts. Thus it is not surprising that her choice of subject for a panel should have been the setting of the

John Hancock House; and the treeless Common, bordering on large pasture lands on the slopes of Beacon Hill, suggested an excellent rural background for a proper pastoral scene. The impression persists in Hannah's family that she prided herself on the originality of her design, and scorned her contemporaries' dependence upon professional designers.

Despite her too easy perspective and casual handling of the Common's sacred contours, there is something of antiquarian interest in the naïve scene. Within the limitations of the craft the Hancock House is rendered faithfully, and can be easily recognized with its adjoining cow pasture, site of Boston's future State House. Downstage center, its builder, the prosperous colonial merchant, Thomas Hancock, and his complacent Lydia contemplate the view over a wall of granite and freestone, a close-up perhaps of a garden "terras" which Hannah has arbitrarily laid across the Common pastures to mark the end of the Hancock lands. Of what he sees Thomas has recorded his satisfaction in a letter to London in 1736: "My Gardens all Lye on the South Side of a hill with the most beautiful Assent to the top and its allowed on all hands the Kingdom of England don't afford so Fine a Prospect as I have both of land & water." Lydia's bead eyes seem to stray in an indulgent way to the handsome mounted youth curvetting across the front plane of the picture. He is their beloved nephew, the future Governor, John Hancock, who had been brought at the age of seven from a simple Braintree parsonage to wealth and position as an adopted heir in their childless home. The pampered and popular young man, just out of Harvard, has a confident seat on his high mettled horse, and an imperious gesture as he cracks his whip in farewell to the worshipful black slavery.

Thomas Hancock built his splendid mansion in 1737, just below the summit of Beacon Hill, dismaying his friends by his independent move from the court end of town to the undeveloped pasture lands beside the Common. Neither money nor effort was spared to make it a dwelling place suitable for Boston's richest merchant. Interior decoration and furnishings were ordered from London, "all to be very rich and beautiful." Shrubs and trees crossed the seas, "Yewes, Holly and Jessamine Vines to Beautifie a flower garden."

West of the Hancock House at this time, there were but three wooden houses, which ultimately came into the possession of John Singleton Copley. In Christian Remick's water-color drawing of *A Prospective View of Part of the Commons in 1768,* owned by the Concord Antiquarian Society, the three Copley houses appear. Comparison of the water-color and the needlework picture shows enough similarities to suggest that the houses west of the Hancock House in Hannah's picture are the same three. The two upper ones were then owned by Doctor Sylvester Gardiner from whom Copley bought them in 1770. The third was owned by Nathaniel Cunningham, father of Hannah's brother James' wife, from whose heirs Copley bought it in 1769.

The land on which this house and orchard stood marked the beginning of real estate history in Boston. This land first belonged to Reverend William Blackstone, a solitary settler on the Shawmut peninsula several years before Governor John Winthrop and his followers tried to establish themselves across the river in Charlestown. Great was their suffering for want of fresh water, so at Blackstone's earnest invitation the thirsty colony followed him to his peninsula, lush and spongy with fresh springs. There they settled, calling the place Boston after Boston in Lincolnshire, England.

That the new town was not unmindful of its debt to Blackstone is established in the *Records* in 1633, where "it is agreed that Mr. Wm. Blackstone shall have 50 acres set out for him near his house in Boston to enjoy forever." Yet a year later, "said inhabitants of Boston did agree with Mr. Wm. Blackstone for the purchase of his estate . . . reserving only about six acres . . . on part whereof his then dwelling house stood, after which purchase the town laid out a place for a training field, which ever since and now is used for that purpose and for the feeding of cattle." So began Boston Common.

As no vestiges of the Hancock House or its appendages remain today, Hannah Otis' quaint record contributes crude testimony to the existence and appearance of ancient landmarks. The hill rises sharply behind Hancock's cow pasture, "so steep as to require some skill even to stand erect on it." On its top is the beacon from which it took its name; it was pulled down in 1790 to make way for a monument to Revolutionary heroes.

With total disregard for the opacity of intervening hills, Hannah has projected upon the sky the graceful spire of the West Church which was to suffer destruction in 1776 at the hands of the irate British in order to stop signals from the Rebels to their friends in Cambridge. Shurtleff, in his *Memorial History of Boston*, cites a Block House, destroyed by fire in 1761, that stood near Powder House Hill on the Common. I have found no early prints or maps that indicate its appearance, and

Hannah's simple version with the king's colors flying may serve at least to suggest its form.

The body of water sprawling through the center plane of the picture is probably the Frog Pond, glorified to meet the appraising gaze of Thomas Hancock, with the old elm which stood by its marshy shelving banks reduced to the simplest needlework terms.

Contemplating the size of Hannah's picture, one marvels at her endurance, for she has used the finest tent stitch from end to end, with only the slight relief of a few French knots for strawberries and an inquisitive goat. For thread there is a lavish use of silks for sky and highlights. These have turned to a lovely ivory which harmonizes with the neutral blues and greens of the faded crewels. Soft reds in strawberries, birds, and costumes scatter bright notes over the whole charming scene.

Though Hannah's design is of her own creation, we know it was embroidered under professional direction in her boarding school in Boston. It is conceivable that it was at the same school where her contemporaries from town and country were at work on their Fishing Lady panels, though the name of the school still eludes us. Some day an old letter or diary may reveal it, or a picture not yet added to the group may tell the secret in embroidered legend or faded writing concealed within the framing.

The photograph collection of the Fishing Lady embroideries, when completed, will be deposited in the Textile Department of the Boston Museum of Fine Arts. The Museum is fortunate in owning several fine originals of the embroideries themselves, in all their brilliant beauty, for the pleasure and inspiration of future students of New England embroidery.

FIG. 5 — NEEDLEWORK PICTURE. The harvest scene recurs twice in the large "chimney pieces" combined with other groups, and twice as the main subject in smaller pictures. *From the collection of Mrs. Stephen Van R. Crosby.*

The Age of Heirloom Quilts

BY FLORENCE PETO

IN CONTRAST WITH *the rare eighteenth-century embroideries, American quilts are a very popular type of textile. Eighteenth-century examples are rarities, but almost everyone has at least one heirloom quilt from the nineteenth century. Mrs. Peto has been studying, collecting, and even making quilts for many years. As lecturer and as author of books and of articles in* ANTIQUES, *she is recognized as the leading authority on the subject. We have selected this article from our July 1942 issue because it gives the sort of practical information about old coverlets that is particularly helpful.*

HOW can one determine the age of an heirloom piece when family history is obscure or lost? Is there something in its appearance that gives the key to its age? It is true that the passage of years induces a mellowing process in both white and dyed fabrics which is comparrable to the patina surfacing old woods and metals. This mellowness is a quality independent of wear. The splendid condition of some quilts bearing indications of great age testifies to care taken of them—they were the "best" or "bride's" spreads and had been used only on occasions of family festivity. A quilt of much later period, by its tatters and shreds, might appear at first glance to be venerable, but spring and fall bed-washings and the romping of sturdy children can effect in a short time a spurious "antiquity."

If condition is not evidence of age, neither is pattern. Traditional geometric compositions and well-known floral motifs went through periods of recurrent popu-

larity. One example: the oldest and simplest version of the eight-pointed star was known to quiltmakers as the *variable star*. Among the heavenly bodies those known as variables are so called because they show distinct changes in brightness from time to time; so in patchwork, accent in coloring gave to this much-used and easily assembled pattern a versatility which led to its apt name. During the William Henry Harrison campaign for the Presidency, the *variable star* sprang into renewed and extraordinary popularity because a contemporary quiltmaker had endowed it with the glamor of a political slogan—it became *Old Tippecanoe and Tyler Too*. Other pattern names changed with migration, current events, and personal adventures, but familiar contours persisted through successive decades of the quiltmaking era. The name your ancestress gave to her handiwork may be your clue to its date.

Methods of construction contribute something to identification of the period of a quilt. Many early bedspreads were made and decorated in one piece or in a series of borders surrounding a central medallion — a cumbersome job for the needleworker. Both appliqué and piecework were used on one spread, making it difficult to answer the oft-repeated question — which is the older technique? Tiny triangles, squares, and hexagons, in all-over effects, appeared on early pieces and such mosaics seem to have been a heritage from England. Generally, it was later that patterns were made in unit blocks, surely for convenience in handling.

Bedcovers were interlined with wool, sometimes with a thin woolen blanket, but cotton was the great favorite. The presence of cotton seeds in an interlining, to determine age, may be taken into account with reservations. A quilt which displays, when held to the light, an interlining thickly studded with cotton seeds is not necessarily earlier than the invention of the cotton gin, for it was a generation after Eli Whitney demonstrated his first device to separate seeds from fiber that the cotton gin came into successful operation. And an interlining free from cotton seeds may exist in a very early southern-made quilt; black hands labored as skillfully as a machine to prepare a padding for the best quilts made in plantation homes.

Bindings furnish interest. Two quilts in my collection made in the first quarter of the nineteenth century show a homespun lining brought over to the face of the quilt and then felled down. Two others of the same period have been bound in tape, or braid, in fancy weaves and in two or more colors. Often such braids were made in the home on tiny hand looms. My handsomest quilted item *(c. 1820)* has both face and lining turned in toward each other

and the two edges whipped together with an over-and-over stitch, forty stitches to the inch on a quilt three yards square! A novelty in the form of a piping of cotton cloth inserted between the face of the quilt and the fold brought over from the back contributes a tailored effect to some early examples. By the middle of the century a simple fold of bias cloth was preferred as a binding; it is still used by modern quiltmakers. Types of binding might be conclusive of periods or years if it were not for the fact that needle-women of a later generation sometimes elected to copy styles favored by their grandmothers. Only a few quiltmakers of any era signed or dated their work; album or autograph quilts are an exception, and because the great majority of these bear dates in the 1840's, they are helpful in placing patterns and textiles in a period.

The average quilt owner is not equipped with the technical training which enables the expert to make deductions from dyes, methods of printing, and processes of weaving, but there are things for which the novice may look. East Indian printed cottons, English or French calicoes and chintzes are not difficult to recognize after study of the helpful reference books on oriental and European fabrics. Foreign cloth was expensive in the Colonies but it was available to women in the coastal towns and was purchased and used by those who could afford it; every inch was utilized and it was often combined with home-woven goods. It was not many years after the Revolution that American manufacturers had advanced to a point where they rivaled each other's output as well as the European importations. The British, unabashed at depicting eagles or other symbols of the late rebels' freedom, had been successful

Fig. 1 — Patches of American Calico (*nineteenth century*). Taken from a friendship patchwork quilt made about 1894 on Long Island.

Fig. 2 — American Cotton Print (*1889*). Commemorating Benjamin Harrison's election as President of the United States. Brown, yellow, and olive drab with flags in natural colors.

FIG. 3 — AMERICAN QUILT (*late nineteenth century*). Material printed in squares to simulate patchwork called *Yankee puzzle. From the Index of American Design, Art Service Project, W.P.A.*

FIG. 4 — SIMULATION OF PATCHWORK (*American, late nineteenth century*). Paisley colors of coppery-red, orange, brown, and white. A dog in each corner completes the repeat.

with historical patterns, and the Yankee states produced patriotic and allusive designs of their own.

As American printers did not use trademarks, nor did early manufacturers keep sample books, an earnest endeavor to identify printed cottons with a specific domestic cotton-printing plant has produced extremely meager results. In Figure 1, picturing a group of swatches of domestic calicoes, there are two with indigo-blue backgrounds and fine, floral patterns of white, yellow and red. Duplicates are to be found in a sample book (*1863*) which had been kept by Borden Mills, Fall River, Rhode Island, and which is now the property of Fruit of the Loom Company. It seems that sample books earlier than that are rare. Manufacturers, then as now, repeated their successes; these particular indigo blues may be earlier than 1863. All of the patches in this group came from a friendship quilt top in my collection. The top had been assembled by the mother of Mrs. Henry Chatfield Smith, of Stony Brook, Long Island; in a letter dated *1894*, Mrs. Smith's mother wrote: "I am finishing that old quilt top . . . some of these calicoes must be over a hundred years old." We must allow for possible exaggeration, but the materials have the appearance of considerable age. The quaint design of pins stuck in cloth, and the graceful horse's heads, are finely engraved, printed in brown on fine white cambric. The latter pattern and the one showing horseshoes, nails, and sledge hammers, were forerunners of the larger horseshoe-and-riding-whip motif and also of the larger horse's heads which prevailed on shirtings for boys in the 1880's and 1890's. The amusing parade of ants (or flies?), the dominoes, the crescents, on three of the other patches, are printed in red and black

on white calico. Tiny florals held their own over a long period even through the decades when the quiltmakers and dressmakers largely favored the flamboyant orange-toned paisleys of the Victorian era. The dainty Persian pear (on which most of the paisleys were based) is shown here with a stippled effect in blue and rose on white. The patch at the left of the Persian pear shows a conventional floral in madder-rose on tan ground. When we attempt to identify the age of a quilt by its textiles, sometimes Grandmother So-and-So's spread (the date of making definitely established) may shed light on the probable age of otherwise elusive domestic cottons. Heirloom quilts may be a valuable source of information on American printed goods; hence it becomes important to record the age of items whose histories are still available.

It may be difficult to link scenic, pictorial, or historical cottons with a specific printworks but they may be classified reasonably as to period. The Centennial brought forth much yardage decorated with Liberty bells, shields, flags, eagles, and the likeness of the Father of his Country. By 1885 the features of Grant and Arthur decorated cotton yard goods; Figure 2 shows portraits of George Washington and Benjamin Harrison, and is dated *1889*. The quiltmakers incorporated these prints in their needlework. Whenever human figures appear on textiles or patchwork, costume and hirsute adornments are nuggets of information.

Often games can be linked with years. A quilt owned in Huntington, Long Island, contains material printed in squares showing children at play — skating, sleighing, rolling hoops, playing hopscotch and London Bridge. Children in many ages have played such games but in this print the

FIG. 5 — COTTON PATCHES (*American, late nineteenth century*). Light piece shows both sides of French franc pieces, dated *1880*, in pink and blue on white ground. Dark swatch reproduces the emblems associated with Horace Greeley and his initials.

FIG. 6 — AMERICAN COTTON PRINT. Attributed to Cranston Print Works, Providence, Rhode Island. On a white ground with brown foliage decoration, medallions of Washington in brown alternate with red shields showing scales and the word *Peace*. The date *1776* suggests that the print was made for the Centennial celebration in 1876. *Illustrations from the author's collection, except Figure 3.*

little girls' bonnets, high buttoned shoes, and clumsy skates tell their own story. This textile bears the name *Merrimack Manufacturing Company* printed on the face of the pattern.

In Figure 3 the grown-up's fondness for a game is pictured in vivid colors. A puzzle keeps the whiskered gentleman, candle in hand, awake in the wee small hours, long after his spouse has given up and gone to sleep. There are fifteen numbered cubes and sixteen square spaces; the trick is to arrange the numbers in proper numerical sequence without lifting the blocks. Notice the late-Victorian details in the furnishings. The printing of cotton cloth to simulate patchwork appeared at least as early as 1849, for a wide border of realistic baby's building blocks or cube work finishes a quilt so dated in my collection. The complete unit in Figure 3, which is of course about thirty years later, simulates a patch pattern known to quiltmakers as the *Yankee puzzle* — appropriate in this case, whether by accident or intention.

In the same coppery-red, orange, brown, and white which are characteristic of the paisleys, Figure 4 displays another expert simulation of patch pattern centered by an engaging feline, smug and happy over a blue ribbon bow. A dog in each corner completes the repeat. Notice the reproduction of early small prints. Pacific Mills manufactured a great many realistic and humorous designs; though those shown here have not been identified as their product, they are considered typical. One cotton-printing plant lost valuable records when a new and over-zealous manager decided that the space occupied by barrels and kegs of "mills" which had been used

in former days was more essential to the company than the out-dated engravings which he sold as junk.

At one time a silk manufacturer made some black necktie silk into which was woven in gold thread a replica of a United States ten-dollar gold piece; it was said he was restrained from putting it on the market, for no one may reproduce Uncle Sam's money in any form! Apparently the restriction did not apply to French money; Figure 5 shows both sides of French franc pieces printed in pink and blue on a white ground. The coins are dated *1880*. Many examples of American historical prints used an entire scene decoratively enclosed by floral and leafy wreaths; in contrast, the dark swatch in Figure 5 has small symbol motifs arranged in half-inch stripes. In color it resembles the paisleys. The initials, *H G*, the spectacles, the white top hat, and the axe and sickle are symbols used to represent Horace Greeley, cartoonist's joy. Charles Dickens once wrote, ". . . Mr. Greeley's white hat has become a sort of proverb among Americans," and he referred to Greeley as "Old White Hat." Greeley advocated an agrarian socialism which recalled his famous advice: "Go west, young man, and know your country." That's where the axe and sickle come in. During the campaign of 1872, Greeley was caricatured by his adversary in a white hat, spectacles, great coat, and boots.

No one factor in determining age of a bedspread is reliable; it is safer to seek evidence in a summary of several — design, methods of construction, trends of style in "sets" and bindings, type of interlinings and the textiles of which the quilt has been fashioned.

FIREARMS

Firearms, from Hall to Garand

BY R. L. DOWLING

To MOST PEOPLE the word antiques is synonymous with furniture or with such domestic items as glass and china. To The Magazine ANTIQUES, it also means all the sorts of things that were made or used in America's early days, from toys to firearms. Collectors of these specialized objects are sometimes inclined to think of them as unrelated to the rest of antiques. In the days of settlement, however, a gun was as essential a part of the home's equipment as a chair or a table, and firearms continued later on to be closely linked with our history. From the various articles in ANTIQUES that have dealt with firearms we have chosen this one from September 1943, which traces American contributions to their development. The author is Honorary Curator of Arms at historic Fort Ticonderoga, which has a firearms collection that is outstanding in this country.

THROUGHOUT the development of American industry, war has served as a stimulus not only to the manufacture of weapons, but to manufacturing generally. It has led to inventions and improvements in war industries that contributed to peacetime industry as well. Many mass-production methods originated in the manufacture of firearms. Among those who made the earliest contributions to quantity production of firearms were Eli Whitney and Captain John H. Hall. Under a contract with the government made in 1798, Whitney devised the first system for the making of each part of the gun separately — the division of labor so essential to mass production. Hall, with a contract signed in 1819, perfected machines so exact that identical parts were produced, interchangeable among any of the Hall rifles.

The methods first utilized successfully in making firearms were later applied to other machines — particularly the improvement of the cotton gin and textile-weaving machinery. The automatic method of carving gunstocks, first used in the early 1830's, at first a government secret, was later utilized in the manufacture of furniture — and marked the end of the old handcraftsmanship to which antique furniture owes its beauty. Another of many examples of the transfer of manufacturing methods from the munitions industry to peacetime industry is the Dalgrin method of hardening the metal in cannon. First used by Dalgrin during the Civil War, this method cooled the cannon from the interior, creating exterior strains which resulted in much stronger casting. It was later employed in the manufacture of heavy-duty engines, railroad locomotives, and so on.

In the earliest days of Colonial settlement the European matchlock and wheel-lock were imported. Both weapons were heavy and cumbersome and it is a matter of record that an Indian could shoot ten aimed arrows at a settler of Plymouth while the latter was loading his gun. At ranges over 50 yards the gun was less accurate than the bow and arrow.

The conditions of forest warfare stimulated the inventive genius of American settlers to develop the so-called Kentucky rifle in the early 1700's. This rifle, distinctly American in every detail, is romantically associated with our early history. The backwoods gunsmiths of Pennsylvania developed it with the crudest of handmade tools, and it became world-famous. The name "Kentucky" has stuck to the gun because so many examples found their way there at a later date, and few people who used them realized that they had been developed and used many years before Kentucky was known. The Kentucky filled the demand, created by conditions in America, for a rifle that could be loaded as quickly as a smoothbore and could shoot into an 8-inch circle at 200 yards. When it left the gunsmith's hands this weapon was the most deadly of its time. The caliber in the early models was from .40 to .45. The rifling was achieved by an ingenious hand process, and all the lining up was done by eye, as no precision tools were available. It required days of hard work and many inspections to make a true bore in exact line with the axis of the barrel.

The Kentucky was, of course, a muzzle loader but could be charged very quickly. Powder was poured down the barrel and a buckskin or linen patch was placed over the muzzle with a round ball on top of it. A wooden ramrod pushed the ball and its surrounding patch down upon the powder charge. The bullet was slightly smaller than the bore and the patch became a perfect gas check. Being wrapped around the bullet it followed the rifling when the gun was fired and imparted a rotary motion to the bullet which left the gun without being distorted.

In contrast, contemporary European rifles were loaded with a heavy ball which was forced down the barrel by blows of a heavy iron ramrod. This was a noisy operation, took considerable time, and resulted in less accurate shooting.

During the Revolution, the original model of the Kentucky was altered. Most specimens were made a little shorter. The greatest invention of the American gunsmiths of that time was the double-barreled model. An over-and-under pair of rifle barrels was secured to an axle at the breech end. The upper barrel was fired first, and both barrels were revolved by hand, after releasing a spring catch, until their positions were reversed. The spring catch snapped into place and the other barrel was ready for use. As a rule, one lock and hammer was used, with a separate flashpan for each barrel. This gun was the backwoods inventor's answer to the Indian's habit of rushing upon a settler after he had fired his gun and before he could reload. Double-barreled guns were known in Europe at this time but none was comparable to the American product.

Another distinctive American gun of the period was the Kentucky fowling piece. In general appearance and in its main features it duplicated the rifle. The difference was in the barrel, which was smooth bore and lighter. The gauge was from 20 to 16. The average barrel was round its entire length. These guns were intended to shoot buckshot or a round ball. They were more

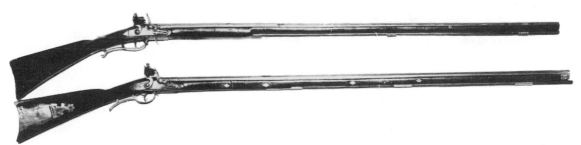

FIG. 1 — "KENTUCKY" RIFLES. *1*, Kentucky fowling piece. *2*, Kentucky rifle (*1750*). *All guns except the Colt revolvers are from the collection of the author. Photographs by John Dowling.*

FIG. 2 — DETAIL OF THE HALL FLINTLOCK. Showing the breech open. Note the slots in the stock to permit escape of gas.

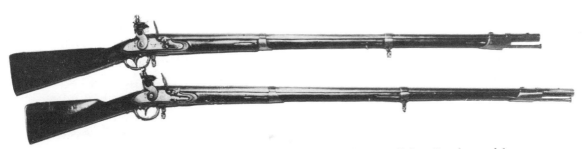

FIG. 4 — SPRINGFIELD FLINTLOCK MUSKETS. *Above,* Special model 1795. *Below,* Regular model 1795.

Fig. 3 — Colt Revolvers. *1*, The "Walker" Model or First Dragoon was used in the Mexican War; all models were used in the Civil War. *2*, Wells Fargo Model. *3*, Second Dragoon. *4*, The Third Dragoon with detachable shoulder stock was the first attempt to convert a pistol into a carbine. *Reproduced by courtesy of the Colt Firearms Company.*

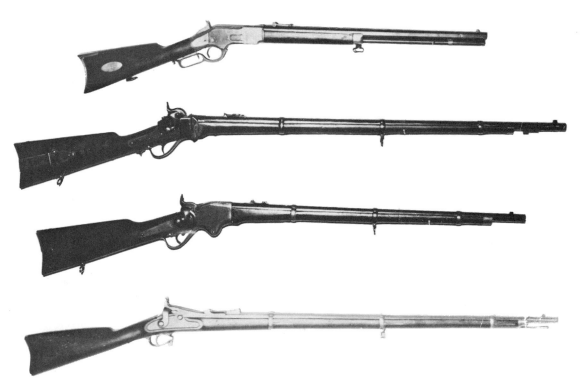

Fig. 5 — American Rifles. *Top to bottom,* Henry repeating rifle. Spencer repeating rifle, model 1865, .56 caliber. Sharps long breech-loading rifle, .52 caliber. U. S. Springfield rifle, model 1865, .58 caliber.

accurate and of better balance than any European fowling pieces of that time.

Both the Kentucky rifle and the fowling piece were extensively used throughout the Colonial period and continued in use in their original form through the Revolution and the War of 1812. The superiority of their workmanship and material is proven by the fact that many of them can shoot nearly as well today as when they were made.

In the early 1830's the Kentucky was modified for service as a saddle gun. These guns were shorter and the stocks no longer had the peculiar curve to the comb found in the early models. Many of them were half-stocked with a rib under the barrel extending to the muzzle.

In the late 1830's the flintlock was discarded in favor of the more dependable caplock. Many of the existing Kentucky rifles were altered to fire by the new system. The alteration consisted in removing the pan, frizzen, and hammer from the lock and substituting a percussion-cap hammer. A lug containing the cap-nipple was screwed into the barrel at the vent-hole. These guns were taken into the West by the early Forty-Niners. They continued to be manufactured up to the time of the Civil War, and some are still in use in backwoods sections of our country.

In 1811 Captain John Hall invented the first American breech-loading army rifle. It was a flintlock of unique design and gave excellent service during the Seminole Indian War and the Mexican War. Some examples were used in the early days of the Civil War but these were of newer design and discharged by the percussion-cap system.

Samuel Colt was another American inventor of this period. He was the most romantic figure of his time in the development of the repeating firearm. In his early boyhood he learned from his grandfather, a veteran of the Revolution, of the exploits of Tim Murphy with his double-barreled Kentucky rifle. From these early impressions sprang the desire to invent a gun that would fire several shots without reloading, and at the age of eleven he began his experiments. In 1830, when he was sixteen years old, he whittled from wood a working model of his first revolver. The great merit of Colt's early model was a system by which the cylinder was revolved automatically, and secured in each firing position by a clutch. This feature became the basic Colt Patent, which was granted February 25, 1836, and is still retained in modern revolvers.

The same year young Colt formed the Patent Arms Company and started manufacture at Paterson, New Jersey. Colt revolvers were made in several models and calibers. The first one was the famous Texas Paterson, .34 caliber, 5 shots, equipped with a concealed trigger. Produced to supply the demand for a repeating weapon for close fighting on the Texas frontier, it marks the revolver as a distinctly American weapon. Nothing like it was manufactured in Europe at that time.

Colt also produced revolving rifles and shotguns of various calibers. All the early Colt arms were loaded with loose powder and a conical ball. The powder was poured in the chambers and the ball pressed down upon it until below the level of the mouth of the chamber, so as not to hinder the rotation of the cylinder. In 1839 a patent was granted to Colt for a loading lever, attached to the frame, and used to ram the bullets into the chambers to a correct and uniform depth. Colt's revolvers were extensively used by our forces in the Seminole Indian War in 1829, and in the Mexican War.

In spite of the excellence of its products, the Paterson plant failed in 1842. In 1847 Colt made a thousand pistols for the United States Government, at the Whitneyville, Connecticut, Armory. This was probably the First Army or Dragoon Pistol (the Walker Model), though some collectors believe this model was first made in Paterson. The following year Colt rented a small factory in Hartford and started the manufacture of the Colt Army Model or the Dragoon Model of 1848. The gold rush of 1849 created a great demand for Colt's arms and he produced several new models at that time. In 1855 the Hartford plant went into mass production as a result of the manufacturing methods of Samuel Colt. He foresaw the coming of the Civil War and was prepared in advance to supply the government. This conflict taxed the capacity of the plant to its utmost, but Colt still sought to improve his weapons. He developed a waterproof cartridge. The charge and bullet were encased in a paper cone, which was inserted and rammed home in each chamber. The paper was impregnated with nitrate of potassium, which made it self-consuming, and left the chamber clean after each discharge. Upwards of 387,000 revolvers as well as a great many carbines were furnished to the United States Government by the Colt plant during the Civil War. Colt's weapons were rated the best of their kind in the world. From the date of the Crimean War they were in great demand by the British armed services because they proved themselves far superior to anything of similar design manufactured in Europe.

In his way Colt was a "visionary" of his

times, and caused contemporary manufacturers to shake their heads in disapproval. The usual workday was then twelve to fourteen hours; Colt gave his workmen the ten-hour day. He also believed in recreational facilities for employees, decent living quarters, sanitary washrooms, and he established pensions for those grown old in his service.

Soon after the introduction of the Colt patents, other revolvers, many of excellent design and performance, were invented and manufactured in this country. Among them was the Remington solid-frame model, patented in 1858, and, next to the Colt, the most popular during the Civil War. It was .44 caliber, 6 shot, percussion. Another of similar design was the Rogers and Spencer, also .44 caliber, 6 shot, and percussion.

The Starr revolver was patented in 1858 and manufactured at Yonkers, New York. The frame, of unique design, was secured just in the rear of the cylinder by a thumbscrew, which allowed the barrel to drop at the muzzle for removing the cylinder. It was .44 caliber, 6 shot, percussion.

These revolvers saw service in the Civil War and were converted to shoot metallic cartridges afterward. Many found their way to the Western frontier in the early 1870's.

The government started the manufacture of muskets at the Springfield Armory with the model 1795, smoothbore flintlock, which was a copy of the French Charleville model 1763. They continued to improve the design as new ideas and current conditions allowed. The workmanship proved superior to contemporary guns manufactured in Europe.

The Civil War proved a great stimulus to American inventors of firearms as well as of many other articles. Models for breech-loading and repeating carbines were introduced, among them the Henry repeating rifle later known as the Winchester. Invented by Tyler Henry in 1860, it was manufactured at New Haven, Connecticut. This typically American rifle filled the demand for a weapon with a large magazine capacity. A tubular metal magazine ran under the barrel and parallel with it to the muzzle. In the early models the magazine was loaded at the muzzle end. The rifle was lever action, .44 caliber. An extension of the trigger guard to the rear, in the form of an oval large enough to accommodate the hand, formed the lever. A carrier operated vertically between the magazine and the chamber. A steel breech block and extractor slid to the rear when the breech was opened, inserted a cartridge, and closed the breech when the lever was returned. The hammer was directly behind the block and was cocked by the action of opening the breech. The barrels were of various lengths, and the calibers with corresponding magazine capacities. A unique feature of this rifle was the bronze receiver and magazine carrier. The Henry saw its first service in the Civil War and was the first repeating rifle used in that conflict. After it, many old Henry rifles found their way to the West and were among the favorite weapons of the scouts and Indian fighters.

The rifle invented by C. M. Spencer was manufactured in 1862 and first appeared in the Civil War in carbine length. It proved most effective throughout the conflict. With the exception of the Springfield muzzle loader the Spencer was the most famous rifle of its time. A tubular metal magazine in the butt stock held seven rim fire metallic cartridges of a .56 caliber.

It had lever action and the hammer had to be cocked by hand at each discharge. Spencers were issued in rifle length to selected regiments of infantry in the latter part of the war and gave excellent service. It has been stated by military authorities that if the French army of Napoleon III had been armed with Spencer rifles the Franco-Prussian War of 1871 would have had a different ending.

Another typically American rifle of this period was the single-shot breech-loading Sharps made in various calibers and various lengths of barrel. The breech block worked vertically in a cavity in the receiver just behind the chamber and was one of the strongest and simplest actions ever made. The original models fired a linen cartridge. Later adapted to shoot metallic cartridges, the Sharps was one of the favorite weapons of the buffalo hunters on the Western plains. One reason for its popularity was its hard hitting and the simplicity of the breech block which enabled it to produce rapid fire in an emergency.

The Starr carbine, made at the same time, was very similar to the Sharps. The principal difference between them was in the breech block. Both weapons were lever action but the Starr block was in two parts. The forward half was hinged and fell back, the rear half worked vertically.

The Remington single-shot breech loader, called the split breech Remington, first appeared during the latter part of the Civil War. Later models were improved and it became known as the most nearly foolproof single-loading rifle made. It was impossible to discharge the weapon until the breech was fully closed because the under body of the block jammed the hammer and locked the trigger. This typically American system was very popular in our service in the 1870's and 1880's. Many thousand specimens were exported to South American countries.

The Buffington rear sight, adapted in the model 1884 Springfield rifle, was another development to improve shooting. But America's greatest contribution to gunmaking at about this time was the Gatling machine gun, invented in 1861. It was of .45 caliber; the mechanism was strong and simple and gave excellent performance under severe service conditions. It was far superior to the French mitrailleuse which came out during the Franco-Prussian War.

All the weapons mentioned above were made to shoot black powder and a lead ball. Americans were the first to perfect a system for drawing brass shells in the manufacture of cartridges, thus making ammunition superior to anything produced abroad at the time.

From Hall to Garand, American firearms have been equal, and often superior, to any in the world. The Springfield rifle model 1903, .30 caliber, was the hardest-hitting, long-range military rifle used in World War I. The Garand rifle, which was used in World War II, is superior to the regulation infantry rifles of all other nations. The underlying reason for this long-time superiority of American arms is traceable to the American capacity for invention, and ingenuity in meeting changing conditions. The system of manufacture and the quality of materials used established the firearms industry in the United States on a firm foundation, and its development has been one of the achievements of American manufacturing methods and business organization.

TOYS

Playthings of the Past

BY ALICE VAN LEER CARRICK

ALICE VAN LEER CARRICK's *series of* Collectors' Luck *(1919), and* Collectors' Luck in France *(1924),* England *(1926), and* Spain *(1930) did much to stimulate interest in antiques in this country, as did also her book on silhouettes,* Shades of Our Ancestors *(1928), and her work while on the staff of* ANTIQUES. *She helped people to realize the fun of collecting through her genial, easy style, while at the same time she emphasized the importance of learning facts instead of fictions. This was her first article in* ANTIQUES, *and it appeared in the very first issue. Other subjects she has written about in the Magazine are glass cup plates and silhouette portraits, as well as numerous minor collectibles that show her appreciation of the unusual.*

THE interest in early playthings is a worthy one. Dolls are as old as mankind, and they and their small belongings mirror the past, mimicking the human beings around them. What dolls did was the usual thing, and just for this very reason they and their houses and their gowns, their prancing horses and minikin toys, are of historical value.

I suppose, if you were very ambitious, you might begin your collection with one of those bead-haired Egyptian dolls, older by a thousand years than the birth of Christ; or a beautifully modeled ivory doll of early Greece; or a royal *poupée* like the one that was given at a cost of 22,000 francs by the Duchesse d'Orleans to the Infanta of Spain in 1722. But for myself, I am more than content with the dolls and their furniture of the eighteenth and early nineteenth centuries which are just about "middling-ly" hard to get, and suited to a "middling"

purse. I am at the beginning of my collection, with a good "low-poster," an admirable ten-inch fiddleback chair, a late eighteenth-century doll, and several pieces of glass and china.

Perhaps I am proudest of my doll, although she is not in the least pretty; papier-mâché is what she is made of, with pipe-stem legs and arms, and a face that is what a North Country acquaintance of mine calls "plain featured" *(Fig. 1)*. But she is engagingly dressed, a little thread-lace cap, a calimanco gown, a printed muslin apron. And, unlike some of the grand French court lady-dolls, she has an abundance of lingerie: "dimothy" petticoats, flannel and cambric petticoats, so that her gown billows amply. On the back of her gown was pinned a slip of paper, and faded formal handwriting told the tale, "Phineas Southworth, born May 12th, 1792. He gave this doll to his youngest sister Fidelia previous to 1817." Further inquiry showed that this same Phineas had lived, a contented daguerreotypist in his native Vermont hill-town, till, caught by the gold fever, he left home, and was lost crossing the Isthmus in '49. I think he gave the doll to little Fidelia earlier than 1817; or perhaps the "storekeeper" had had it a long time, for all the characteristics are eighteenth century.

I prize my little china vases, too, and my Queensware pitcher, prettily sprigged; my dainty glass tureen, my bowl, and sparkling snowflake plates. Deming Jarves must have had an interest in children, for so many toys were made at his glass factory. Of course time has swept away many pieces of such fragility.

In a large collection, like that at the Essex Institute in Salem, one can see dolls of every kind — little ones, big ones, pretty ones and plain. I remember particularly a lady-doll with a lovely serene face, her dress a long-waisted, caped affair of azure and green figured poplin. On a clothes horse two feet high hung checked and figured petticoats that she might have worn. and a very grand plaid silk jacket for best. (Were those two bureaus, each a little more than nine inches high, where she kept her clothes, I wonder?) Scotch dolls and sailor dolls; dolls with checked dresses and dolls with spotted dresses, and a few wearing modest, concealing pantalettes. Two of my favorites from that collection are a demure lady of 1840 with a sprigged gown edged with tatting and a straw bonnet tied with ribbons under the chin, and "Annie, 1847," a cheerful, red-cheeked black-haired lassie in a crimson checked silk gown and cap trimmed with black lace.

Among special curiosities are the cleverly made doll groups of old Mrs. Cleve-land — the *Abolition Dolls*, the *Sick Chamber*, and *The Second Wife*. I am told that she was most particular to choose smooth white kid for the children's faces so that a completely unwrinkled effect might be obtained. In a private collection I saw a small group of hers, *The Old Woman Who Lived in a Shoe*, meticulous even to the children's toys. Beginning in 1840, Mrs. Cleveland amused herself by this work until her death in 1865, accompanying each group with an original poem.

It is no wonder that the ladies of olden days sewed so skilfully: they began when they were tiny things, working for their dolls. Such stitchery as they accomplished! Such delicately embroidered bonnets and tiny handkerchiefs marked quite as real people's were. Even gentleman-dolls were considered, for I have seen a very fine waistcoat and minute stocks and ruffled shirt-fronts. Mittens and socks, too — my thumb would go in one comfortably! They must have been knitted from gossamer floss on all but invisible needles; not only knitted, but purled, and bordered with color in the most elegant manner. Oh, I assure you, those old dolls were well dressed *(Fig. 3)*. Shoes and stockings they had, and aprons and silk gowns and calimanco gowns, embroidered dresses and highwaisted frocks of white muslin. They were neat and orderly, too: "a place for everything and everything in its place." One tiny trunk at the Essex Institute — an engaging thing any child would love — is covered with browned French paper which shows a gay carnival scene, and written inside are the words, *Mary Sutton, her trunk, 1773*. There is also a delightful miniature hatbox, 3½ inches long, with a cover design of a pheasant on a flowering bough. Pretty enough as it is, but open it and you

FIG. 1 — LATE EIGHTEENTH-CENTURY DOLL. Made of papier mâché and dressed, like the "babies" of the time, as a mature woman. *Author's collection.*

FIG. 2 — FANCHON, A DOLL OF 1875, showing part of her carefully designed wardrobe, and her bureau. *Philadelphia Museum of Art.*

will see its *raison d'être*, a captivating little Leghorn bonnet with pink "taffetas" ribbon.

I am sure the dolls of old were excellent housekeepers. I know, for I have seen some of their stencil trays and tea caddies and kettles, skillets and spiders and sad irons, andirons and burnished coalhods, not to mention their sets of dishes in old Nankin and printed Staffordshire. Of course they had a great deal of furniture *(Fig. 4)*. One of the most elegant pieces I have seen is a highboy in the Essex Institute, so engaging that it charms you into playing with it *(Fig. 5)*. Ample bandy legs and Dutch feet, and plenty of drawers to serve as hiding places for treasures of satinettes and cassimers and bits of "patch." It is quite a large piece, 22½ inches high by 12 wide, and in the days of its youth it was decorated in green and gold lacquer.

Among old-time playthings, special interest attaches to those which might be called "Sunday toys." Noah's Ark, for instance, because of its scriptural value, could be produced for sedate amusement when other playthings were deemed light and frivolous *(Fig. 6)*. I think that a game called "The Mansion of Happiness" must also have been intended for a Sunday toy. It is played with counters somewhat resembling faded tiddlywinks, and the Mansion itself is a bower with dancing damsels, the title printed on a waving ribbon held by an American eagle. There you seek to arrive, having stopped at the Inn, escaped the Stocks and Pillory, avoided the Whipping Post and the Road to Folly, and, most dangerous of all, the Summit of Dissipation — this last menace being represented by a sumptuous parlor where a violent man is hurling about decanters and wine bottles. Another Sunday toy is "The Game of Pope and Pagan, or Siege of the Stronghold of Satan by the Christian Army" illustrated by such cheerful pictures as "A Hindoo Woman on the Funeral Pile of her Husband" and "Missionaries Landing on a Foreign Shore." Further description adds, "This simple amusement exhibits a band of devoted missionaries attacking the stronghold of Satan, defended by the Pope and Pagan Antichrist."

Toys designed especially for boys are

FIG. 3 — DOLL'S BED, BUREAUS, AND TWO CHAIRS. The high-post, chintz-covered bed is a late eighteenth-century expression, while the two bureaus are probably early nineteenth, the Hepplewhite piece being earlier than the scrolled front. Chairs, early nineteenth century. *Essex Institute.*

rarer than those for girls, perhaps because they played outdoors so much more. But still, there are ships, marbles, balls of hard gum rubber, engines, martial peep-shows, and tumbling toys. And there are wooden horses, of course, and carriages *(Fig. 7)*. Among the latter the most appealing to me are two small, gaily painted coaches brought from Leghorn in 1804 for a little boy who died the year they came. One is red and one is green, and the galloping horses are yellow-spotted and black-plumed. I am convinced that some other little lad must have loved them and played with them, so that they carried their passengers of the imagination after all.

Some old games were undoubtedly de-signed to make learning easy. There is an Alphabet Game, done in such crude colors and limping rhyme that I wonder how much effect it really had. Yet childhood is endowed with a magic vision, and

> Q is a Queen who looks very grand
> R is a Reaper who reaps from the land

may have opened doors for them.

I have spent many a happy day with old playthings — old dolls, many of them still very lovable, creaking carriages, outworn games. In so doing I have stretched out my hands to the past, far beyond my own youth to my great-grandmother's little girlhood. Even more, I have learned much of the dailiness of our ancestors' lives.

FIG. 4 — HORSE AND CARRIAGES. The toy horse, hand-carved, and an excellent piece of work, stands fifteen inches high; its date is very early nineteenth century. The toy phaeton was made before 1800, and the barouche was a little model made after the first real barouche that appeared in Salem in 1822. The legend is that it created great excitement. *Essex Institute*.